INTRODUCTION

The essential information required to intelligently buy or sell U.S. coins and paper money is presented in this handbook. Aimed primarily at fulfilling the needs of beginning, novice and occasional collectors, it features side by side buying and selling price comparisons.

Selling prices - generally indicated in five or six grades of preservation ranging from good to extremely fine or uncirculated - provide the user with an indication of what dealers can be expected to charge for a specific coin in a given grade. The indicated buying prices - AVERAGE BUYING PRICE (ABP) - are accurate reflections of what dealers generally will pay for a given coin in average condition.

Anyone using this handbook should take careful heed to ascertaining a coin's condition in fixing thereto the valuations indicated, as the demand for careful consideration of this factor can not be overstated. The determination of condition - aside from attributing the date, mintmark and in some instances variety of an issue - is the most important factor which must be established in pegging the value of a given coin.

The average buying prices - indicated in the shaded ABP columns - listed are for coins in the conditions they are most likely to be encountered in finds from circulation, or those lucky finds which repose in family coin accumulations which have been handed down through the years. As these values represent coins in average circulated condition - most 19th century issues are represented in good; early 20th century, good to very good; post-World War I, fine to very fine; post-World War II, very fine to extremely fine; gold commencing in the mid-1800s, fine to very fine - specimens in better or lesser conditions command proportionately higher or lower premiums, as indicated by the companion selling price ranges.

Most modern silver dimes, quarters and halves - 1934 through 1964 - in average condition command premiums commensurate with the value of their bullion content, causing their value to fluctuate in line with the daily changes in silver prices on the bullion markets. The same factors are applicable to common date $5, $10 and $20 gold pieces dating after the mid-1870s. The majority of coins encountered in daily change are "silverless" pieces minted in 1965 and subsequently, along with cents and nickels dating from the mid-1950s. Few of these issues, except in proof or sometime choice uncirculated conditions, command premiums from dealers.

The presence of a dash (—) in the ABP column indicates that one of the two conditions prevail. In the case of high value coins, particularly those described as "rare" or "very rare", which fall in the uncollectable class for the average collector and is unlikely to be found in a coin accumulation, it indicates the piece is offered so seldom that it is not possible to establish a reliable buy or sell price. Where relatively common issues are concerned, the

---

STANDARD GUIDE TO U.S. COIN AND PAPER MONEY VALUATIONS

Published by Krause Publications, Inc., Iola, WI 54990. All rights reserved. No portion of the contents or illustrations may be reproduced or used in any manner without written permission, except in the case of reviews or price analysis. The publisher assumes no responsibility for errors.

COPYRIGHT MCMLXXXI BY KRAUSE PUBLICATIONS, INC

Library of Congress Catalog Card Number: 79-67100.

International Standard Book Number: 0-87341-065-3.

dash indicates a collectable specimen, but one which is normally not actively sought by dealers because their stocks are adequate to supply the collector demand.

Comparison of the selling and ABP prices is intended to allow the individual to determine if the price a dealer offers to pay for a coin, or is asking for a given issue is fair. It should be remembered that both the buying and selling prices indicated in the listings which follow are accurate reflections of the current market. However, as averages, they may be at slight variance with actual market conditions in a given area or where a given dealer is concerned, due to variations in supply and demand or popularity factors.

P9-CAF-273

Silver and Gold Coin Bullion Values

Many U.S. gold and silver coins minted over the last 100 years bear a premium value related to their precious metal content rather than their value as numismatic items. The ABP premiums of these coins is closely tied to the fluctuations of the gold and silver bullion markets. The charts below indicate the bullion value of common date U.S. gold and silver coins at various price per ounce precious metal values. Persons desiring to buy or sell bullion coins should always make themselves aware of the current gold and silver market levels before any transaction.

Silver Bullion Value	$ 8.00	$ 9.00	$10.00	$11.00	$12.00	$13.00	$14.00
☐ Dimes thru 1964	.58	.66	.72	.80	.86	.94	1.01
☐ Quarters thru 1964	1.45	1.62	1.80	1.98	2.16	2.35	2.53
☐ Halves thru 1964	2.89	3.26	3.62	3.98	4.34	4.70	5.06
☐ Halves, 1965-1970	1.18	1.34	1.48	1.62	1.78	1.92	2.07
☐ Dollars thru 1935	6.19	6.96	7.74	8.50	9 28	10.06	10.83

Gold Bullion Value	$400	$450	$500	$550	$600	$650	$700
☐ $5, Half Eagles	96.75	108.85	120.94	135.45	145.13	157.22	169.32
☐ $10, Eagles	193.50	217.69	241.88	270.90	290.25	314.44	338.63
☐ $20, Double Eagles	387.00	435.38	483.76	541.81	580.51	628.88	677.26

HOW TO GRADE YOUR COINS

PROOF (Prf-65) - Specially struck coins, generally with a mirror-like finish and sometimes with the highlight areas frosted, produced on selected planchets with highly polished dies.

UNCIRCULATED - Two qualities; MS-65 and MS-60. Choice uncirculated (MS-65) specimens have only the slightest weakness or blemish, or a few scattered, barely noticeable bag marks or edge nicks detracting from a perfect coin with full mint luster, but perhaps uneven toning or light fingermarking. Typical uncirculated (MS-60) pieces must evidence no wear, although a moderate number of surface bag marks, minor edge nicks or similar abrasions resulting from bulk handling are permissible; may lack full mint luster, and surfaces may be dull or spotted.

AU-50 (About Uncirculated) - Just a slight trace of wear may be present, generally with at least half of the original mint luster remaining.

XF-40 (Extremely Fine) - Only the slightest evidence of wear is detectable on the highest points of the design, particularly in the hair lines of portraits, eagle feathers, wreath leaves and the like.

VF-20 (Very Fine) - Wear is obvious at the fine points of the design, with some details slightly smoothed, though the overall quality is still sharp.

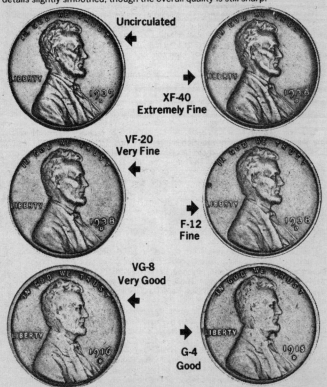

Uncirculated

XF-40
Extremely Fine

VF-20
Very Fine

F-12
Fine

VG-8
Very Good

G-4
Good

F-12 (Fine) - There is readily descernible wear on all high points, though all elements of the design and lettering remain readily distinguishable. Where "LIBERTY" appears in a headband it must be fully visible, and the rim must be fully raised and sharp on 20th century types.

VG-8 (Very Good) - Considerable wear is obvious, with most points of detail worn smooth. Where "LIBERTY" appears in a headband at least three letters must show, and the rim is starting to merge with the lettering on 20th century types.

G-4 (Good) - All points of detail are worn smooth, with only the basic design readily distinguishable. "LIBERTY" has disappeared and rims are nearly merged with adjoining lettering. On early mint issues only an outline of the major design elements is evident.

PAPER MONEY

The paper money section of this handbook is arranged along the same general lines as those already outlined for the coin section. As in the coin section, the ABP column indicates the price a dealer can generally be expected to pay for a given note in the average condition of specimens most often recovered from accumulations or circulation. This condition is generally very good; that is, a rather limp textured note which has been heavily folded or creased, resulting in substantial loss of design details.

Retail valuations are generally provided in one or two of the more desirable collector grades. These grades are: Fine - substantial evidence of circulation will be present, but the note will still be fairly crisp, intact and without evidence of major abuse, fading or staining: Very Fine - only slight evidence of circulation or handling, including faint folds or creases, will be present on an otherwise crips note; Uncirculated - a perfectly preserved note which does not evidence any indications of circulation or mishandling.

MINTS AND MINTMARKS

Established at Philadelphia in 1792, the first U.S. Mint did not begin producing coins for circulation until 1793, although several pattern issues were produced that first year.

The Philadelphia Mint has been the nation's major coinage source through the years, although its production supremacy has, from time to time, been surpassed by its sister facility in Denver. Coins from the Philadelphia Mint are generally distinguished by the absence of a mintmark. However, the silver-content wartime nickel issues of 1942-45 bear a large "P" over the dome of Monticello on the reverse; and, beginning in 1980, the five-cent through $1 coins produced at the Philadelphia Mint also carry the "P" mintmark (Philadelphia-struck cents do not have the mintmark). Since 1974, a portion of the nation's cent and quarter requirements have been met by striking them at the West Point (N.Y.) Bullion Depository, operating as an annex to the Philadelphia Mint. Coins struck there are indistinguishable from those struck at Philadelphia.

Coins struck at the Denver Mint, opened in 1906, bear a "D" mintmark. San Francisco Mint issues, including collector silver coin issues and proof sets produced since 1968, generally bear a "S" mintmark. However, during the years of acute coin shortage (1965-67) all denominations were also struck there for circulation issue without the distinguishing mintmark, as were dimes in 1975.

Several other branch mints have operated in other cities at different times in our history. These mints and their mintmarks were:

C - Charlotte, N.C. (1838-1861); O - New Orleans, La. (1838-1909)
D - Dahlonega, Ga. (1838-1861); CC - Carson City, Nev. (1870-93)

Proper mintmark identification is generally vital to coin value determination. The mints at which each coin date was struck is indicated by the mint letter incorporated with the date listings in this handbook. Mintmark locations are illustrated or described at the beginning of each coin type listing.

REGULAR ISSUE U.S. COINS

HALF CENTS

Although it survived as a regular issue for 65 years, the half cent was never a popular issue with the public. In total face value less than $40,000 of half cents were issued from 1793 through 1857 when it was discontinued in accordance with an act dated February 21, 1857. In most years 100,000 or less examples were issued, and for 20 years, 1830 through 1849, excepting 1832-35, none were actually struck for circulation, while the coinage was suspended completely from 1812 through 1824, and in only two years did the production exceed one million examples ($5,000).

With approximately 85 percent of the production concentrated in no less than nine years - 1804, 1805, 1806, 1807, 1808, 1809, 1828, 1829, and 1835 - many half cent dates and varieties are extremely scarce. Authorized as a 132 grain issue by the original coinage law of 1792, the half cent's weight was reduced to 104 grains by a January 14, 1793 law before coinage commenced, and further to 84 grains by an act of March 3, 1795.

Date	Mintage	G-4	VG-8	F-12	VF-20	XF-40	ABP
☐ 1793 Head L	35,334	2500.	2900.	3500.	4500.	8000.	1500.
☐ 1794 Head R	81,600	350.	550.	750.	1500.	2500.	210.
☐ 1795 Lettered Edge, Pole	25,600	275.	475.	650.	1150.	2000.	165.
☐ 1795 Plain Edge, No Pole	109,000	275.	475.	650.	1150.	2000.	165.
☐ 1795 Lettered Edge, Punctuated Date	Inc. Ab.	275.	475.	650.	1150.	2000.	165.
☐ 1795 Plain Edge, Punctuated Date	Inc. Ab.	275.	475.	650.	1150.	2000.	165.
☐ 1796 W/Pole	5,090	2450.	3600.	6500.	9500.	13,000.	1450.
☐ 1796 No Pole	1,390	—	—	—	Rare	—	—
☐ 1797 Pl. Edge	119,215	275.	475.	650.	1150.	2000.	165.
☐ 1797 Let. Edge	Inc. Ab.	350.	550.	750.	1600.	2300.	210.
☐ 1797 1 Above 1	Inc. Ab.	275.	475.	650.	1150.	2000.	165.

Stems

Stemless

Draped Bust

Date	Mintage	G-4	VG-8	F-12	VF-20	XF-40	ABP
☐ 1800	211,530	25.00	38.00	45.00	65.00	110.	15.00
☐ 1802/0 Rev. 1800	14,366	1750.	2500.	3500.	—	—	1050.
☐ 1802/0 Rev. 1802	Inc. Ab.	200.	275.	500.	1150.	—	120.
☐ 1803	97,900	20.00	38.00	45.00	50.00	110.	13.50
☐ 1804 Plain 4, Stemless Wreath	1,055,312	20.00	38.00	45.00	50.00	110.	12.00
☐ 1804 Plain 4, Stems	Inc. Ab.	20.00	38.00	45.00	50.00	110.	12.00
☐ 1804 Cross 4, Stemless	Inc. Ab.	20.00	38.00	45.00	50.00	110.	12.00
☐ 1804 Cross 4, Stems	Inc. Ab.	20.00	38.00	45.00	50.00	110.	12.00
☐ 1804 Spiked Chin	Inc.Ab.	20.00	38.00	45.00	50.00	125.	12.00
☐ 1805 Small 5, Stemless	814,464	20.00	38.00	45.00	75.00	120.	12.00
☐ 1805 Small 5, Stems	Inc. Ab.	75.00	125.	350.	600.	—	45.00
☐ 1805 Large 5, Stems	Inc. Ab.	20.00	38.00	45.00	60.00	110.	12.00
☐ 1806 Small 6, Stems	356,000	30.00	45.00	85.00	150.	230.	18.00
☐ 1806 Small 6, Stemless	Inc. Ab.	20.00	38.00	45.00	55.00	110.	12.00
☐ 1806 Large 6, Stems	Inc. Ab.	20.00	38.00	45.00	55.00	105.	12.00
☐ 1807	476,000	20.00	38.00	45.00	70.00	130.	12.00
☐ 1808 Over 7	400,000	45.00	60.00	115.	225.	—	27.00
☐ 1808	Inc. Ab.	20.00	38.00	45.00	65.00	125.	12.00

Classic Head

Date	Mintage	G-4	VG-8	F-12	VF-20	XF-40	MS-60	ABP
☐ 1809 Over 6	1,154,572	20.00	30.00	35.00	45.00	60.00	290.	12.00
☐ 1809	Inc. Ab.	20.00	30.00	35.00	45.00	60.00	300.	12.00
☐ 1810	215,000	20.00	35.00	45.00	75.00	90.00	400.	12.00

Date	Mintage	G-4	VG-8	F-12	VF-20	XF-40	MS-60	ABP
☐ 1811	63,140	65.00	80.00	150.	450.	1100.	1250.	40.00
☐ 1811 Restrike, Reverse Of 1802, Uncirculated	—	—	—	—	—	2500.		
☐ 1825	63,000	25.00	30.00	35.00	45.00	75.00	450.	15.00
☐ 1826	234,000	20.00	23.00	25.00	30.00	42.50	285.	12.00
☐ 1828 13 Stars	606,000	20.00	23.00	25.00	30.00	42.50	285.	12.00
☐ 1828 12 Stars	Inc. Ab.	20.00	23.00	25.00	40.00	60.00	400.	12.00
☐ 1829	487,000	20.00	23.00	25.00	30.00	42.50	285.	12.00
☐ 1831 Original	2,200	—	—	—	800.	1000.	2000.	—
☐ 1831 Restrike, Lg. Berries, Reverse Of 1836, Proof					—	—	1750.	1000.
☐ 1831 Restrike, Sm. Berries, Reverse Of 1852, Proof					—	—	3000.	1800.
☐ 1832	154,000	20.00	23.00	25.00	30.00	42.50	285.	12.00
☐ 1833	120,000	20.00	23.00	25.00	30.00	42.50	285.	12.00
☐ 1834	141,000	20.00	23.00	25.00	30.00	42.50	285.	12.00
☐ 1835	398,000	20.00	23.00	25.00	30.00	42.50	285.	12.00
☐ 1836 Original	—	—	Proof	Only	—	—	1400.	800.
☐ 1836 Restrike, Reverse Of 1852, Proof Only					—	—	2500.	1500.

Braided Hair

Date	Mintage	G-4	VG-8	F-12	VF-20	XF-40	MS-60	ABP
☐ 1840 Original	—	—	—	Proof	Only	—	3500.	2100.
☐ 1840 Restrike	—	—	—	Proof	Only	—	3500.	2100.
☐ 1841 Original	—	—	—	Proof	Only	—	3500.	2100.
☐ 1841 Restrike	—	—	—	Proof	Only	—	3500.	2100.
☐ 1842 Original	—	—	—	Proof	Only	—	4000.	2400.
☐ 1842 Restrike	—	—	—	Proof	Only	—	3500.	2100.
☐ 1843 Original	—	—	—	Proof	Only	—	3600.	2150.
☐ 1843 Restrike	—	—	—	Proof	Only	—	3500.	2100.
☐ 1844 Original	—	—	—	Proof	Only	—	4000.	2400.
☐ 1844 Restrike	—	—	—	Proof	Only	—	3600.	2150.
☐ 1845 Original	—	—	—	Proof	Only	—	4500.	2700.
☐ 1845 Restrike	—	—	—	Proof	Only	—	3600.	2150.
☐ 1846 Original	—	—	—	Proof	Only	—	3600.	2150.
☐ 1846 Restrike	—	—	—	Proof	Only	—	3500.	2100.
☐ 1847 Original	—	—	—	Proof	Only	—	3600.	2150.
☐ 1847 Restrike	—	—	—	Proof	Only	—	3600.	2150.
☐ 1848 Original	—	—	—	Proof	Only	—	3600.	2150.
☐ 1848 Restrike	—	—	—	Proof	Only	—	3500.	2100.
☐ 1849 Original Small Date		—	Proof	Only	—	4500.	2700.	
☐ 1849 Restrike Small Date		—	Proof	Only	—	3600.	2150.	

NOTE: The so-called 'original' and 'restrike' half cent proof coins of the 1840-49 period were produced utilizing indistinguishable obverse dies. The distinction between the two versions is evidenced by the size of the berries on the reverse wreath. Relatively large berries are present on the originals, small berries on the restrikes.

Date	Mintage	G-4	VG-8	F-12	VF-20	XF-40	MS-60	ABP
☐ 1849 Lg. Date	39,864	25.00	30.00	35.00	45.00	58.00	375.	15.00
☐ 1850	39,812	25.00	30.00	35.00	45.00	68.00	375.	15.00

Date	Mintage	G-4	VG-8	F-12	VF-20	XF-40	MS-60	ABP
☐ 1851	147,672	22.00	30.00	35.00	45.00	59.00	285.	13.00
☐ 1852	—	—	—	Proof	Only	—	2500.	—
☐ 1853	129,694	22.00	30.00	35.00	45.00	59.00	285.	13.00
☐ 1854	55,358	23.00	30.00	35.00	45.00	62.00	285.	13.50
☐ 1855	56,500	23.00	30.00	35.00	45.00	62.00	285.	13.50
☐ 1856	40,430	27.50	32.00	35.00	45.00	70.00	285.	16.00
☐ 1857	35,180	30.00	35.00	40.00	50.00	75.00	300.	18.00

NOTE: Brilliant original uncirculated half cents command substantially higher prices.

LARGE CENTS

The early years of our coinage found the mint concentrating on the minting of cents, the coin most needed for daily commercial transactions. Most mintages were substantial and varieties numerous. Like a number of coin issues which would follow, the original chain cent design was subjected to much criticism and abandoned in favor of the wreath reverse. Although the chain's links were intended to represent the solidarity of the states then in the union, it was interpeted as representing the chains of bondage.

The large cent, at double the weight of the half cent, was subjected to the same weight changes as the latter, with mintages being produced in every year except 1815. The weight changes in both the cent and half cent during this period were necessitated by rising copper prices. The 1795 change was substantial enough to prevent the need for further adjustments for more than 60 years, but ultimately the unprofitable nature of the large cent, coupled with its inconvenient, cumbersome size, forced the introduction of the small cent.

Flowing Hair

Date	Mintage	G-4	VG-8	F-12	VF-20	XF-40	ABP
☐ 1793 Chain	36,103	3000.	3750.	4500.	9500.	20,000.	1800.
		Auction 80, Aug. 1980, MS-65 $120,000.					
☐ 1793 Wreath	63,353	1500.	1900.	2500.	4400.	9500.	900.

Liberty Cap

Date	Mintage	G-4	VG-8	F-12	VF-20	XF-40	ABP
☐ 1793 Cap	11,056	2450.	3200.	4500.	6000.	—	1400.
☐ 1794	918,521	165.	235.	335.	800.	1200.	100.
☐ 1794 Head '93	Inc. Ab.	325.	500.	1100.	2000.	—	195.
☐ 1795	501,500	160.	250.	325.	700.	1400.	95.00
☐ 1795 Lettered Edge, One Cent High In Wreath							
	37,000	180.	275.	375.	600.	975.	110.
☐ 1796 Lib. Cap	109,825	175.	260.	390.	900.	1650.	105.

Draped Bust

Date	Mintage	G-4	VG-8	F-12	VF-20	XF-40	ABP
☐ 1796	363,375	75.00	110.	165.	335.	750.	45.00
☐ 1797	897,510	40.00	60.00	125.	200.	650.	24.00

Stems   Stemless

Date	Mintage	G-4	VG-8	F-12	VF-20	XF-40	ABP
☐ 1797 Stemless	Inc. Ab.	75.00	125.	200.	1500.	2250.	45.00
☐ 1798	1,841,745	35.00	50.00	75.00	185.	600.	21.00
☐ 1798/97	Inc. Ab.	70.00	115.	185.	450.	800.	42.00
☐ 1799	42,540	700.	1250.	2100.	3000.	—	420.
☐ 1800	2,822,175	29.00	45.00	65.00	165.	565.	17.00
☐ 1801	1,362,837	29.00	45.00	65.00	165.	565.	17.00

Date	Mintage	G-4	VG-8	F-12	VF-20	XF-40	ABP
☐ 1801 3 Errors 1/000, One Stem, IINITED							
	Inc. Ab.	30.00	50.00	125.	300.	600.	18.00
☐ 1802	3,435,100	23.00	35.00	50.00	140.	320.	13.50
☐ 1803	2,471,353	23.00	35.00	50.00	140.	320.	13.50
☐ 1804	756,838	450.	695.	1250.	2000.	3500.	270.
☐ 1805	941,116	28.00	40.00	58.00	170.	500.	16.50
☐ 1806	348,000	40.00	65.00	100.	270.	750.	24.00
☐ 1807	727,221	30.00	45.00	75.00	195.	350.	18.00

Classic Head

Date	Mintage	G-4	VG-8	F-12	VF-20	XF-40	MS-60	ABP
☐ 1808	1,109,000	33.00	55.00	85.00	265.	600.	—	19.50
☐ 1809	222,867	80.00	145.	235.	565.	1500.	—	48.00
☐ 1810	1,458,500	30.00	50.00	80.00	250.	550.	3800.	18.00
☐ 1811	218,025	65.00	105.	165.	445.	700.	—	39.00
☐ 1812	1,075,500	30.00	50.00	80.00	250.	550.	3800.	18.00
☐ 1813	418,000	45.00	72.00	115.	325.	650.	—	27.00
☐ 1814	357,830	30.00	50.00	80.00	250.	550.	3800.	18.00

Coronet Type

Date	Mintage	G-4	VG-8	F-12	VF-20	XF-40	MS-60	ABP
☐ 1816	2,820,982	12.50	17.00	22.00	45.00	95.00	275.	7.50
☐ 1817	3,948,400	11.00	13.00	16.00	35.00	80.00	250.	6.50
☐ 1817 15 Stars	Inc. Ab.	12.00	20.00	30.00	60.00	130.	450.	7.00
☐ 1818	3,167,000	10.00	13.00	16.00	35.00	80.00	250.	6.00
☐ 1819	2,671,000	11.00	13.00	16.00	35.00	80.00	250.	6.50
☐ 1820	4,407,550	11.00	13.00	16.00	35.00	80.00	250.	6.50
☐ 1821	389,000	17.50	30.00	45.00	100.	250.	—	10.50
☐ 1822	2,072,339	11.00	15.00	19.00	41.00	110.	350.	6.50

Date	Mintage	G-4	VG-8	F-12	VF-20	XF-40	MS-60	ABP
☐ 1823	Inc. 1824	35.00	55.00	90.00	235.	650.	—	21.00
☐ 1823/22	Inc. 1824	27.00	45.00	65.00	175.	350.	1750.	16.00
☐ 1824	1,262,000	11.50	16.00	23.00	55.00	80.00	1000.	6.75
☐ 1824/22	Inc. Ab.	20.00	35.00	55.00	115.	275.	1500.	12.00
☐ 1825	1,461,100	10.50	14.00	19.00	50.00	115.	350.	6.25
☐ 1826	1,517,425	10.50	14.00	19.00	45.00	105.	300.	6.25
☐ 1826/25	Inc. Ab.	18.00	30.00	60.00	115.	250.	500.	10.50
☐ 1827	2,357,732	10.50	12.50	15.00	40.00	90.00	300.	6.25
☐ 1828	2,260,624	11.00	14.00	20.00	45.00	90.00	300.	6.50
☐ 1829	1,414,500	10.50	13.00	16.00	40.00	95.00	350.	6.25
☐ 1830	1,711,500	10.50	13.00	15.00	35.00	85.00	300.	6.25
☐ 1831	3,359,260	9.50	11.00	13.00	30.00	75.00	315.	5.75
☐ 1832	2,362,000	10.00	12.00	14.00	35.00	80.00	315.	6.00
☐ 1833	2,739,000	9.50	11.00	13.00	30.00	75.00	300.	5.75
☐ 1834	1,855,100	10.50	13.00	16.00	35.00	75.00	350.	6.25
☐ 1835	3,878,400	10.50	13.00	16.00	35.00	80.00	285.	6.25
☐ 1836	2,111,000	9.50	11.00	16.00	32.50	70.00	275.	5.75
☐ 1837	5,558,300	9.50	11.00	16.00	27.00	65.00	260.	5.75
☐ 1838	6,370,200	9.50	11.00	16.00	20.00	55.00	250.	5.75
☐ 1839	3,128,661	10.50	11.00	16.00	38.00	80.00	350.	6.25
☐ 1839/36	Inc. Ab.	125.	195.	300.	600.	1200.	—	75.00

Braided Hair

Date	Mintage	G-4	VG-8	F-12	VF-20	XF-40	MS-60	ABP
☐ 1840	2,462,700	9.50	10.00	11.50	19.00	58.00	250.	5.75
☐ 1841	1,597,367	9.50	11.00	13.00	23.00	68.00	275.	5.75
☐ 1842	2,383,390	9.50	10.00	11.50	18.00	55.00	250.	5.75

Small Date

Large Date

Large cents of 1840 and 1842 are known with both small and large dates, with little differential in value.

Date	Mintage	G-4	VG-8	F-12	VF-20	XF-40	MS-60	ABP
☐ 1843	2,425,342	9.50	12.50	17.00	25.00	65.00	250.	5.75
☐ 1843 Obverse 1842 With Reverse Of 1844								
	Inc. Ab.	10.00	18.00	35.00	45.00	80.00	350.	6.00

Date	Mintage	G-4	VG-8	F-12	VF-20	XF-40	MS-60	ABP
☐ 1844	2,398,752	9.00	9.75	11.00	17.00	49.00	250.	5.25
☐ 1844/81	Inc. Ab.	12.00	20.00	28.00	60.00	130.	450.	7.20
☐ 1845	3,894,804	9.00	9.50	10.00	15.00	45.00	250.	5.25
☐ 1846	4,120,800	9.00	9.50	10.00	15.00	45.00	250.	5.25
☐ 1847	6,183,669	9.00	9.50	10.00	15.00	45.00	250.	5.25
☐ 1848	6,415,799	9.00	9.50	10.00	15.00	45.00	250.	5.25
☐ 1849	4,178,500	9.00	9.50	10.00	16.50	45.00	275.	5.25
☐ 1850	4,426,844	9.00	9.50	10.00	15.00	45.00	275.	5.25
☐ 1851	9,889,707	9.00	9.50	10.00	15.00	45.00	275.	5.25
☐ 1851/81	Inc. Ab.	10.00	12.50	18.00	35.00	95.00	400.	6.00
☐ 1852	5,063,094	9.00	9.50	10.00	15.00	45.00	250.	5.25
☐ 1853	6,641,131	9.00	9.50	10.00	15.00	45.00	250.	5.25
☐ 1854	4,236,156	9.00	9.50	10.00	15.00	45.00	250.	5.25

Slanting 5's   Upright 5's

Large cents of 1855 and 1856 are known with both slanting and upright 5's, with little differential in value.

Date	Mintage	G-4	VG-8	F-12	VF-20	XF-40	MS-60	ABP
☐ 1855	1,574,829	9.00	9.50	10.00	15.00	45.00	250.	5.25
☐ 1856	2,690,463	9.00	9.50	10.00	15.00	45.00	250.	5.25
☐ 1857	333,456	20.00	25.00	32.00	42.00	65.00	300.	12.00

NOTE: Brilliant original uncirculated cents command substantially higher prices.

FLYING EAGLE CENTS

The short-lived Flying Eagle cent was conceived as the replacement for the large cent, offering the public a more convenient, cleaner and more durable coin than the old coppers. It was made of an alloy of 88 percent copper and 12 percent nickel; its 72 grain weight being less than half that of its predecessor, and 12 grains less than the half cent. In the strictest sense, the 1856 issue is a pattern, produced in large numbers so that the proposed new issue could be offered in sample form to legislators. A substantial quantity of the 1856 Flying Eagle cents eventually found their way into circulation.

Date	Mintage	G-4	VG-8	F-12	VF-20	XF-40	MS-60	MS-65	ABP
☐ 1856	Est. 1,000	825.	1100.	1450.	1750.	2100.	3800.	6600.	495.
☐ 1857	17,450,000	9.00	11.00	12.50	25.00	60.00	380.	1900.	5.25

Large Letters	Small Letters
AM Connected	AM Separated

Date	Mintage	G-4	VG-8	F-12	VF-20	XF-40	MS-60	MS-65	ABP
☐ 1858LL	24,600,000	9.00	11.00	12.50	25.00	60.00	380.	1900.	5.25
☐ 1858SL	Inc. Ab.	9.00	11.00	12.50	25.00	60.00	380.	1900.	5.25

INDIAN HEAD CENTS

After just two years of regular production, James B. Longacre's flying eagle design on the cent (which he had copied from Gobrecht's pattern dollars of 1836-39) was replaced by his more famous Indian head design. Two major changes were instituted during the life of this type; the first being in 1860 when, after one year of production, the laurel wreath reverse was replaced with an oak wreath and shield device. Then, in 1864, the metallic composition of the cent was changed to bronze and the weight reduced to 48 grains, in accordance with a law enacted on April 22, 1864, designed to halt the practice of cent hoarding during the Civil War.

1859   1860-1909   Mintmark

COPPER-NICKEL

Date	Mintage	G-4	VG-8	F-12	VF-20	XF-40	MS-60	MS-65	ABP
☐ 1859	36,400,000	5.00	6.00	9.00	20.00	60.00	380.	1900.	3.00
☐ 1860	20,566,000	3.50	4.75	7.00	12.00	22.00	225.	1200.	1.75
☐ 1861	10,100,000	8.00	10.00	16.50	23.00	40.00	325.	1300.	4.50
☐ 1862	28,075,000	3.00	3.50	5.75	8.50	19.00	200.	1125.	1.50
☐ 1863	49,840,000	2.75	3.50	4.75	7.50	17.00	170.	1000.	1.50
☐ 1864	13,740,000	7.00	8.00	12.50	18.00	32.00	250.	1300.	3.75

BRONZE

Date	Mintage	G-4	VG-8	F-12	VF-20	XF-40	MS-60	MS-65	ABP
☐ 1864	39,233,714	3.00	4.50	7.50	15.00	25.00	80.00	800.	1.50
☐ 1864L	Inc. Ab.	25.00	32.00	55.00	90.00	135.	400.	1700.	12.00

Designer Longacre's Initial added, 1864-1909.

Date	Mintage	G-4	VG-8	F-12	VF-20	XF-40	MS-60	MS-65	ABP
☐ 1865	35,429,286	2.75	3.25	6.50	20.00	30.00	100.	800.	1.50
☐ 1866	9,826,500	21.00	25.00	33.00	55.00	90.00	260.	1000.	12.00
☐ 1867	9,821,000	21.00	25.00	33.00	55.00	90.00	260.	1000.	12.00
☐ 1868	10,266,500	21.00	25.00	33.00	55.00	90.00	260.	1000.	12.00
☐ 1869/8	6,420,000	80.00	100.	215.	325.	480.	1150.	4000.	48.00
☐ 1869	Inc. Ab.	30.00	40.00	70.00	110.	160.	400.	1500.	18.00
☐ 1870	5,275,000	23.00	28.00	50.00	70.00	110.	280.	1325.	13.00
☐ 1871	3,929,500	27.00	35.00	57.00	75.00	100.	275.	1275.	16.00
☐ 1872	4,042,000	41.00	50.00	80.00	120.	165.	400.	1700.	24.00
☐ 1873	11,676,500	7.00	8.50	16.00	25.00	42.00	150.	1100.	4.00
☐ 1874	14,187,500	7.00	8.50	14.50	24.00	40.00	150.	750.	4.00
☐ 1875	13,528,000	7.00	8.50	14.50	.25.00	41.00	125.	750.	4.00
☐ 1876	7,944,000	10.50	13.00	22.50	30.00	50.00	180.	800.	6.00
☐ 1877	852,500	325.	350.	500.	650.	900.	1800.	5000.	195.
☐ 1878	5,799,850	10.50	13.00	25.00	40.00	55.00	200.	700.	6.00
☐ 1879	16,231,200	3.25	4.00	8.00	12.00	20.00	80.00	650.	2.00
☐ 1880	38,964,955	1.25	2.00	4.00	5.75	15.00	75.00	475.	.65
☐ 1881	39,211,575	1.25	2.00	3.50	5.75	15.00	75.00	450.	.65
☐ 1882	38,581,100	1.25	2.00	3.50	5.75	15.00	75.00	450.	.65
☐ 1883	45,589,109	1.25	2.00	3.50	5.75	15.00	75.00	450.	.65
☐ 1884	23,261,742	2.00	3.00	6.50	10.00	18.00	80.00	450.	1.00
☐ 1885	11,765,384	3.25	6.25	9.00	18.00	30.00	90.00	450.	2.00
☐ 1886	17,654,290	2.25	3.25	6.50	10.00	25.00	80.00	450.	1.00
☐ 1887	45,226,483	1.00	1.25	2.50	3.50	10.00	70.00	425.	.50
☐ 1888	37,494,414	1.00	1.25	2.50	3.50	10.00	70.00	425.	.50
☐ 1889	48,869,361	1.00	1.25	2.50	3.50	10.00	50.00	425.	.50
☐ 1890	57,182,854	.85	1.25	2.25	3.25	10.00	50.00	400.	.40
☐ 1891	47,072,350	.85	1.25	2.25	3.25	10.00	50.00	400.	.40
☐ 1892	37,649,832	.85	1.25	2.25	3.25	10.00	50.00	400.	.40
☐ 1893	46,642,195	.85	1.25	2.25	3.25	10.00	50.00	400.	.40
☐ 1894	16,752,132	1.75	4.00	7.00	10.00	19.00	70.00	500.	.90
☐ 1895	38,343,636	.85	1.00	1.75	3.75	7.50	50.00	390.	.40
☐ 1896	39,057,293	.85	1.00	1.75	3.75	7.50	50.00	390.	.40
☐ 1897	50,466,330	.85	1.00	1.50	3.00	7.50	50.00	390.	.40
☐ 1898	49,823,079	.85	1.00	1.50	3.00	7.50	50.00	390.	.40
☐ 1899	53,600,031	.85	1.00	1.50	3.00	7.50	50.00	390.	.40
☐ 1900	66,833,764	.80	.90	1.50	3.00	7.00	38.00	380.	.40
☐ 1901	79,611,143	.75	.85	1.50	2.75	7.00	38.00	380.	.40
☐ 1902	87,376,722	.75	.85	1.50	2.75	7.00	38.00	380.	.40
☐ 1903	85,094,493	.75	.85	1.50	2.75	7.00	38.00	380.	.40
☐ 1904	61,328,015	.75	.85	1.50	2.75	7.00	38.00	380.	.40
☐ 1905	80,719,163	.75	.85	1.50	2.75	7.00	38.00	380.	.40
☐ 1906	96,022,255	.75	.85	1.50	2.75	7.00	38.00	380.	.40
☐ 1907	108,138,618	.75	.85	1.50	2.75	7.00	38.00	380.	.40
☐ 1908	32,327,987	.75	.85	1.50	2.75	7.00	40.00	380.	.40
☐ 1908S	1,115,000	23.00	24.00	25.00	31.00	42.00	225.	1300.	13.00
☐ 1909	14,370,645	1.00	1.50	2.00	3.00	8.00	60.00	615.	.50
☐ 1909S	309,000	125.	170.	180.	200.	260.	500.	2000.	75.00

LINCOLN CENTS

In 1909, on the occasion of the 100th anniversary of Abraham Lincoln's birth, the introduction of Victor D. Brenner's Lincoln cent ended the life of the Indian head design at 50 years. In another 50 years a new reverse featuring Frank Gasparro's engraving of the Lincoln Memorial was mated to Brenner's obverse. In 1969, Mint artisans refurbished Brenner's Lincoln portrait which had deteriorated badly during 60 years of use.

Through the years the 95 percent copper, 5 percent tin and zinc cent alloy specified in the coinage law of April 22, 1864, was altered in its latter proportions, with tin being permanently eliminated after September 5, 1962. An order of the Secretary of the Treasury dated December 16, 1943, which carried through December 31, 1946, allowed the mint to produce its cents from salvaged shell cases. This action was taken after the zinc coated steel cent issue of 1943, which had lawful weights of both 41.5 and 42.5 grains, proved unsatisfactory.

1909-Date

V.D.B.

1909-1958

Mintmark

Date	Mintage	G-4	VG-8	F-12	VF-20	XF-40	MS-60	MS-65	ABP
☐ 1909	72,702,618	.30	.40	.50	.60	1.25	20.00	90.00	—
☐ 1909VDB	27,995,000	1.50	1.85	2.00	2.25	3.00	19.00	75.00	.75
☐ 1909S	1,825,000	50.00	55.00	60.00	75.00	100.	200.	600.	30.00
☐ 1909SVDB	484,000	350.	375.	425.	500.	600.	825.	1850.	210.
☐ 1910	146,801,218	.15	.25	.35	.50	1.50	20.00	75.00	—
☐ 1910S	6,045,000	7.75	8.50	9.75	11.00	19.00	80.00	400.	4.50
☐ 1911	101,177,787	.15	.30	.65	1.25	2.00	25.00	100.	—
☐ 1911D	12,672,000	2.50	3.50	4.50	9.00	17.50	90.00	450.	1.50
☐ 1911S	4,026,000	11.00	12.50	14.00	17.00	29.00	150.	575.	6.50
☐ 1912	68,153,060	.25	.45	1.65	3.75	6.00	30.00	125.	—
☐ 1912D	10,411,000	2.50	3.00	4.50	10.00	20.00	125.	450.	1.50
☐ 1912S	4,431,000	10.00	11.00	12.50	17.00	25.00	125.	515.	6.00
☐ 1913	76,532,352	.15	.35	1.25	2.00	5.75	40.00	125.	—
☐ 1913D	15,804,000	1.35	1.75	3.75	7.50	17.50	80.00	365.	.50
☐ 1913S	6,101,000	7.00	7.75	8.50	11.00	19.00	125.	625.	4.00
☐ 1914	75,238,432	.20	.35	1.25	3.00	4.50	100.	250.	—
☐ 1914D	1,193,000	90.00	105.	125.	185.	365.	1175.	2975.	54.00
☐ 1914S	4,137,000	8.75	9.75	11.00	18.00	26.00	250.	3100.	4.25
☐ 1915	29,092,120	.75	1.00	4.25	9.00	25.00	120.	350.	.30
☐ 1915D	22,050,000	.50	.80	1.05	5.00	11.00	50.00	325.	.25
☐ 1915S	4,833,000	7.75	8.50	9.00	12.00	20.00	95.00	625.	4.50
☐ 1916	131,833,677	.15	.20	.35	.75	3.00	15.00	100.	—
☐ 1916D	35,956,000	.25	.50	1.00	1.50	5.50	40.00	290.	—
☐ 1916S	22,510,000	.75	1.00	1.25	1.50	5.50	85.00	350.	.30
☐ 1917	196,429,785	.15	.20	.35	.60	2.00	20.00	100.	—
☐ 1917D	55,120,000	.25	.45	.65	2.75	4.50	75.00	335.	—
☐ 1917S	32,620,000	.25	.45	.65	2.50	4.00	85.00	400.	—
☐ 1918	288,104,634	.15	.20	.35	.60	2.00	20.00	95.00	—
☐ 1918D	47,830,000	.25	.45	.60	2.25	5.00	75.00	375.	—
☐ 1918S	34,680,000	.25	.45	.60	2.25	5.00	85.00	325.	—

Date	Mintage	G-4	VG-8	F-12	VF-20	XF-40	MS-60	MS-65	ABP
☐ 1919	392,021,000	.15	.20	.30	.50	1.75	15.00	90.00	—
☐ 1919D	57,154,000	.20	.30	.65	2.75	5.25	45.00	300.	—
☐ 1919S	139,760,000	.20	.30	.40	.75	2.00	65.00	325.	—
☐ 1920	310,165,000	.15	.20	.30	.50	1.75	20.00	80.00	—
☐ 1920D	49,280,000	.15	.20	.55	1.25	4.00	60.00	375.	—
☐ 1920S	46,220,000	.15	.20	.50	1.25	4.00	95.00	475.	—
☐ 1921	39,157,000	.20	.25	.50	1.00	4.25	65.00	195.	—
☐ 1921S	15,274,000	.60	.75	1.00	2.25	9.00	225.	1100.	.25
☐ 1922D	7,160,000	4.00	4.50	5.50	7.50	12.00	65.00	450.	2.50
☐ 1922	Inc. Ab.	240.	275.	350.	425.	700.	3100.	13,000.	145.
☐ 1923	74,723,000	.15	.20	.35	.60	2.00	20.00	65.00	—
☐ 1923S	8,700,000	1.50	1.75	2.25	4.00	10.00	250.	1500.	.75
☐ 1924	75,178,000	.15	.20	.35	.60	3.50	50.00	180.	—
☐ 1924D	2,520,000	8.25	9.00	11.00	13.00	35.00	250.	1175.	5.00
☐ 1924S	11,696,000	.50	.75	1.00	2.25	6.50	150.	650.	.25
☐ 1925	139,949,000	.15	.20	.35	.60	2.00	15.00	65.00	—
☐ 1925D	22,580,000	.25	.35	.55	1.10	4.00	50.00	240.	—
☐ 1925S	26,380,000	.15	.25	.40	1.00	3.00	85.00	500.	—
☐ 1926	157,088,000	.15	.20	.35	.50	2.00	15.00	80.00	—
☐ 1926D	28,020,000	.20	.25	.45	.80	3.00	70.00	375.	—
☐ 1926S	4,550,000	2.75	3.25	4.50	6.00	9.50	200.	750.	1.90
☐ 1927	144,440,000	.15	.20	.30	.40	2.00	15.00	55.00	—
☐ 1927D	27,170,000	.15	.20	.30	.40	2.50	45.00	230.	—
☐ 1927S	14,276,000	.25	.35	.50	1.65	4.00	85.00	360.	—
☐ 1928	134,116,000	.15	.20	.30	.40	1.50	15.00	55.00	—
☐ 1928D	31,170,000	.20	.25	.30	.60	1.50	30.00	160.	—
☐ 1928S	17,266,000	.25	.30	.35	.65	2.00	80.00	340.	—
☐ 1929	185,262,000	.15	.20	.30	.40	1.25	15.00	45.00	—
☐ 1929D	41,730,000	.15	.20	.30	.40	1.25	20.00	70.00	—
☐ 1929S	50,148,000	.15	.20	.30	.40	1.25	17.00	70.00	—
☐ 1930	157,415,000	.10	.15	.20	.30	1.00	15.00	38.00	—
☐ 1930D	40,100,000	.10	.15	.20	.40	1.00	15.00	44.00	—
☐ 1930S	24,286,000	.10	.15	.20	.40	1.00	20.00	65.00	—
☐ 1931	19,396,000	.20	.25	.30	.40	1.50	20.00	80.00	—
☐ 1931D	4,480,000	2.25	2.50	2.75	3.50	4.75	55.00	310.	1.65
☐ 1931S	866,000	33.00	35.00	37.50	43.00	50.00	85.00	270.	18.00
☐ 1932	9,062,000	1.25	1.50	1.75	2.00	2.75	19.00	85.00	.75
☐ 1932D	10,500,000	.65	.75	1.25	2.00	2.50	18.00	90.00	.25
☐ 1933	14,360,000	.50	.60	.70	.90	2.00	16.00	100.	.20
☐ 1933D	6,200,000	1.85	2.00	2.25	2.75	4.00	20.00	115.	1.00
☐ 1934	219,080,000	.10	.15	.20	.30	.50	5.00	12.00	—
☐ 1934D	28,446,000	.15	.20	.25	.30	1.00	20.00	60.00	—
☐ 1935	245,338,000	—	.10	.15	.20	.25	3.80	5.50	—
☐ 1935D	47,000,000	.15	.20	.25	.30	.45	5.00	16.00	—
☐ 1935S	38,702,000	.15	.20	.25	.30	.45	10.00	30.00	—
☐ 1936	309,637,569	—	.10	.15	.20	.25	1.70	3.00	—
☐ 1936D	40,620,000	.15	.20	.25	.30	.35	2.00	5.50	—
☐ 1936S	29,130,000	.15	.20	.25	.30	.35	2.25	5.50	—
☐ 1937	309,179,320	—	—	.10	.15	.20	1.75	5.00	—
☐ 1937D	50,430,000	—	.10	.15	.20	.25	1.50	4.50	—
☐ 1937S	34,500,000	—	.10	.15	.20	.25	1.70	3.50	—
☐ 1938	156,696,734	—	—	—	.10	.15	2.20	3.75	—
☐ 1938D	20,010,000	.15	.20	.25	.30	.50	3.00	6.00	—
☐ 1938S	15,180,000	.20	.30	.40	.50	.60	2.40	5.50	—
☐ 1939	316,479,520	—	—	—	.10	.15	1.25	2.00	—
☐ 1939D	15,160,000	.30	.35	.50	.60	.75	4.00	9.00	—
☐ 1939S	52,070,000	—	.10	.15	.20	.25	1.80	3.75	—

Date	Mintage	G-4	VG-8	F-12	VF-20	XF-40	MS-60	MS-65	ABP
☐ 1940	586,825,872	—	—	—	.10	.15	1.00	1.50	—
☐ 1940D	81,390,000	—	—	—	.10	.15	2.50	3.75	—
☐ 1940S	112,940,000	—	—	—	.10	.15	1.50	2.25	—
☐ 1941	887,039,100	—	—	—	.10	.15	1.60	2.35	—
☐ 1941D	128,700,000	—	—	—	.10	.15	3.25	5.50	—
☐ 1941S	92,360,000	—	—	—	.10	.15	4.50	11.50	—
☐ 1942	657,828,600	—	—	—	.10	.15	.75	1.00	—
☐ 1942D	206,698,000	—	—	—	.10	.15	.75	1.40	—
☐ 1942S	85,590,000	—	—	—	.15	.25	5.50	10.00	—

Date	Mintage	MS-60	ABP
☐ 1943	684,628,670	1.20	—
☐ 1943D	217,660,000	2.20	—
☐ 1943S	191,550,000	5.00	—
☐ 1944	1,435,400,000	.40	—
☐ 1944D	430,578,000	1.00	—
☐ 1944D, D/S	—	225.	35.00
☐ 1944S	282,760,000	.75	—
☐ 1945	1,040,515,000	.30	—
☐ 1945D	226,268,000	.80	—
☐ 1945S	181,770,000	.50	—
☐ 1946	991,655,000	.30	—
☐ 1946D	315,690,000	.35	—
☐ 1946S	198,100,000	.85	—
☐ 1947	190,555,000	.85	—
☐ 1947D	194,750,000	.70	—
☐ 1947S	99,000,000	.75	—
☐ 1948	317,570,000	.75	—
☐ 1948D	172,637,000	.80	—
☐ 1948S	81,735,000	1.00	—
☐ 1949	217,775,000	1.50	—
☐ 1949D	153,132,000	.90	—
☐ 1949S	64,290,000	2.50	—
☐ 1950	272,686,386	.90	—
☐ 1950D	334,950,000	.70	—
☐ 1950S	118,505,000	.60	—
☐ 1951	295,633,500	.75	—
☐ 1951D	625,355,000	.35	—
☐ 1951S	136,010,000	1.70	—
☐ 1952	186,856,980	.60	—
☐ 1952D	746,130,000	.25	—
☐ 1952S	137,800,004	1.00	—
☐ 1953	256,883,800	.20	—
☐ 1953D	700,515,000	.20	—
☐ 1953S	181,835,000	.45	—
☐ 1954	71,873,350	.45	—
☐ 1954D	251,552,500	.25	—
☐ 1954S	96,190,000	.35	—

Date	Mintage	MS-60	ABP
☐ 1955	330,958,000	.20	—
☐ 1955D	563,257,500	.20	—
☐ 1955S	44,610,000	.60	—
☐ 1956	421,414,384	.15	—
☐ 1956D	1,098,201,100	.15	—
☐ 1957	283,787,952	.15	—
☐ 1957D	1,051,342,000	.15	—
☐ 1958	253,400,652	.15	—
☐ 1958D	800,953,300	.15	—

LINCOLN MEMORIAL REVERSE INTRODUCED 1959

Date	Mintage	MS-60	ABP
☐ 1959	610,864,291	.15	—
☐ 1959D	1,279,760,000	.15	—

Small Date

Large Date

Date	Mintage	MS-60	ABP
☐ 1960SD	588,096,602	4.50	1.00
☐ 1960LD	Inc. Ab.	.10	—
☐ 1960D SD	1,580,884,000	.30	—
☐ 1960D LD	Inc. Ab.	.15	—
☐ 1961	756,373,244	.10	—

1955 Double Die

Date	VF-20	XF-40	ABP
☐ 1955 Double Die	425.	465.	225.

Date	Mintage	MS-60	ABP		Date	Mintage	MS-60	ABP
□ 1961D	1,753,266,700	.10	—		□ 1963D	1,774,020,400	.10	—
□ 1962	609,263,019	.10	—		□ 1964	2,652,525,762	.10	—
□ 1962D	1,793,148,400	.10	—		□ 1964D	3,799,071,500	.10	—
□ 1963	757,185,645	.10	—					

Commencing 1965 — See Modern Singles — Page 117

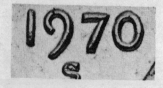

Large Date

Small Date

Date	MS-60	ABP		Date	MS-60	ABP
□ 1970S LD	.15	—		1970S SD	10.00	5.00

Date	MS-60	ABP
□ 1972 Double Die	325.	195.

HANDLING COINS

In addition to possessing the greatly improved ability to house his collection, today's collector has a number of other aids at his disposal which allow him to better enjoy the hobby.

There are even tongs and vinyl gloves for handling coins. Such devices are particularly useful in the handling of uncirculated and proof coins, as their use prevents the deposit of oils from the hands, which cause tarnishing. All coins, but particularly uncirculated and proof specimens, should be handled with utmost care, and this includes gripping them by the edge to prevent marring the surface. No collector's coin, regardless of its condition, should be held except by the edge.

This rule on handling is an important one to remember; even for those who begin collecting by removing coins from circulation, some of which may be quite valuable, as it will prevent needless damage and loss of value when the individual graduates to the selection of more choice pieces.

TWO CENT

Authorized by the same law which provided for the change to a bronze composition for the cent, the two cent piece had a weight (96 grains) exactly twice that of the cent. It served to fill the vital need for small change in expediting the replacement of monetary substitutes then in circulation, but soon outlived its usefulness, and its issue was halted by the major revision in the nation's coinage laws instituted in 1873. This coin, at the instigation of the Reverend Mark R. Watkinson, with the support of Lincoln's Secretary of the Treasury Salmon P. Chase, became the first to carry the motto "In God We Trust".

Date	Mintage	G-4	VG-8	F-12	VF-20	XF-40	MS-60	ABP
☐ 1864SM	42.00	55.00	80.00	100.	165.	220.	500.	30.00
☐ 1864LM	Inc. Ab.	5.00	6.00	7.50	12.50	28.00	215.	3.00

SMALL MOTTO

LARGE MOTTO

Date	Mintage	G-4	VG-8	F-12	VF-20	XF-40	MS-60	ABP
☐ 1865	13,640,000	4.00	4.50	6.00	12.50	28.00	215.	2.50
☐ 1866	3,177,000	4.50	5.00	7.00	12.50	30.00	230.	2.50
☐ 1867	2,938,750	4.50	5.00	6.00	12.50	30.00	230.	2.50
☐ 1868	2,803,750	4.75	5.50	6.00	12.50	30.00	230.	2.75
☐ 1869	1,546,500	5.50	6.50	8.50	14.50	35.00	250.	3.25
☐ 1870	861,250	6.50	8.00	50.00	28.00	50.00	325.	4.00
☐ 1871	721,250	8.00	10.00	17.00	35.00	65.00	350.	4.50
☐ 1872	65,000	75.00	95.00	145.	220.	325.	900.	40.00
☐ 1873	Est. 1100	—	—	Proof	Only	—	—	—

THREE CENT SILVER

Although the denomination seems today to be quite odd, it was a well conceived issue which gained immediate public popularity. During the first three years of issue it was produced at a then unbelievable rate of about a million examples per month (half dimes of the period were being produced at a rate of substantially less than a million pieces per year).

Mintmark

TYPE 1 - NO OUTLINES TO STAR

Date	Mintage	G-4	VG-8	F-12	VF-20	XF-40	MS-60	ABP
☐ 1851	5,447,400	8.00	10.00	12.00	24.00	50.00	380.	4.75
☐ 1851O	720,000	12.00	15.00	24.00	45.00	75.00	600.	7.25
☐ 1852	18,663,500	8.00	10.00	12.50	24.00	50.00	380.	4.75
☐ 1853	11,400,000	8.00	10.00	12.50	24.00	50.00	380.	4.75

TYPE 2 - THREE OUTLINES TO STAR

Date	Mintage	G-4	VG-8	F-12	VF-20	XF-40	MS-60	ABP
☐ 1854	671,000	11.50	14.00	20.00	30.00	80.00	535.	6.50
☐ 1855	139,000	15.00	20.00	32.50	50.00	140.	900.	9.00
☐ 1856	1,458,000	11.50	14.50	20.00	30.00	80.00	535.	6.00
☐ 1857	1,042,000	11.50	14.50	20.00	30.00	80.00	535.	6.00
☐ 1858	1,604,000	11.50	14.50	20.00	30.00	80.00	535.	6.00

TYPE 3 - TWO OUTLINES TO STAR

Date	Mintage	G-4	VG-8	F-12	VF-20	XF-40	MS-60	ABP
☐ 1859	365,000	13.50	15.00	20.00	35.00	60.00	380.	7.50
☐ 1860	287,000	13.50	15.00	20.00	35.00	60.00	380.	7.50
☐ 1861	498,000	13.50	15.00	20.00	35.00	60.00	380.	7.50
☐ 1862	343,550	13.50	15.00	20.00	35.00	60.00	380.	7.50
☐ 1863	21,460	—	—	—	—	275.	500.	165.
☐ 1864	12,470	—	—	—	—	285.	525.	170.
☐ 1865	8,500	—	—	—	—	295.	575.	175.
☐ 1866	22,725	—	—	—	—	275.	525.	165.
☐ 1867	4,625	—	—	—	—	325.	575.	195.
☐ 1868	4,100	—	—	—	—	325.	575.	195.
☐ 1869	5,100	—	—	—	—	295.	575.	175.
☐ 1870	4,000	—	—	—	—	325.	575.	195.
☐ 1871	4,360	—	—	—	—	325.	575.	195.
☐ 1872	1,950	—	—	—	—	325.	675.	195.
☐ 1873	600	—	—	Proof	Only	—	—	—

THREE CENT NICKEL

Faced with the fact that the silver trime was not circulating, the Congress moved in an act dated March 3, 1865, to authorize the introduction of a nickel composition three cent piece. The series enjoyed an uneventful history stretching over 25 years, although the annual quantities of issue after 1874 were largely insignificant. When the series was closed out in 1889, the quantities produced in any of the last 13 years exceeded 41,200 only in 1881 when over a million examples were offered.

Date	Mintage	G-4	VG-8	F-12	VF-20	XF-40	MS-60	ABP
☐ 1865	11,382,000	6.00	6.50	7.50	11.00	21.00	215.	3.50
☐ 1866	4,801,000	6.00	6.50	7.50	11.00	21.00	215.	3.50
☐ 1867	3,915,000	6.00	6.50	7.50	11.00	21.00	215.	3.50
☐ 1868	3,252,000	6.00	6.50	7.50	11.00	21.00	215.	3.50
☐ 1869	1,604,000	6.00	7.00	8.50	11.00	21.00	215.	3.50
☐ 1870	1,335,000	6.50	7.50	9.00	12.00	21.00	225.	3.75
☐ 1871	604,000	6.50	7.50	9.75	12.50	22.50	250.	3.75
☐ 1872	862,000	6.50	7.50	9.75	12.50	22.50	250.	3.75
☐ 1873	1,173,000	6.50	7.50	9.00	12.00	21.50	215.	3.75
☐ 1874	790,000	6.50	7.50	9.00	12.00	21.00	215.	3.75
☐ 1875	228,000	7.50	9.75	13.50	18.50	30.00	275.	4.00
☐ 1876	162,000	11.00	13.50	16.00	20.00	31.50	275.	6.00
☐ 1877	Est. 900	—	—	Proof	Only	—	—	1500.
	Impaired Proof	600.		650.	725.	850.	—	—
☐ 1878	2,350	—	—	Proof	Only	—	—	950.
	Impaired Proof	215.		235.	265.	300.	—	—
☐ 1879	41,200	72.50	82.50	95.00	110.	125.	400.	42.00
☐ 1880	24,955	90.00	97.50	110.	135.	165.	500.	54.00
☐ 1881	1,080,575	6.00	6.50	7.50	10.00	19.50	215.	3.50
☐ 1882	25,300	85.00	92.50	100.	120.	150.	500.	50.00
☐ 1883	10,609	200.	225.	260.	300.	350.	650.	120.
☐ 1884	5,642	385.	425.	485.	525.	575.	800.	230.
☐ 1885	4,790	550.	600.	650.	700.	800.	1200.	330.
☐ 1886	4,290	—	—	Proof	Only	—	—	800.
	Impaired Proof	575.		625.	675.	725.	—	325.
☐ 1887/6	7,961	—	—	Proof	Only	—	—	500.
	Impaired Proof	650.		725.	775.	850.	—	375.
☐ 1887	Inc. Ab.	325.	350.	375.	410.	450.	600.	195.
☐ 1888	41,083	65.00	72.50	85.00	95.00	110.	425.	39.00
☐ 1889	21,561	85.00	92.50	100.	115.	140.	475.	50.00

HALF DIMES

These were the silver predecessors of today's nickel. The basic history of this series throughout its 80 year mintage closely parallels that of its sister fractional silver issues of the period, excepting the fact that its coinage was suspended during the years 1806 through 1828. Although the first issue is dated 1794, it was not produced until early the following year.

Originally authorized, like the nation's other silver coins, as a .8924 fine issue with a proportionate weight of 20.8 grains, the fineness was increased to .900 and the grain weight reduced to 20-5/8 by a January 18, 1837, law which similarly influenced the other denominations. The weight of the coin was reduced more substantially to 19.2 grains by the February 21, 1853, coinage law. To emphasize this change arrows were placed either side of the date on the affected 1853 coins, and all issues of 1854 and 1855. The half dime series was terminated as a result of the coinage law revisions of 1873, eight years after the first nickel five cent piece was issued.

Flowing Hair Half-Dimes

Date		Mintage	G-4	VG-8	F-12	VF-20	XF-40	MS-60	ABP
☐	1794	86.416	1450.	1850.	3375.	4850.	6500.	12,000.	850.
☐	1795	Inc. Ab.	1250.	1500.	2500.	4000.	5500.	10,000.	750.

Draped Bust Half-Dimes

Date		Mintage	G-4	VG-8	F-12	VF-20	XF-40	MS-60	ABP
☐	1796	10,230	1175.	1500.	2400.	3600.	5100.	11,600.	700.
☐	1796 Liberty	Inc. Ab.	1175.	1500.	2450.	3700.	5300.	—	700.
☐	1796/5	Inc. Ab.	1250.	1650.	2750.	4000.	5500.	13,000.	750.
☐	1797 13 Stars	44,527	1200.	1700.	2800.	4500.	6500.	17,500.	725.
☐	1797 15 Stars	Inc. Ab.	1175.	1500.	2650.	3600.	5100.	11,600.	700.
☐	1797 16 Stars	Inc. Ab.	1175.	1500.	2650.	3600.	5100.	11,600.	700.

LIBEKTY

HERALDIC EAGLE INTRODUCED

Date	Mintage	G-4	VG-8	F-12	VF-20	XF-40	MS-60	ABP
☐ 1800	24,000	850.	1200.	1650.	2750.	4500.	10,750.	500.
☐ 1800 Libekty	Inc. Ab.	850.	1200.	1650.	2750.	4500.	10,750.	500.
☐ 1801	33,910	900.	1300.	1650.	2750.	5000.	13,000.	525.
☐ 1802	13,010	2950.	3500.	8000.	12,000.	45,000.	—	1700.
☐ 1803	37,850	850.	1200.	1650.	2750.	4500.	10,750.	500.
☐ 1805	15,600	1000.	1500.	2500.	3500.	6500.	—	600.

Liberty Cap Half-Dimes

Date	Mintage	G-4	VG-8	F-12	VF-20	XF-40	MS-60	ABP
☐ 1829	1,230,000	16.00	18.00	25.00	50.00	125.	630.	9.50
☐ 1830	1,240,000	16.00	18.00	25.00	50.00	125.	630.	9.50
☐ 1831	1,242,700	16.00	18.00	25.00	50.00	125.	630.	9.50
☐ 1832	965,000	16.00	18.00	25.00	50.00	125.	630.	9.50
☐ 1833	1,370,000	16.00	18.00	25.00	50.00	125.	630.	9.50
☐ 1834	1,480,000	16.00	18.00	25.00	50.00	125.	630.	9.50
☐ 1835 Large Date, Large 5C.	2,760,000	16.00	18.00	25.00	50.00	125.	630.	9.50
☐ 1835 Large Date, Small 5C.	Inc. Ab.	16.00	18.00	25.00	50.00	125.	630.	9.50
☐ 1835 Small Date, Large 5C.	Inc. Ab.	16.00	18.00	25.00	50.00	125.	630.	9.50
☐ 1835 Small Date, Small 5C.	Inc. Ab.	16.00	18.00	25.00	50.00	125.	630.	9.50
☐ 1836 Large 5C.	1,900,000	16.00	18.00	25.00	50.00	125.	630.	9.50
☐ 1836 Sm. 5C.	I.A.	16.00	18.00	25.00	50.00	125.	630.	9.50
☐ 1837 Large 5C.	2,276,000	16.00	18.00	25.00	50.00	125.	630.	9.50
☐ 1837 Sm. 5C.	I.A.	22.00	30.00	55.00	85.00	150.	700.	12.00

MINTMARK ABOVE AND BELOW WREATH TIE

Liberty Seated Half-Dimes

WITHOUT STARS AROUND RIM

Date	Mintage	G-4	VG-8	F-12	VF-20	XF-40	MS-60	ABP
☐ 1837 Sm. Date	Inc. Ab.	40.00	55.00	80.00	150.	400.	950.	36.00
☐ 1837 Lg. Date	Inc. Ab.	24.00	35.00	45.00	85.00	225.	785.	14.00
☐ 1838O	70,000	125.	175.	300.	500.	1000.	—	75.00

STARS ADDED AROUND RIM

Date	Mintage	G-4	VG-8	F-12	VF-20	XF-40	MS-60	ABP
☐ 1838	2,255,000	7.00	9.00	10.00	20.00	50.00	600.	4.25

Date	Mintage	G-4	VG-8	F-12	VF-20	XF-40	MS-60	ABP
☐ 1838 sm.stars	Inc. Ab.	20.00	30.00	50.00	80.00	200.	1200.	12.00
☐ 1839	1,069,150	7.00	9.00	10.00	20.00	50.00	600.	4.25
☐ 1839O	1,034,039	15.00	18.00	25.00	45.00	90.00	975.	9.00
☐ 1839O Rev. 1838O		75.00	100.	175.	250.	500.	—	40.00
☐ 1840	1,344,085	7.00	9.00	10.00	20.00	60.00	600.	4.25
☐ 1840O	935,000	15.00	20.00	30.00	50.00	100.	1000.	9.00

Without Drapery   With Drapery

DRAPERY ADDED TO LIBERTY

Date	Mintage	G-4	VG-8	F-12	VF-20	XF-40	MS-60	ABP
☐ 1840	Inc. Ab.	50.00	75.00	200.	400.	650.	1800.	30.00
☐ 1840O	Inc. Ab.	40.00	60.00	200.	400.	750.	—	24.00
☐ 1841	1,150,000	10.00	15.00	20.00	35.00	70.00	430.	6.00
☐ 1841O	815,000	12.00	18.00	25.00	40.00	85.00	650.	7.00
☐ 1842	815,000	10.00	15.00	20.00	35.00	60.00	430.	6.00
☐ 1842O	350,000	35.00	60.00	125.	225.	500.	—	21.00
☐ 1843	1,165,000	10.00	15.00	20.00	35.00	60.00	430.	6.00
☐ 1844	430,000	10.00	15.00	20.00	35.00	60.00	430.	6.00
☐ 1844O	220,000	100.	150.	350.	650.	1500.	—	60.00
☐ 1845	1,564,000	10.00	15.00	20.00	35.00	60.00	430.	6.00
☐ 1845/1845	Inc. Ab.	20.00	30.00	50.00	90.00	175.	550.	12.00
☐ 1846	27,000	135.	225.	275.	475.	875.	—	80.00
☐ 1847	1,274,000	10.00	15.00	20.00	35.00	60.00	430.	6.00
☐ 1848 Medium Date								
	668,000	10.00	15.00	20.00	35.00	70.00	430.	6.00
☐ 1848 Lg. Date	Inc. Ab.	15.00	20.00	30.00	60.00	120.	600.	9.00
☐ 1848O	600,000	15.00	20.00	30.00	60.00	120.	800.	9.00
☐ 1849/8	1,309,000	18.00	25.00	30.00	45.00	90.00	700.	10.00
☐ 1849/6	Inc. Ab.	12.00	18.00	25.00	40.00	80.00	650.	7.00
☐ 1849	Inc. Ab.	10.00	15.00	20.00	35.00	70.00	600.	6.00
☐ 1849O	140,000	45.00	55.00	125.	375.	700.	—	27.00
☐ 1850	955,000	10.00	15.00	20.00	35.00	70.00	600.	6.00
☐ 1850O	690,000	15.00	20.00	30.00	45.00	90.00	800.	9.00
☐ 1851	781,000	10.00	15.00	20.00	35.00	70.00	600.	6.00
☐ 1851O	860,000	12.00	18.00	30.00	50.00	100.	800.	7.00
☐ 1852	1,000,500	10.00	15.00	20.00	35.00	70.00	430.	6.00
☐ 1852O	260,000	40.00	60.00	100.	175.	350.	—	24.00
☐ 1853	135,000	30.00	50.00	75.00	125.	200.	800.	18.00
☐ 1853O	160,000	115.	135.	250.	400.	800.	—	70.00

ARROWS AT DATE

Date	Mintage	G-4	VG-8	F-12	VF-20	XF-40	MS-60	ABP
☐ 1853	13,210,020	5.50	8.00	8.50	17.00	44.00	440.	3.50
☐ 1853O	2,200,000	10.00	12.00	15.00	35.00	80.00	450.	6.00

Date	Mintage	G-4	VG-8	F-12	VF-20	XF-40	MS-60	ABP
☐ 1854	5,740,000	7.00	8.00	9.00	17.00	50.00	440.	4.25
☐ 1854O	1,560,000	15.00	20.00	30.00	60.00	120.	900.	9.00
☐ 1855	1,750,000	7.00	8.00	9.00	17.00	50.00	440.	4.25
☐ 1855O	600,000	20.00	30.00	50.00	75.00	125.	1000.	12.00

ARROWS AT DATE REMOVED

Date	Mintage	G-4	VG-8	F-12	VF-20	XF-40	MS-60	ABP
☐ 1856	4,880,000	6.00	7.25	8.75	18.00	40.00	430.	3.50
☐ 1856O	1,100,000	15.00	20.00	30.00	60.00	100.	600.	9.00
☐ 1857	7,280,000	6.00	7.25	8.75	18.00	40.00	430.	3.50
☐ 1857O	1,380,000	15.00	20.00	30.00	60.00	100.	600.	9.00
☐ 1858	3,500,000	6.00	7.25	8.75	18.00	40.00	430.	3.50
☐ 1858 Inverted Date	Inc. Ab.	30.00	35.00	70.00	115.	225.	700.	18.00
☐ 1858 Double Date	Inc. Ab.	40.00	60.00	80.00	200.	400.	1200.	25.00
☐ 1858O	1,660,000	15.00	20.00	30.00	60.00	100.	600.	9.00
☐ 1859	340,000	15.00	25.00	50.00	65.00	130.	430.	9.00
☐ 1859O	560,000	15.00	20.00	30.00	75.00	125.	700.	9.00

TRANSITIONAL PATTERNS

Date	Mintage	G-4	VG-8	F-12	VF-20	XF-40	MS-60	ABP
☐ 1859 Obverse Of 1859, Reverse 1860					—	—	—	—
☐ 1860 Obverse Of 1859, Reverse 1860					—	—	4000.	—

Mintmark   ONLY 1871-72

OBVERSE LEGEND REPLACES STARS

Date	Mintage	G-4	VG-8	F-12	VF-20	XF-40	MS-60	ABP
☐ 1860	799,000	5.50	7.00	8.00	14.00	31.50	360.	3.00
☐ 1860O	1,060,000	5.50	7.00	25.00	35.00	60.00	420.	3.00
☐ 1861	3,361,000	5.50	7.00	8.00	14.00	31.50	360.	3.00
☐ 1861/0	Inc. Ab.	20.00	30.00	60.00	120.	250.	800.	12.00
☐ 1862	1,492,550	5.50	7.00	8.00	14.00	31.50	360.	3.00
☐ 1863	18,460	100.	125.	175.	225.	400.	800.	60.00
☐ 1863S	100,000	15.00	20.00	30.00	65.00	150.	900.	9.00
☐ 1864	48,470	250.	300.	375.	425.	650.	1200.	150.
☐ 1864S	90,000	25.00	35.00	95.00	150.	300.	1200.	15.00
☐ 1865	13,500	150.	175.	200.	275.	500.	900.	90.00
☐ 1865S	120,000	15.00	20.00	30.00	75.00	200.	975.	9.00
☐ 1866	10,725	175.	200.	250.	350.	525.	1000.	100.
☐ 1866S	120,000	15.00	20.00	30.00	75.00	200.	950.	9.00
☐ 1867	8,625	200.	225.	300.	375.	600.	1100.	120.
☐ 1867S	120,000	15.00	20.00	35.00	70.00	200.	900.	9.00
☐ 1868	89,200	40.00	65.00	95.00	150.	250.	600.	24.00
☐ 1868S	280,000	15.00	20.00	25.00	40.00	80.00	500.	9.00
☐ 1869	208,600	15.00	20.00	30.00	50.00	95.00	475.	9.00
☐ 1869S	230,000	15.00	20.00	25.00	40.00	80.00	500.	9.00
☐ 1870	536,600	10.00	15.00	20.00	30.00	60.00	450.	6.00

Date	Mintage	G-4	VG-8	F-12	VF-20	XF-40	MS-60	ABP
☐ 1870S	Unique, 1	Known	In	Unc.	Private	Sale,	Apr.1980	$425,000.
☐ 1871	1,873.960	5.50	7.00	8.00	30.00	60.00	425.	3.00
☐ 1871S	161.000	20.00	30.00	50.00	85.00	170.	675.	12.00
☐ 1872	2,947.950	5.50	7.00	8.00	30.00	60.00	425.	3.00
☐ 1872S Mintmark In Wreath								
	837.000	10.00	15.00	20.00	30.00	50.00	425.	6.00
☐ 1872S Mintmark Below Wreath								
	Inc. Ab.	10.00	15.00	20.00	30.00	60.00	450.	6.00
☐ 1873	712.600	5.50	7.00	8.00	30.00	70.00	425.	3.00
☐ 1873S	324.000	10.00	15.00	20.00	30.00	60.00	475.	6.00

SHIELD NICKELS

Issue of the nickel-composition five-cent coin was authorized by an Act of May 16, 1866, as a companion coin to the smaller three-cent nickel authorized a little over a year earlier. Originally approved as a substitute for the silver half dime during the period following the Civil War when specie payments were suspended, the five-cent nickel ultimately brought on the demise of its silver counterpart. The Shield nickel designs were the work of the Mint's chief engraver, James B. Longacre.

Date	Mintage	G-4	VG-8	F-12	VF-20	XF-40	MS-60	ABP
☐ 1866	14,742.500	11.50	14.00	25.00	35.00	115.	600.	6.50
☐ 1867 With Rays								
	2,019.000	13.50	16.50	27.00	40.00	125.	280.	8.00
☐ 1867 Without Rays								
	28,890.500	7.50	9.00	12.50	17.50	30.00	250.	4.50
☐ 1868	28,817.000	7.50	9.00	12.50	17.50	30.00	250.	4.50
☐ 1869	16,395.000	7.50	9.00	12.50	17.50	30.00	250.	4.50
☐ 1870	4,806.000	10.00	11.50	14.50	20.00	35.00	300.	6.00
☐ 1871	561.000	33.00	38.00	45.00	60.00	95.00	400.	19.50
☐ 1872	6,036.000	10.00	11.50	14.50	20.00	40.00	250.	6.00
☐ 1873	4,550.000	10.00	11.50	14.50	20.00	40.00	300.	6.00
☐ 1874	3,538.000	10.00	12.00	16.00	22.50	40.00	290.	6.00
☐ 1875	2,097.000	12.00	15.00	20.00	30.00	50.00	300.	7.25
☐ 1876	2,530.000	11.50	14.00	20.00	28.00	47.00	300.	6.50
☐ 1877	Est. 500	—	—	Proof	Only	—	—	2100.
	Impaired Proof	1000.	1250.	1500.	1950.		—	600.
☐ 1878	2,350	—	—	Proof	Only	—	—	600.
	Impaired Proof	350.	475.	575.	695.		—	200.
☐ 1879	29,100	245.	295.	395.	450.	550.	800.	145.
☐ 1880	19,995	285.	345.	400.	465.	595.	975.	170.
☐ 1881	72,375	225.	265.	325.	385.	445.	750.	135.
☐ 1882	11,476.600	7.50	9.00	12.50	17.50	30.00	250.	4.50
☐ 1883	1,456.919	10.00	11.00	12.50	17.50	30.00	250.	6.00

LIBERTY HEAD NICKELS

Charles E. Barber executed the designs for the Liberty nickel introduced in 1883. His initial design offered only the large "V" inside the wreath as an indication of denomination. This was too much for those of deceitful intent, who, finding the coin so similar in size to the half eagle, gave them a reeded edge and gold plating so that they might be passed on the unsuspecting as $5 instead of 5¢. This fault was quickly corrected with the addition of the word "CENTS" below the wreath in place of "E PLURIBUS UNUM", which was incorporated above the wreath.

The Liberty nickel series also encompasses one of the most famous American coins, the clandestine 1913 nickel made famous in nationwide numismatic promotions conducted by B. Max Mehl, in which he offered to pay $50 for specimens of the issue. Mehl never owned one of the coins, but knowing that the only five produced rested in collections he could make the offer without fear of its being accepted. The originals were produced in secrecy at the instigation of Samuel Brown, a one time mint employee, and they later passed into the possession of the rich eccentric Col. E.H.R. Green, the son of Hetty Green.

Untold thousands of 1903, 1910 and 1912 Liberty nickels have been industriously altered with varying degrees of skill through the years by those who would pass them as authentic issues. Mehl was undoubtedly on the receiving end of many such specimens. One which was authentic was owned for some twenty-five years by coin dealer J.V. McDermott of Milwaukee, Wis., who offered his $900 purchase for display at coin events throughout the country. Following his death, the coin was sold to another dealer, Aubrey E. Bebee of Omaha, for $46,000.

Without Cents   Mintmark   With Cents

Date	Mintage	G-4	VG-8	F-12	VF-20	XF-40	MS-60	MS-65	ABP
☐ 1883 NC	5,479,519	2.00	3.00	4.75	7.50	11.00	60.00	500.	1.00
☐ 1883 WC	16,032,983	6.00	8.50	17.50	26.00	44.00	300.	1450.	3.25
☐ 1884	11,273,942	7.00	8.75	20.00	28.00	46.00	310.	1600.	3.50
☐ 1885	1,476,490	365.	415.	550.	725.	850.	1325.	3000.	220.
☐ 1886	3,330,290	49.00	58.00	105.	140.	240.	600.	2300.	29.00
☐ 1887	15,263,652	4.00	5.50	18.00	27.00	45.00	290.	1500.	2.25
☐ 1888	10,720,483	6.00	10.00	21.00	30.00	47.00	310.	1600.	3.25
☐ 1889	15,881,361	4.00	5.50	18.00	27.00	45.00	300.	1500.	2.25
☐ 1890	16,259,272	4.00	5.50	17.00	26.00	44.00	300.	1550.	2.25
☐ 1891	16,834,350	3.75	5.50	16.50	25.00	43.00	300.	1500.	2.00
☐ 1892	11,699,642	4.50	7.00	19.00	27.50	45.00	300.	1500.	2.25
☐ 1893	13,370,195	4.25	6.00	18.00	27.00	44.00	300.	1600.	2.00

Date	Mintage	G-4	VG-8	F-12	VF-20	XF-40	MS-60	MS-65	ABP
☐ 1894	5,413,132	7.00	9.50	25.00	38.00	75.00	350.	1700.	3.50
☐ 1895	9,979,884	5.50	6.50	21.00	30.00	48.00	300.	1500.	3.00
☐ 1896	8,842,920	5.75	7.00	22.00	32.00	50.00	325.	1650.	3.25
☐ 1897	20,428,735	1.00	2.00	5.50	10.00	30.00	190.	1000.	.50
☐ 1898	12,532,087	1.25	2.25	5.75	11.00	32.00	255.	1000.	.60
☐ 1899	26,029,031	.85	1.75	4.00	9.00	27.00	190.	1000.	.40
☐ 1900	27,255,995	.75	1.25	3.50	9.00	27.00	190.	1000.	.35
☐ 1901	26,480,213	.75	1.25	3.50	9.00	27.00	190.	1000.	.35
☐ 1902	31,480,579	.75	1.15	3.25	8.00	25.00	190.	1000.	.35
☐ 1903	28,006,725	.75	1.25	3.50	8.50	26.00	190.	1000.	.35
☐ 1904	21,404,984	.80	1.30	3.75	10.00	30.00	190.	1000.	.35
☐ 1905	29,827,276	.75	1.15	3.25	8.00	25.00	190.	1000.	.35
☐ 1906	38,613,725	.65	.90	3.00	7.00	25.00	190.	1000.	.35
☐ 1907	39,214,800	.65	.90	3.00	7.00	25.00	190.	1000.	.35
☐ 1908	22,686,177	.75	1.10	3.50	8.00	27.00	190.	1000.	.35
☐ 1909	11,590,526	.85	1.20	3.75	10.00	30.00	190.	1000.	.35
☐ 1910	30,169,353	.65	.90	3.00	7.00	25.00	190.	1000.	.35
☐ 1911	39,559,372	.65	.90	3.00	7.00	25.00	190.	1000.	.35
☐ 1912	26,236,714	.70	1.10	3.25	8.00	27.00	190.	1000.	.35
☐ 1912D	8,474,000	.95	1.50	5.50	17.00	57.00	450.	2100.	.50
☐ 1912S	238,000	48.00	58.00	75.00	195.	375.	800.	2800.	28.00

☐ 1913 Only 5 known, last sold in private sale at $200,000.

Authentic   Altered Date

The above enlargements of the date areas of authentic and altered date 1913 Liberty Head nickels illustrate the normal differences in the configuration of the 3.

BUFFALO NICKELS

The Buffalo or Indian head nickel designed by James E. Fraser features the profile of an Indian head on the obverse and a likeness of the American bison Black Diamond from the New York Zoological Gardens on the reverse. Through the years many Indians have claimed to have been one of the three models Fraser stated he used in forming the obverse design, who were chiefs John Tree, Iron Tail and Two Moon.

One of only four overdates among the U.S. 20th century coins is included in this series. It also includes a "D" over "S" mintmark variety, and one of the most popular mint error coins, the three-legged buffalo of 1937 from the Denver Mint. This error was created when the die was over polished in the area of the buffalo's front right leg, making it disappear. This error is easily faked, but there are several distinguishing marks on authentic specimens, including an irregular row of raised dots arching to the ground below the belly of the buffalo.

Mound Type   Line Type

Mintmark   Overdate — 18D / 17

MOUND TYPE

Date	Mintage	G-4	VG-8	F-12	VF-20	XF-40	MS-60	MS-65	ABP
☐ 1913	30,993,520	3.00	3.50	4.50	7.50	12.50	63.00	425.	1.25
☐ 1913D	5,337,000	6.00	7.50	9.50	13.50	24.00	105.	750.	3.00
☐ 1913S	2,105,000	9.00	11.00	16.00	25.00	45.00	190.	900.	5.00

LINE-TYPE

Date	Mintage	G-4	VG-8	F-12	VF-20	XF-40	MS-60	MS-65	ABP
☐ 1913	29,858,700	3.50	4.00	5.00	7.50	13.50	70.00	480.	2.00
☐ 1913D	4,156,000	44.00	48.00	55.00	70.00	105.	290.	1000.	26.00
☐ 1913S	1,209,000	95.00	115.	135.	165.	225.	500.	1400.	57.00
☐ 1914	20,665,738	4.00	5.00	6.50	8.00	15.00	95.00	525.	2.25
☐ 1914D	3,912,000	29.00	34.00	45.00	65.00	105.	380.	1550.	17.00
☐ 1914S	3,470,000	4.50	6.00	12.00	17.50	40.00	190.	1125.	2.50
☐ 1915	20,987,270	2.00	2.50	4.50	6.50	12.00	88.00	480.	1.10
☐ 1915D	7,569,500	6.00	8.00	12.50	33.00	50.00	225.	1250.	3.25
☐ 1915S	1,505,000	11.00	14.50	25.00	55.00	95.00	450.	1650.	6.50
☐ 1916	63,498,066	.60	.85	1.25	2.50	6.00	60.00	420.	—
☐ 1916/16	Inc. Ab.	—	100.	210.	300.	500.	1425.	3950.	—
☐ 1916D	13,333,000	4.50	6.00	9.00	22.00	45.00	220.	1350.	2.25
☐ 1916S	11,860,000	3.00	4.00	6.50	19.00	45.00	220.	1175.	1.75
☐ 1917	51,424,029	.75	1.00	1.75	3.00	10.00	65.00	465.	—
☐ 1917D	9,910,800	4.50	6.50	12.00	40.00	85.00	350.	1500.	2.50
☐ 1917S	4,193,000	4.50	5.50	10.00	35.00	75.00	375.	1700.	2.50
☐ 1918	32,086,314	.65	1.25	2.50	6.00	15.00	130.	700.	—
☐ 1918D/17	8,362,314	600.	750.	1000.	2000.	4000.	13,000.	35,000.	360.
☐ 1918D	Inc. Ab.	5.00	7.00	11.00	65.00	90.00	440.	4500.	3.00
☐ 1918S	4,882,000	3.50	5.50	10.00	40.00	85.00	400.	3375.	1.75
☐ 1919	60,868,000	.60	.75	1.00	3.00	8.50	58.00	450.	—
☐ 1919D	8,006,000	5.00	6.50	15.00	78.00	125.	500.	5500.	3.00
☐ 1919S	7,521,000	3.00	5.00	10.00	50.00	90.00	400.	4500.	1.75
☐ 1920	63,093,000	.50	.70	1.00	3.00	8.50	60.00	450.	—
☐ 1920D	9,418,000	3.50	5.00	10.00	63.00	120.	500.	4500.	1.75
☐ 1920S	9,689,000	2.00	3.00	7.00	32.00	85.00	450.	6000.	1.10
☐ 1921	10,663,000	.80	1.00	2.50	7.50	18.50	125.	475.	—
☐ 1921S	1,557,000	12.00	16.00	32.50	85.00	235.	775.	3900.	7.00
☐ 1923	35,715,000	.50	.75	1.00	3.00	7.50	60.00	400.	—

Date	Mintage	G-4	VG-8	F-12	VF-20	XF-40	MS-60	MS-65	ABP
☐ 1923S	6,142,000	1.25	2.50	5.00	27.00	65.00	300.	4500.	.75
☐ 1924	21,620,000	.50	.75	1.25	3.00	10.00	75.00	475.	—
☐ 1924D	5,258,000	2.50	3.50	8.00	48.00	85.00	385.	2800.	1.25
☐ 1924S	1,437,000	5.00	6.75	15.00	98.00	240.	850.	7500.	3.00
☐ 1925	35,565,100	.40	.60	1.00	2.50	10.00	265.	400.	—
☐ 1925D	4,450,000	3.75	6.50	12.00	60.00	100.	445.	4000.	1.75
☐ 1925S	6,256,000	2.25	4.00	7.00	25.00	55.00	380.	4600.	1.15
☐ 1926	44,693,000	.35	.50	.75	2.00	5.00	55.00	300.	—
☐ 1926D	5,638,000	2.00	4.00	9.50	55.00	100.	320.	4500.	1.10
☐ 1926S	970,000	5.25	8.00	13.00	65.00	280.	975.	7000.	3.00
☐ 1927	37,981,000	.30	.40	.75	1.50	5.00	50.00	300.	—
☐ 1927D	5,730,000	1.00	1.50	2.75	11.50	40.00	180.	1000.	.40
☐ 1927S	3,430,000	.90	1.25	2.50	15.00	65.00	320.	1750.	—
☐ 1928	23,411,000	.30	.40	.75	2.00	5.00	60.00	295.	—
☐ 1928D	6,436,000	.75	.90	2.00	5.00	11.50	80.00	475.	—
☐ 1928S	6,936,000	.50	.70	1.25	2.50	10.00	175.	950.	—
☐ 1929	36,446,000	.30	.40	.75	1.50	4.50	50.00	290.	—
☐ 1929D	8,370,000	.75	.85	1.35	3.50	10.00	90.00	885.	—
☐ 1929S	7,754,000	.40	.50	.75	2.00	9.50	69.00	450.	—
☐ 1930	22,849,000	.30	.50	.75	1.50	4.00	60.00	200.	—
☐ 1930S	5,435,000	.50	.60	1.00	1.75	7.50	82.00	575.	—
☐ 1931S	1,200,000	3.00	3.50	3.75	5.25	12.50	82.00	480.	1.75
☐ 1934	20,213,003	.30	.40	.60	1.50	3.50	60.00	180.	—
☐ 1934D	7,480,000	.45	.55	.85	1.50	4.00	125.	325.	—
☐ 1935	58,264,000	.30	.35	.40	.75	2.00	38.00	90.00	—
☐ 1935D	12,092,000	.35	.45	.60	2.00	6.00	125.	600.	—
☐ 1935S	10,300,000	.35	.40	.50	1.25	3.00	60.00	135.	—
☐ 1936	119,001,420	.30	.35	.40	.75	1.50	35.00	85.00	—
☐ 1936D	24,814,000	.30	.40	.50	1.00	3.00	38.00	90.00	—
☐ 1936S	14,930,000	.30	.40	.50	1.00	3.00	32.00	130.	—
☐ 1937	79,485,769	.30	.35	.40	.75	1.50	30.00	90.00	—
☐ 1937D	17,826,000	.30	.40	.55	1.00	2.00	27.50	40.00	—
☐ 1937D 3LEG Inc. Ab.		180.	210.	250.	350.	450.	900.	5000.	100.

Three-Legged
Buffalo Enlargements

Date	Mintage	G-4	VG-8	F-12	VF-20	XF-40	MS-60	MS-65	ABP
☐ 1937S	5,635,000	.40	.45	.50	1.00	1.75	27.50	40.00	—
☐ 1938D	7,020,000	.40	.45	.55	1.00	1.75	27.50	40.00	—
☐ 1938D/S	Inc. Ab.	—	—	6.00	7.50	10.00	35.00	100.	3.50

JEFFERSON NICKELS

This design resulted from a public competition in which Felix Schlag bested some 390 artists for a $1,000 cash award. Although Schlag's obverse was largely retained in the production design, a completely new reverse was prepared by the Mint's engraving staff. The design went unsigned for nearly 30 years, until a small "FS" was added below the bust in 1966, in tribute to the last private artist to conceive a regular issue U.S. coin design. Mint engravers prepared new master dies, sharpening the features on this coin for the 1971 edition.

Mintmarks

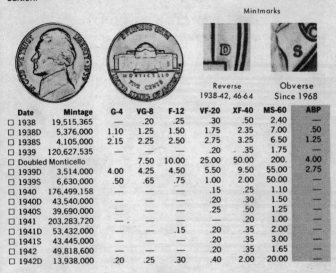

| | | Reverse 1938-42, 46-64 | Obverse Since 1968 |

Date	Mintage	G-4	VG-8	F-12	VF-20	XF-40	MS-60	ABP
☐ 1938	19,515,365	—	.20	.25	.30	.50	2.40	—
☐ 1938D	5,376,000	1.10	1.25	1.50	1.75	2.35	7.00	.50
☐ 1938S	4,105,000	2.15	2.25	2.50	2.75	3.25	6.50	1.25
☐ 1939	120,627,535	—	—	—	.20	.35	1.75	—
☐ Doubled Monticello			7.50	10.00	25.00	50.00	200.	4.00
☐ 1939D	3,514,000	4.00	4.25	4.50	5.50	9.50	55.00	2.75
☐ 1939S	6,630,000	.50	.65	.75	1.00	2.00	50.00	—
☐ 1940	176,499,158	—	—	—	.15	.25	1.10	—
☐ 1940D	43,540,000	—	—	—	.20	.30	1.50	—
☐ 1940S	39,690,000	—	—	—	.25	.50	1.25	—
☐ 1941	203,283,720	—	—	—	—	.20	1.00	—
☐ 1941D	53,432,000	—	—	.15	.20	.35	2.00	—
☐ 1941S	43,445,000	—	—	—	.20	.35	3.00	—
☐ 1942	49,818,600	—	—	—	.20	.35	1.65	—
☐ 1942D	13,938,000	.20	.25	.30	.40	2.00	20.00	—

SILVER WARTIME NICKELS

During the World War II years, the nickel composition of the five-cent coin was abandoned in favor of a copper-silver-manganese alloy containing 35 percent silver. By the early '60s the bullion value of these coins exceeded their face value. To distinguish these issues from the nickel version, large mintmarks were placed above the dome of Monticello on the reverse, including a "P" for Philadelphia, the first time the U.S. mother mint has placed a mintmark on her domestic issues.

Date	Mintage	G-4	VG-8	F-12	VF-20	XF-40	MS-60	ABP
☐ 1942P	57,900,600	—	—	—	.60	2.50	14.00	.35
☐ 1942S	32,900,000	—	—	—	.60	.80	8.00	.35

Date	Mintage	G-4	VG-8	F-12	VF-20	XF-40	MS-60	ABP
☐ 1943P	271,165,000	—	—	—	.60	—	2.50	.35
☐ 1943P 3/2 Inc. Ab.		35.00	45.00	55.00	100.	165.	475.	20.00
☐ 1943D	15,294,000	—	—	—	.60	.80	4.25	.35
☐ 1943S	104,060,000	—	—	—	.60	.80	4.50	.35
☐ 1944P	119,150,000	—	—	—	.60	.80	4.35	.35
☐ 1944D	32,309,000	—	—	—	.60	.80	5.50	.35
☐ 1944S	21,640,000	—	—	—	.60	.80	5.50	.35
☐ 1945P	119,408,100	—	—	—	.60	.80	4.75	.35
☐ 1945D	37,158,000	—	—	—	.60	.80	3.00	.35
☐ 1945S	58,939,000	—	—	—	.60	.80	2.75	.35

PRE-WAR COMPOSITION

Date	Mintage	G-4	VG-8	F-12	VF-20	XF-40	MS-60	ABP
☐ 1946	161,116,000	—	—	—	—	.15	.75	—
☐ 1946D	45,292,200	—	—	—	—	.20	.85	—
☐ 1946S	13,560,000	—	—	—	—	.40	1.00	—
☐ 1947	95,000,000	—	—	—	—	.15	.85	—
☐ 1947D	37,822,000	—	—	—	—	.30	1.35	—
☐ 1947S	24,720,000	—	—	—	.25	.40	1.00	—
☐ 1948	89,348,000	—	—	—	—	.15	.75	—
☐ 1948D	44,734,000	—	—	—	—	.30	1.00	—
☐ 1948S	11,300,000	—	—	.20	.30	.50	1.00	—
☐ 1949	60,652,000	—	—	—	—	.15	1.65	—
☐ 1949D	36,498,000	—	—	—	.25	.30	1.90	—
☐ 1949 D/S Inc. Ab.		—	—	20.00	30.00	65.00	280.	12.00
☐ 1949S	9,716,000	—	.25	.30	.40	.75	2.50	—
☐ 1950	9,847,386	—	.30	.40	.50	.90	1.60	—
☐ 1950D	2,630,030	—	7.50	7.75	8.00	8.25	10.00	6.00
☐ 1951	28,609,500	—	—	—	—	.35	1.25	—
☐ 1951D	20,460,000	—	—	—	—	.30	1.25	—
☐ 1951S	7,776,000	—	.35	.40	.50	.90	3.75	—
☐ 1952	64,069,980	—	—	—	—	.15	.90	—
☐ 1952D	30,638,000	—	—	—	—	.65	2.25	—
☐ 1952S	20,572,000	—	—	—	—	.20	.95	—
☐ 1953	46,772,800	—	—	—	—	—	.30	—
☐ 1953D	59,878,600	—	—	—	—	—	.30	—
☐ 1953S	19,210,900	—	—	—	—	.20	.50	—
☐ 1954	47,917,350	—	—	—	—	—	.35	—
☐ 1954D	117,136,560	—	—	—	—	—	.35	—
☐ 1954S	29,384,000	—	—	—	—	—	.40	—
☐ 1954S S/D Inc. Ab.		—	—	5.00	6.50	11.50	25.00	3.00
☐ 1955	8,266,200	—	.35	.40	.50	.60	1.00	—
☐ 1955D	74,464,100	—	—	—	—	—	.25	—
☐ 1956	35,885,384	—	—	—	—	—	.25	—
☐ 1956D	67,222,940	—	—	—	—	—	.20	—
☐ 1957	39,655,952	—	—	—	—	—	.25	—
☐ 1957D	136,828,900	—	—	—	—	—	.20	—
☐ 1958	17,963,652	—	—	—	.20	.25	.35	—
☐ 1958D	168,249,120	—	—	—	—	—	.20	—

Date	Mintage	MS-60	ABP	Date	Mintage	MS-60	ABP
☐ 1959	28,397,291	.25	—	☐ 1962	100,602,019	.15	—
☐ 1959D	160,738,240	.15	—	☐ 1962D	280,195,720	.15	—
☐ 1960	57,107,602	.15	—	☐ 1963	178,851,645	.15	—
☐ 1960D	192,582,180	.15	—	☐ 1963D	276,829,460	.15	—
☐ 1961	76,668,244	.15	—	☐ 1964	1,028,622,762	.15	—
☐ 1961D	229,342,760	.15	—	☐ 1964D	1,787,297,160	.15	—

Commencing 1965 See Modern Singles — Page 117

DIMES

During the early years of U.S. coinage, the concentration on dime production was minimal, with only slightly more than a million pieces ($102,279.60) being struck up to 1820, as coins were issued in only 13 of 25 possible years. By the time the Liberty cap design was abandoned in 1837 the total had grown to only about 12.8 million pieces.

Draped Bust Dimes

Date	Mintage	G-4	VG-8	F-12	VF-20	XF-40	MS-60	ABP
☐ 1796	22,135	1700.	2100.	3350.	4700.	6900.	15,000.	1000.
☐ 1797 13 Stars	25,261	1700.	2100.	3350.	4700.	6900.	15,000.	1000.
☐ 1797 16 Stars	Inc. Ab.	1700.	2100.	3350.	4700.	6900.	15,000.	1000.

HERALDIC EAGLE INTRODUCED

Date	Mintage	G-4	VG-8	F-12	VF-20	XF-40	MS-60	ABP
☐ 1798	27,550	800.	950.	1650.	2200.	3250.	7000.	475.
☐ 1798/97 13 Stars	Inc. Ab.	1650.	2000.	2750.	4000.	5000.	—	975.
☐ 1798/97 16 Stars	Inc. Ab.	850.	1095.	2000.	2500.	3500.	6750.	500.
☐ 1798 Small 8	Inc. Ab.	—	—	Rare	—	—	—	
☐ 1800	21,760	800.	950.	1675.	2200.	3250.	6500.	475.
☐ 1801	34,640	800.	950.	1695.	2200.	3500.	—	475.
☐ 1802	10,975	850.	1250.	2100.	3000.	4500.	—	500.
☐ 1803	33,040	800.	950.	1650.	2150.	3150.	7000.	475.
☐ 1804 13 Stars	8,265	1500.	2000.	3500.	5500.	—	—	900.
☐ 1804 14 Stars	Inc. Ab.	1500.	2000.	3500.	5500.	—	—	900.
☐ 1805 4 Berries	120,780	800.	950.	1550.	2100.	3150.	6500.	475.
☐ 1805 5 Berries	Inc. Ab.	800.	950.	1550.	2100.	3150.	6500.	475.
☐ 1807	165,000	800.	950.	1550.	2100.	3150.	6500.	475.

Liberty Cap Dimes

Date	Mintage	G-4	VG-8	F-12	VF-20	XF-40	MS-60	ABP
☐ 1809	51,065	75.00	100.	165.	225.	375.	4200.	45.00
☐ 1811/9	65,180	45.00	65.00	85.00	150.	325.	4000.	27.00
☐ 1814 Sm. Dt.	421,500	25.00	35.00	55.00	90.00	300.	2500.	15.00
☐ 1814 Lg. Dt.	Inc. Ab.	25.00	30.00	45.00	80.00	300.	2500.	15.00
☐ 1820 Lg. O	942,587	22.00	27.50	40.00	95.00	300.	2450.	13.00
☐ 1820 Sm. O	Inc. Ab.	22.50	28.00	40.00	95.00	300.	2500.	13.50
☐ 1821 Lg. Dt.	1,186,512	22.50	28.00	40.00	100.	300.	2500.	13.50
☐ 1821 Sm. Dt.	Inc. Ab.	22.50	30.00	45.00	100.	300.	2500.	13.50
☐ 1822	100,000	75.00	95.00	175.	275.	475.	4000.	45.00
☐ 1823/22 Lg.E'S	440,000	22.00	27.50	40.00	100.	275.	2500.	13.00
☐ 1823/22 Sm.E'S	Inc. Ab.	22.00	27.50	40.00	100.	275.	2500.	13.00
☐ 1824/22 Undetermined		22.00	27.50	40.00	100.	275.	2500.	13.00
☐ 1825	510,000	21.00	26.00	37.50	95.00	275.	2450.	12.50
☐ 1827	1,215,000	20.00	24.50	32.00	95.00	275.	2450.	12.00
☐ 1828 Lg.Dt.	125,000	35.00	45.00	69.00	120.	350.	3000.	21.00

COIN SIZE REDUCED SLIGHTLY

Date	Mintage	G-4	VG-8	F-12	VF-20	XF-40	MS-60	ABP
☐ 1828 Sm.Dt.	Inc. Ab.	25.00	30.00	40.00	85.00	225.	2250.	15.00
☐ 1829 Lg. 10C.	770,000	22.50	28.00	40.00	75.00	200.	2100.	13.50
☐ 1829 Med. 10C.	Inc. Ab.	14.00	16.00	25.00	55.00	190.	1900.	8.00
☐ 1829 Sm. 10C.	Inc. Ab.	14.00	16.00	25.00	55.00	190.	1900.	8.00
☐ 1830 Lg. 10C.	510,000	14.00	16.00	25.00	55.00	190.	2000.	8.00
☐ 1830 Sm. 10C.	Inc. Ab.	14.00	16.00	25.00	55.00	190.	2000.	8.00
☐ 1830/29	Inc. Ab.	—	75.00	125.	200.	300.	2500.	45.00
☐ 1831	771,350	14.00	16.00	25.00	55.00	190.	1900.	8.00
☐ 1832	522,500	14.00	16.00	25.00	55.00	190.	2150.	8.00
☐ 1833	485,000	14.00	16.00	25.00	55.00	190.	2100.	8.00
☐ 1833 High 3	Inc. Ab.	14.00	16.00	25.00	55.00	190.	2100.	8.00
☐ 1834 Lg. 4	635,000	14.00	16.00	25.00	55.00	190.	2000.	8.00
☐ 1834 Sm. 4	Inc. Ab.	14.00	16.00	25.00	55.00	190.	2000.	8.00
☐ 1835	1,410,000	14.00	16.00	26.00	55.00	190.	1825.	8.00
☐ 1836	1,190,000	14.00	16.00	25.00	55.00	190.	1825.	8.00
☐ 1837	1,042,000	14.00	16.00	25.00	55.00	190.	1825.	8.00

LIBERTY SEATED DIMES

Introduction of the Liberty seated dime series, and half dimes, quarters and halves as well, followed on the heels of the enactment of a January 18, 1837, law which reduced its weight to 41.25 grains from 41.6, in conformity with a 3.5 grain weight reduction for the silver dollar standard. This change in the law also provided for the fineness of silver coins to be increased from .8924 to .900.

An act of February 21, 1853, reduced the weight of all fractional silver coins by nearly seven percent, to 38.4 grains for the dime, so that they could be maintained in circulation in the face of the growing disparity between the relative values of silver and gold brought on by the California gold discoveries. Arrows were placed either side of the date on most 1853, and all 1854 and 1855 issues to note this change. A similar step was taken twenty years later when the weight of the dime, and the quarter and half proportionately, was increased slightly to 38.58 grains.

MINTMARK
ABOVE AND BELOW
WREATH TIE

WITHOUT STARS AROUND RIM

Date	Mintage	G-4	VG-8	F-12	VF-20	XF-40	MS-60	ABP
☐ 1837 Sm.Date	Inc. Ab.	24.00	35.00	50.00	120.	290.	1400.	14.00
☐ 1837 Lg.Date	Inc. Ab.	24.00	35.00	50.00	120.	290.	1400.	14.00
☐ 1838O	406,034	45.00	80.00	125.	350.	650.	4000.	27.50

STARS ADDED AROUND RIM

Date	Mintage	G-4	VG-8	F-12	VF-20	XF-40	MS-60	ABP
☐ 1838 Sm.Stars	1,992,500	35.00	50.00	75.00	150.	300.	2000.	21.00
☐ 1838 Lg.Stars	Inc. Ab.	10.00	15.00	20.00	40.00	80.00	880.	6.00
☐ 1838 Partial Drapery	Inc. Ab.	40.00	65.00	100.	175.	400.	1500.	25.00
☐ 1839	1,053,115	10.00	15.00	20.00	40.00	80.00	625.	6.00
☐ 1839O	1,323,000	15.00	20.00	25.00	60.00	125.	950.	9.00
☐ 1839O Rev. 1838O		120.	300.	450.	600.	1500.	—	72.00
☐ 1840	1,358,580	6.00	7.00	8.00	18.00	54.00	625.	3.50
☐ 1840O	1,175,000	15.00	30.00	45.00	65.00	125.	1500.	9.00

DRAPERY ADDED TO LIBERTY

Date	Mintage	G-4	VG-8	F-12	VF-20	XF-40	MS-60	ABP
☐ 1840	Inc. Ab.	50.00	75.00	175.	250.	500.	—	30.00
☐ 1841	1,622,500	8.00	15.00	25.00	35.00	70.00	485.	4.50
☐ 1841O	2,007,500	15.00	20.00	30.00	70.00	150.	1500.	9.00
☐ 1842	1,887,500	8.00	15.00	25.00	35.00	70.00	485.	4.50
☐ 1842O	2,020,000	15.00	20.00	30.00	70.00	150.	—	9.00
☐ 1843	1,370,000	8.00	10.00	15.00	35.00	70.00	485.	4.50
☐ 1843/1843	—	15.00	20.00	30.00	70.00	150.	800.	9.00
☐ 1843O	150,000	50.00	65.00	125.	250.	800.	—	30.00
☐ 1844	72,500	28.00	40.00	75.00	175.	300.	2000.	16.00
☐ 1845	1,755,000	8.00	15.00	25.00	35.00	70.00	485.	4.50
☐ 1845/1845	Inc. Ab.	55.00	110.	175.	250.	500.	—	—
☐ 1845O	230,000	18.00	32.00	75.00	150.	800.	—	10.00
☐ 1846	31,300	90.00	110.	165.	325.	850.	—	54.00
☐ 1847	245,000	15.00	25.00	50.00	75.00	200.	1200.	9.00
☐ 1848	451,500	10.00	15.00	25.00	50.00	80.00	750.	6.00
☐ 1849	839,000	8.00	15.00	25.00	45.00	70.00	725.	4.50
☐ 1849/8	Inc. Ab.	50.00	75.00	250.	400.	600.	—	30.00
☐ 1849O	300,000	15.00	20.00	35.00	150.	350.	—	9.00
☐ 1850	1,931,500	8.00	15.00	25.00	35.00	70.00	485.	4.50
☐ 1850O	510,000	12.00	16.00	30.00	75.00	150.	1000.	7.00
☐ 1851	1,026,500	8.00	15.00	25.00	35.00	80.00	485.	4.50
☐ 1851O	400,000	12.00	16.00	30.00	75.00	150.	1500.	7.00

Date	Mintage	G-4	VG-8	F-12	VF-20	XF-40	MS-60	ABP
☐ 1852	1,535,500	8.00	15.00	25.00	35.00	80.00	485.	4.50
☐ 1852O	430,000	15.00	20.00	40.00	125.	250.	1800.	9.00
☐ 1853	95,000	50.00	75.00	95.00	150.	350.	1000.	30.00

ARROWS AT DATE

ARROWS AT DATE

Date	Mintage	G-4	VG-8	F-12	VF-20	XF-40	MS-60	ABP
☐ 1853	12,078,010	5.00	6.00	7.25	16.00	44.00	535.	3.00
☐ 1853O	1,100,000	5.00	15.00	25.00	40.00	150.	1000.	3.00
☐ 1854	4,470,000	5.00	10.00	15.00	25.00	65.00	1000.	3.00
☐ 1854O	1,770,000	5.00	12.00	20.00	35.00	115.	1000.	3.00
☐ 1855	2,075,000	5.00	10.00	15.00	22.00	65.00	1100.	3.00

ARROWS AT DATE REMOVED

Date	Mintage	G-4	VG-8	F-12	VF-20	XF-40	MS-60	ABP
☐ 1856 Small Date								
	5,780,000	8.00	15.00	25.00	30.00	60.00	565.	4.50
☐ 1856 Large Date								
	Inc. Ab.	15.00	18.00	20.00	50.00	85.00	750.	9.00
☐ 1856O	1,180,000	15.00	20.00	25.00	40.00	85.00	750.	9.00
☐ 1856S	70,000	50.00	75.00	100.	225.	450.		30.00
☐ 1857	5,580,000	5.00	6.00	7.00	12.50	31.00	485.	3.00
☐ 1857O	1,540,000	5.00	6.00	7.00	16.00	85.00	750.	3.00
☐ 1858	1,540,000	5.00	6.00	7.00	12.50	31.00	485.	3.00
☐ 1858O	290,000	20.00	30.00	50.00	100.	200.	1200.	12.00
☐ 1858S	60,000	50.00	75.00	125.	250.	500.		30.00
☐ 1859	430,000	5.00	6.00	7.00	12.50	65.00	1000.	3.00
☐ 1859O	480,000	10.00	20.00	30.00	50.00	100.	1100.	6.00
☐ 1859S	60,000	100.	125.	175.	325.	600.		60.00
☐ 1860S	140,000	25.00	30.00	45.00	75.00	185.		15.00

TRANSITIONAL PATTERN

Date	Mintage	G-4	VG-8	F-12	VF-20	XF-40	MS-60	ABP
☐ 1859 Obverse Of 1859, Reverse Of 1860					—	—		—

Mintmark

LEGEND REPLACES STARS ON OBVERSE

Date	Mintage	G-4	VG-8	F-12	VF-20	XF-40	MS-60	ABP
☐ 1860	607,000	10.00	15.00	20.00	35.00	55.00	525.	6.00
☐ 1860O	40,000	400.	500.	700.	1500.	2200.		240.

Date	Mintage	G-4	VG-8	F-12	VF-20	XF-40	MS-60	ABP
☐ 1861	1,884,000	10.00	15.00	20.00	25.00	50.00	500.	6.00
☐ 1861S	172,500	20.00	25.00	45.00	100.	225.	—	12.00
☐ 1862	847,550	8.00	10.00	15.00	25.00	50.00	500.	4.50
☐ 1862S	180,750	20.00	25.00	40.00	75.00	150.	—	12.00
☐ 1863	14,460	150.	175.	200.	300.	550.	1300.	90.00
☐ 1863S	157,500	22.00	35.00	45.00	100.	225.	1200.	13.00
☐ 1864	11,470	150.	175.	200.	300.	550.	1300.	90.00
☐ 1864S	230,000	18.00	20.00	40.00	50.00	140.	1200.	10.00
☐ 1865	10,500	175.	200.	225.	375.	600.	1100.	105.
☐ 1865S	175,000	20.00	25.00	30.00	75.00	180.	—	12.00
☐ 1866	8,725	200.	250.	300.	450.	650.	1300.	120.
☐ 1866S	135,000	30.00	40.00	50.00	75.00	225.	1500.	18.00
☐ 1867	6,625	250.	300.	400.	550.	750.	1800.	150.
☐ 1867S	140,000	30.00	35.00	40.00	85.00	225.	1200.	18.00
☐ 1868	464,600	6.00	10.00	25.00	50.00	125.	700.	3.50
☐ 1868S	260,000	20.00	30.00	40.00	85.00	195.	1000.	12.00
☐ 1869	256,600	6.00	10.00	25.00	75.00	140.	725.	3.50
☐ 1869S	450,000	8.00	12.00	18.00	50.00	95.00	825.	4.50
☐ 1870	471,500	6.00	10.00	18.00	50.00	100.	450.	3.50
☐ 1870S	50,000	60.00	75.00	165.	250.	500.	3200.	35.00
☐ 1871	907,710	6.00	9.00	12.00	20.00	55.00	350.	3.50
☐ 1871CC	20,100	300.	400.	850.	1100.	3000.	—	180.
☐ 1871S	320,000	15.00	25.00	40.00	75.00	140.	1000.	9.00
☐ 1872	2,396,450	6.00	9.00	12.00	20.00	50.00	350.	3.50
☐ 1872CC	35,480	200.	300.	550.	750.	2100.	—	120.
☐ 1872S	190,000	25.00	40.00	80.00	125.	250.	1100.	15.00
☐ 1873 Closed 3								—
	1,568,600	18.00	25.00	35.00	60.00	85.00	350.	10.00
☐ 1873 Open 3								—
	Inc. Ab.	25.00	45.00	65.00	100.	150.	—	15.00
☐ 1873CC	12,400	—	—	—	Only One Known		—	—

ARROWS AT DATE

Date	Mintage	G-4	VG-8	F-12	VF-20	XF-40	MS-60	ABP
☐ 1873	2,378,500	15.00	18.00	27.50	45.00	115.	750.	9.00
☐ 1873CC	18,791	375.	500.	675.	1300.	2800.	13,000.	225.
☐ 1873S	455,000	16.00	20.00	32.00	60.00	125.	1500.	9.50
☐ 1874	2,940,700	15.00	18.00	27.50	45.00	115.	750.	9.00
☐ 1874CC	10,817	900.	1500.	2000.	2500.	4300.	—	540.
☐ 1874S	240,000	30.00	50.00	100.	150.	300.	1500.	18.00

ARROWS AT DATE REMOVED

Date	Mintage	G-4	VG-8	F-12	VF-20	XF-40	MS-60	ABP
☐ 1875	10,350,700	5.00	5.50	6.25	9.00	22.00	350.	3.00
☐ 1875CC Mintmark In Wreath								—
	4,645,000	15.00	20.00	25.00	45.00	75.00	350.	9.00
☐ 1875CC Mintmark Under Wreath								—
	Inc. Ab.	15.00	18.00	30.00	50.00	85.00	350.	9.00

Date	Mintage	G-4	VG-8	F-12	VF-20	XF-40	MS-60	ABP
☐ 1875S Mintmark In Wreath								—
	9,070,000	25.00	40.00	85.00	150.	215.	350.	15.00
☐ 1875S Mintmark Under Wreath								—
	Inc. Ab.	5.00	5.50	6.25	9.00	22.00	350.	3.00
☐ 1876	11,461,150	5.00	5.50	6.25	9.00	22.00	350.	3.00
☐ 1876CC	8,270,000	5.00	5.50	6.25	9.00	22.00	350.	3.00
☐ 1876CC (Double obv.)								
	Inc. Ab.	50.00	75.00	125.	350.	550.	—	30.00
☐ 1876S	10,420,000	5.00	5.50	6.25	9.00	22.00	350.	3.00
☐ 1877	7,310,510	5.00	5.50	6.25	9.00	22.00	350.	3.00
☐ 1877CC	7,700,000	5.00	5.50	6.25	9.00	22.00	350.	3.00
☐ 1877S	2,340,000	5.00	5.50	6.25	9.00	22.00	350.	3.00
☐ 1878	1,678,800	5.00	5.50	6.25	9.00	22.00	350.	3.00
☐ 1878CC	200,000	50.00	75.00	100.	150.	300.	900.	30.00
☐ 1879	15,100	100.	150.	200.	325.	450.	500.	60.00
☐ 1880	37,335	100.	125.	175.	275.	350.	450.	60.00
☐ 1881	24,975	100.	150.	200.	300.	400.	475.	60.00
☐ 1882	3,911,100	5.00	5.50	6.25	9.00	22.00	350.	3.00
☐ 1883	7,675,712	5.00	5.50	6.25	9.00	22.00	350.	3.00
☐ 1884	3,366,380	5.00	5.50	6.25	9.00	22.00	350.	3.00
☐ 1884S	564,969	15.00	20.00	25.00	35.00	95.00	450.	9.00
☐ 1885	2,533,427	5.00	5.50	6.25	9.00	22.00	350.	3.00
☐ 1885S	43,690	120.	150.	220.	325.	500.	3000.	70.00
☐ 1886	6,377,570	5.00	5.50	6.25	9.00	22.00	350.	3.00
☐ 1886S	206,524	15.00	20.00	30.00	45.00	90.00	500.	9.00
☐ 1887	11,283,939	5.00	5.50	6.25	9.00	22.00	350.	3.00
☐ 1887S	4,454,450	5.00	5.50	6.25	9.00	22.00	350.	3.00
☐ 1888	5,496,487	5.00	5.50	6.25	9.00	22.00	350.	3.00
☐ 1888S	1,720,000	5.00	5.50	6.25	9.00	22.00	350.	3.00
☐ 1889	7,380,711	5.00	5.50	6.25	9.00	22.00	350.	3.00
☐ 1889S	972,678	10.00	15.00	25.00	40.00	85.00	475.	6.00
☐ 1890	9,911,541	5.00	5.50	6.25	9.00	22.00	350.	3.00
☐ 1890S	1,423,076	10.00	15.00	20.00	40.00	80.00	475.	6.00
☐ 1890S/S	Inc. Ab.	10.00	20.00	75.00	150.	275.	—	6.00
☐ 1891	15,310,600	5.00	5.50	6.25	9.00	22.00	350.	3.00
☐ 1891O	4,540,000	5.00	5.50	6.25	9.00	22.00	475.	3.00
☐ 1891-O/S	Inc. Ab.	30.00	50.00	125.	200.	350.	—	18.00
☐ 1891O/horz. O								
	Inc. Ab.	40.00	70.00	150.	275.	425.	—	24.00
☐ 1891S	3,196,116	5.00	5.50	6.25	9.00	22.00	500.	3.00

BARBER DIMES

After a run of more than half a century, the nation's Liberty seated silver coin designs were supplanted by the classical Liberty head designs prepared by Charles E. Barber in 1892. His initial, "B" appears at the truncation of the neck. The change was instituted, in large part, due to the mounting public criticism of the old designs.

Mintmark

41

Date	Mintage	G-4	VG-8	F-12	VF-20	XF-40	MS-60	MS-65	ABP
☐ 1892	12,121,245	3.50	5.00	8.00	16.00	35.00	250.	950.	2.00
☐ 1892O	3,841,700	4.50	9.00	15.00	23.00	41.00	410.	2200.	2.50
☐ 1892S	990,710	33.00	50.00	66.00	96.00	125.	440.	2850.	19.00
☐ 1893	3,340,792	4.75	10.00	17.50	28.00	50.00	325.	1700.	2.75
☐ 1893O	1,760,000	14.00	22.00	33.00	48.00	84.00	535.	2800.	8.00
☐ 1893S	2,491,401	7.00	11.00	20.00	35.00	55.00	410.	2200.	3.50
☐ 1894	1,330,972	8.00	14.00	24.00	38.00	70.00	440.	2400.	4.50
☐ 1894O	720,000	33.00	55.00	85.00	120.	200.	3150.	9500.	19.00
☐ 1894S	24	—		Proof Only	—	—	—	—	
☐ 1895	690,880	55.00	88.00	110.	175.	300.	1075.	4400.	30.00
☐ 1895O	440,000	170.	190.	250.	350.	525.	2600.	7500.	100.
☐ 1895S	1,120,000	15.00	29.00	41.00	60.00	95.00	535.	2650.	9.00
☐ 1896	2,000,762	7.50	15.00	27.50	45.00	65.00	300.	1700.	4.00
☐ 1896O	610,000	45.00	68.00	100.	150.	225.	1275.	5000.	25.00
☐ 1896S	575,056	40.00	65.00	95.00	140.	220.	760.	3100.	22.00
☐ 1897	10,869,264	2.50	4.50	11.00	20.00	40.00	250.	1260.	1.50
☐ 1897O	666,000	38.00	62.00	90.00	130.	210.	1900.	5350.	20.00
☐ 1897S	1,342,844	7.50	14.00	27.00	55.00	85.00	535.	2800.	4.00
☐ 1898	16,320,735	2.00	3.25	8.00	16.00	38.00	250.	1260.	1.20
☐ 1898O	2,130,000	4.50	8.00	22.50	40.00	75.00	575.	3800.	2.50
☐ 1898S	1,702,507	4.00	7.50	15.00	26.00	43.00	410.	2800.	2.25
☐ 1899	19,580,846	2.00	3.25	7.50	14.00	35.00	250.	1260.	1.20
☐ 1899O	2,650,000	4.25	8.50	22.00	34.00	64.00	410.	3800.	2.50
☐ 1899S	1,867,493	4.00	7.50	15.00	29.00	48.00	410.	2500.	2.25
☐ 1900	17,600,912	2.25	3.75	7.50	15.00	36.00	250.	1260.	1.35
☐ 1900O	2,010,000	6.00	10.00	24.00	42.00	76.00	660.	4100.	3.50
☐ 1900S	5,168,270	2.60	4.25	8.00	15.00	34.00	410.	2500.	1.50
☐ 1901	18,860,478	2.00	3.50	6.00	14.00	34.00	250.	1260.	1.20
☐ 1901O	5,620,000	2.50	4.00	7.50	20.00	50.00	660.	4100.	1.50
☐ 1901S	593,022	42.00	64.00	100.	150.	250.	1850.	6300.	24.00
☐ 1902	21,380,777	1.50	3.25	6.00	13.00	30.00	250.	1260.	.90
☐ 1902O	4,500,000	2.75	5.00	8.00	20.00	42.00	500.	3300.	1.50
☐ 1902S	2,070,000	4.00	8.00	19.00	32.00	63.00	600.	3000.	2.25
☐ 1903	19,500,755	1.50	3.75	6.50	14.00	32.00	250.	1260.	.90
☐ 1903O	8,180,000	2.45	4.25	7.50	19.00	40.00	500.	2800.	1.45
☐ 1903S	613,300	33.00	54.00	69.00	115.	205.	1500.	5350.	20.00
☐ 1904	14,601,027	2.00	4.00	6.75	14.50	33.00	250.	1260.	1.20
☐ 1904S	800,000	25.00	47.00	64.00	105.	180.	1500.	5000.	15.00
☐ 1905	14,552,350	1.95	3.50	6.00	14.00	32.00	250.	1260.	.95
☐ 1905O	3,400,000	2.50	6.50	16.00	30.00	60.00	475.	2500.	1.50
☐ 1905S	6,855,199	2.10	4.00	9.00	19.00	40.00	475.	2500.	1.20
☐ 1906	19,958,406	1.50	2.25	5.00	13.00	30.00	250.	1260.	.90
☐ 1906D	4,060,000	2.75	4.50	9.00	20.00	42.00	380.	1900.	1.65
☐ 1906O	2,610,000	3.50	6.50	17.50	30.00	51.00	475.	2150.	2.00
☐ 1906S	3,136,640	2.75	5.00	9.50	21.00	43.00	475.	2150.	1.65
☐ 1907	22,220,575	1.50	2.25	5.00	13.00	30.00	250.	1260.	.90
☐ 1907D	4,080,000	2.70	4.50	9.00	20.00	42.00	500.	2250.	1.60
☐ 1907O	5,058,000	2.10	4.00	8.50	20.00	42.00	380.	1600.	1.25
☐ 1907S	3,178,470	2.25	4.50	9.50	21.00	45.00	500.	2450.	1.35
☐ 1908	10,600,545	1.50	2.25	5.50	14.50	33.00	250.	1260.	.90
☐ 1908D	7,490,000	1.50	2.20	5.00	13.50	32.00	250.	1500.	.90
☐ 1908O	1,789,000	3.50	7.50	16.00	28.00	50.00	475.	2300.	2.00
☐ 1908S	3,220,000	2.00	4.50	8.00	20.00	42.00	475.	2300.	1.20
☐ 1909	10,240,650	2.00	2.50	6.00	15.00	35.00	250.	1260.	1.20
☐ 1909D	954,000	3.50	8.00	19.00	37.00	65.00	500.	2400.	2.00
☐ 1909O	2,287,000	2.00	4.50	8.50	22.00	44.00	325.	2000.	1.20
☐ 1909S	1,000,000	4.50	11.00	24.00	45.00	70.00	500.	2250.	2.50

Date	Mintage	G-4	VG-8	F-12	VF-20	XF-40	MS-60	MS-65	ABP
☐ 1910	11,520,551	1.50	2.25	5.50	14.00	34.00	250.	1260.	.90
☐ 1910D	3,490,000	2.00	4.50	7.50	18.00	39.00	500.	2400.	.90
☐ 1910S	1,240,000	3.50	6.00	11.00	22.00	45.00	475.	2000.	2.00
☐ 1911	18,870,543	1.50	2.10	4.25	11.50	29.00	250.	1260.	.90
☐ 1911D	11,209,000	1.50	2.20	4.50	12.00	30.00	250.	1400.	.90
☐ 1911S	3,520,000	2.00	2.75	6.50	18.00	40.00	430.	1700.	1.20
☐ 1912	19,350,700	1.50	2.10	4.25	11.50	29.00	250.	1260.	.90
☐ 1912D	11,760,000	1.50	2.10	4.25	11.50	29.00	315.	1325.	.90
☐ 1912S	3,420,000	2.00	3.50	5.75	17.00	39.00	430.	1775.	1.20
☐ 1913	19,760,622	1.50	2.10	4.25	11.50	29.00	250.	1260.	.90
☐ 1913S	510,000	7.50	14.00	35.00	70.00	160.	630.	2650.	4.50
☐ 1914	17,360,655	1.50	2.10	4.25	11.50	29.00	250.	1260.	.90
☐ 1914D	11,908,000	1.50	2.10	4.25	11.50	29.00	250.	1325.	.90
☐ 1914S	2,100,000	2.00	3.25	5.50	18.00	40.00	430.	1850.	1.20
☐ 1915	5,620,450	2.00	3.25	5.50	15.00	38.00	315.	1260.	1.20
☐ 1915S	960,000	2.75	5.00	11.00	22.00	49.00	475.	2000.	1.65
☐ 1916	18,490,000	1.50	2.10	4.25	11.50	29.00	250.	1260.	.90
☐ 1916S	5,820,000	2.00	4.00	5.50	13.50	35.00	315.	1300.	1.20

MERCURY DIMES

The nation's fractional silver coin issues were redesigned in 1916 when the Barber designs were 25 years old. A.A. Weinman, whose monogram appears in the field behind the neck of the Mercury-winged head of Liberty on the obverse, designed this coin which carries a fasces on the reverse. This series offers two of the five overdates in 20th century U.S. coinage.

Mintmark

Date	Mintage	G-4	VG-8	F-12	VF-20	XF-40	MS-60	MS-65	ABP
☐ 1916	22,180,080	2.75	3.50	4.50	6.00	10.00	32.00	70.00	.80
☐ 1916D	264,000	595.	750.	1150.	1500.	2150.	3000.	5250.	350.
☐ 1916S	10,450,000	2.75	3.75	6.00	7.50	13.00	45.00	185.	.80
☐ 1917	55,230,000	1.75	2.50	3.50	4.50	6.50	27.50	70.00	.80
☐ 1917D	9,402,000	2.50	3.75	7.75	12.00	30.00	150.	450.	.80
☐ 1917S	27,330,000	2.00	3.00	4.00	6.00	9.00	60.00	225.	.80
☐ 1918	26,680,000	2.00	3.00	4.00	9.50	22.00	70.00	250.	.80
☐ 1918D	22,674,800	2.20	3.25	4.00	7.50	18.00	95.00	375.	.80
☐ 1918S	19,300,000	2.20	3.25	3.75	5.50	11.00	80.00	300.	.80
☐ 1919	35,740,000	2.00	2.50	3.50	4.75	7.50	38.00	110.	.80
☐ 1919D	9,939,000	2.50	3.75	5.25	13.00	32.50	175.	525.	.80
☐ 1919S	8,850,000	2.40	3.60	5.00	12.00	27.00	200.	650.	.80
☐ 1920	59,030,000	1.75	2.50	3.50	4.25	7.00	28.00	75.00	.80
☐ 1920D	19,171,000	2.00	3.25	4.00	6.25	13.00	100.	315.	.80
☐ 1920S	13,820,000	2.00	3.25	3.75	6.00	12.00	90.00	290.	.80
☐ 1921	1,230,000	28.00	35.00	85.00	155.	475.	1400.	2600.	18.00
☐ 1921D	1,080,000	40.00	55.00	110.	215.	525.	1350.	2400.	28.00
☐ 1923	50,130,000	1.75	2.50	3.25	3.75	7.00	24.00	70.00	.80
☐ 1923S	6,440,000	2.00	3.50	4.00	7.00	18.00	135.	475.	.80

Date	Mintage	G-4	VG-8	F-12	VF-20	XF-40	MS-60	MS-65	ABP
☐ 1924	24,010,000	1.75	2.50	3.25	4.25	7.00	50.00	125.	.80
☐ 1924D	6,810,000	1.75	3.25	4.00	6.50	17.00	150.	450.	.80
☐ 1924S	7,120,000	2.00	3.25	3.75	6.00	15.00	145.	500.	.80
☐ 1925	25,610,000	1.75	2.50	3.25	4.00	7.00	45.00	125.	.80
☐ 1925D	5,117,000	4.50	5.50	8.50	20.00	60.00	325.	825.	2.50
☐ 1925S	5,850,000	2.00	3.25	3.75	6.25	16.00	170.	600.	.80
☐ 1926	32,160,000	1.75	2.25	3.00	3.50	6.00	24.00	70.00	.80
☐ 1926D	6,828,000	2.00	3.00	4.00	5.50	13.50	100.	375.	.80
☐ 1926S	1,520,000	8.00	10.00	15.00	30.00	95.00	525.	1950.	5.00
☐ 1927	28,080,000	1.75	2.25	3.00	3.75	5.75	24.00	70.00	.80
☐ 1927D	4,812,000	2.50	3.25	5.00	12.00	30.00	275.	700.	.80
☐ 1927S	4,770,000	2.25	3.00	3.50	5.00	14.00	125.	475.	.80
☐ 1928	19,480,000	1.75	2.25	2.75	3.50	4.50	25.00	75.00	.80
☐ 1928D	4,161,000	2.50	3.50	6.00	12.00	30.00	170.	500.	.80
☐ 1928S	7,400,000	2.00	3.00	3.50	4.50	10.00	75.00	285.	.80
☐ 1929	25,970,000	1.75	2.25	2.75	3.50	4.00	20.00	60.00	.80
☐ 1929D	5,034,000	2.25	3.50	4.00	5.75	9.00	40.00	155.	.80
☐ 1929S	4,730,000	2.00	3.00	3.50	4.00	6.00	48.00	185.	.80
☐ 1930	6,770,000	2.00	2.75	3.25	3.75	5.00	30.00	100.	.80
☐ 1930S	1,843,000	3.00	4.00	4.50	5.50	11.00	115.	350.	.80
☐ 1931	3,150,000	2.00	3.25	3.50	4.25	8.00	60.00	145.	1.40
☐ 1931D	1,260,000	8.50	9.50	11.50	17.50	32.00	135.	375.	5.50
☐ 1931S	1,800,000	3.00	4.00	5.00	7.00	11.50	115.	335.	1.80
☐ 1934	24,080,000	1.50	1.80	2.00	2.25	2.50	17.50	85.00	.80
☐ 1934D	6,772,000	1.50	1.80	2.00	2.25	5.00	70.00	185.	.80
☐ 1935	58,830,000	1.50	1.80	2.00	2.25	2.50	14.50	46.00	.80
☐ 1935D	10,477,000	—	1.00	1.25	2.25	7.00	130.	280.	.80
☐ 1935S	15,840,000	—	1.00	1.25	1.80	5.00	45.00	135.	.80
☐ 1936	87,504,130	—	1.00	1.25	1.80	2.50	15.00	45.00	.80
☐ 1936D	16,132,000	—	1.00	1.25	1.80	4.00	70.00	170.	.80
☐ 1936S	9,210,000	—	1.00	1.25	1.80	2.50	37.50	100.	.80
☐ 1937	56,865,756	—	1.00	1.25	1.80	2.50	15.00	45.00	.80
☐ 1937D	14,146,000	—	1.00	1.25	1.80	2.50	55.00	145.	.80
☐ 1937S	9,740,000	—	1.00	1.25	1.80	2.50	45.00	100.	.80
☐ 1938	22,198,728	—	1.00	1.25	1.80	2.50	18.50	55.00	.80
☐ 1938D	5,537,000	—	1.00	1.25	1.80	5.00	60.00	150.	.80
☐ 1938S	8,090,000	—	1.00	1.25	1.80	5.00	30.00	50.00	.80
☐ 1939	67,749,321	—	1.00	1.25	1.80	2.50	13.50	25.00	.80
☐ 1939D	24,394,000	—	1.00	1.25	1.80	2.50	12.00	28.00	.80
☐ 1939S	10,540,000	—	1.00	1.25	1.80	2.50	37.50	80.00	.80
☐ 1940	65,361,827	—	1.00	1.25	1.80	2.50	10.00	18.00	.80
☐ 1940D	21,198,000	—	1.00	1.25	1.80	2.50	30.00	60.00	.80
☐ 1940S	21,560,000	—	1.00	1.25	1.80	2.50	12.25	27.00	.80
☐ 1941	175,106,557	—	1.00	1.25	1.80	2.50	10.00	15.00	.80
☐ 1941D	45,634,000	—	1.00	1.25	1.80	2.50	27.00	28.00	.80
☐ 1941S	43,090,000	—	1.00	1.25	1.75	2.00	11.00	23.00	.80

Date	Mintage	G-4	VG-8	F-12	VF-20	XF-40	MS-60	MS-65	ABP
☐ 1942/41	Unrecorded	335.	350.	400.	425.	500.	1600.	4500.	200.
☐ 1942	205,432,329	—	—	1.00	1.25	1.50	10.00	14.00	.80

Date	Mintage	G-4	VG-8	F-12	VF-20	XF-40	MS-60	MS-65	ABP
☐ 1942D	60,740,000	—	—	1.00	1.25	1.50	18.00	22.00	.80
☐ 1942/41D									
	Unrecorded	335.	350.	400.	425.	500.	1800.	4500.	200.
☐ 1942S	49,300,000	—	—	1.00	1.25	1.50	23.00	48.00	.80
☐ 1943	191,710,000	—	—	1.00	1.25	1.50	10.00	14.00	1.40
☐ 1943D	71,949,000	—	—	1.00	1.25	1.50	8.00	21.00	1.40
☐ 1943S	60,400,000	—	—	1.00	1.25	1.50	21.00	28.00	1.40
☐ 1944	231,410,000	—	—	1.00	1.25	1.50	9.00	14.00	1.40
☐ 1944D	62,224,000	—	—	1.00	1.25	1.50	8.00	21.00	1.40
☐ 1944S	49,490,000	—	—	1.00	1.25	1.50	8.00	18.00	1.40
☐ 1945	159,130,000	—	—	1.00	1.25	1.50	9.00	14.00	1.40
☐ 1945D	40,245,000	—	—	1.00	1.25	1.50	9.00	20.00	1.40
☐ 1945S	41,920,000	—	—	1.00	1.25	1.50	9.00	18.00	1.40
☐ 1945S Micro	Inc.Ab.	—	—	1.50	1.75	2.00	15.00	48.00	1.40

ROOSEVELT DIMES

National sentiment following the death of President Franklin D. Roosevelt on April 12, 1945, led to the creation of the Roosevelt dime which was introduced in 1946. It was fitting that the dime be used for the Roosevelt memorial issue, as the former President was so closely associated with the March of Dimes. The designs were executed by John R. Sinnock, whose initials "JS" appear at the base of the bust. On July 23, 1965, Congress authorized the introduction of a cupronickel clad copper dime to replace the silver standard composition which had gone unchanged for more than 90 years.

1946 - 1964
Reverse

Since 1968
Obverse

Date	Mintage	G-4	VG-8	F-12	VF-20	XF-40	MS-60	MS-65	ABP
☐ 1946	225,250,000	—	—	—	.85	1.00	2.10	4.25	.75
☐ 1946D	61,043,500	—	—	—	.85	1.00	3.20	9.00	.75
☐ 1946S	27,900,000	—	—	—	.85	1.00	5.80	8.25	.75
☐ 1947	121,520,000	—	—	—	.85	1.00	3.80	8.25	.75
☐ 1947D	46,835,000	—	—	.85	1.25	1.70	10.00	14.00	.75
☐ 1947S	34,840,000	—	—	—	.85	1.00	4.70	8.80	.75
☐ 1948	74,950,000	—	—	—	.85	1.00	6.30	7.60	.75
☐ 1948D	52,841,000	—	—	.85	1.25	1.70	14.00	22.00	.75
☐ 1948S	35,520,000	—	—	—	.85	1.00	6.90	14.25	.75
☐ 1949	30,940,000	—	1.25	1.70	2.50	4.00	15.00	29.00	.75
☐ 1949D	26,034,000	—	—	.85	1.00	1.70	12.75	18.00	.75
☐ 1949S	13,510,000	—	1.25	1.70	2.75	4.25	35.00	70.00	.75
☐ 1950	50,181,500	—	—	—	.85	1.00	5.60	7.30	.75
☐ 1950D	46,803,000	—	—	—	.85	1.00	4.00	6.90	.75
☐ 1950S	20,440,000	—	.85	1.25	1.70	2.50	27.50	35.00	.75
☐ 1951	102,937,602	—	—	—	.85	1.00	2.50	6.00	.75
☐ 1951D	56,529,000	—	—	—	.85	1.00	2.50	7.00	.75
☐ 1951S	31,630,000	—	.85	1.25	1.70	1.90	19.50	24.00	.75

Date	Mintage	G-4	VG-8	F-12	VF-20	XF-40	MS-60	MS-65	ABP
☐ 1952	99,122,073	—	—	—	.85	1.00	3.50	5.80	.75
☐ 1952D	122,100,000	—	—	—	.85	1.00	2.80	6.30	.75
☐ 1952S	44,419,500	—	.85	1.25	1.70	1.90	7.25	9.50	.75
☐ 1953	53,618,920	—	—	—	.85	1.00	2.30	5.60	.75
☐ 1953D	136,433,000	—	—	—	.85	1.00	2.80	5.00	.75
☐ 1953S	39,180,000	—	—	—	.85	1.00	2.50	5.00	.75
☐ 1954	114,243,503	—	—	—	.85	1.00	1.80	2.00	.75
☐ 1954D	106,397,000	—	—	—	.85	1.00	2.00	3.00	.75
☐ 1954S	22,860,000	—	—	—	.85	1.00	3.00	5.00	.75
☐ 1955	12,828,381	—	—	1.25	1.50	2.00	3.50	5.90	.75
☐ 1955D	13,959,000	—	—	—	1.30	1.45	2.40	4.00	.75
☐ 1955S	18,510,000	—	—	1.25	1.40	1.40	2.10	6.60	.75
☐ 1956	109,309,384	—	—	—	.85	1.00	1.80	3.75	.75
☐ 1956D	108,015,100	—	—	—	.85	1.00	2.10	4.30	.75
☐ 1957	161,407,952	—	—	—	.85	1.00	1.55	3.75	.75
☐ 1957D	113,354,330	—	—	—	.85	1.00	2.60	5.50	.75
☐ 1958	32,785,652	—	—	—	.85	1.00	2.00	4.25	.75
☐ 1958D	136,564,600	—	—	—	.85	1.00	2.10	3.10	.75
☐ 1959	86,929,291	—	—	—	.85	1.00	2.25	3.00	.75
☐ 1959D	164,919,790	—	—	—	.85	1.00	1.40	1.90	.75
☐ 1960	72,081,602	—	—	—	.85	1.00	1.40	1.90	.75
☐ 1960D	200,160,400	—	—	—	.85	1.00	1.40	1.90	.75
☐ 1961	96,758,244	—	—	—	.85	1.00	1.40	1.90	.75
☐ 1961D	209,146,550	—	—	—	.85	1.00	1.40	1.90	.75
☐ 1962	75,668,019	—	—	—	.85	1.00	1.40	1.90	.75
☐ 1962D	334,948,380	—	—	—	.85	1.00	1.40	1.90	.75
☐ 1963	126,725,645	—	—	—	.85	1.00	1.40	1.90	.75
☐ 1963D	421,476,530	—	—	—	.85	1.00	1.40	1.90	.75
☐ 1964	933,310,762	—	—	—	.85	1.00	1.40	1.90	.75
☐ 1964D	1,357,517,180	—	—	—	.85	1.00	1.40	1.90	.75

Commencing 1965 - See Modern Singles — Page 117

EDUCATIONAL AIDS

With graduation from the novice class, most collectors find it beneficial to subscribe to one of the leading publications which can provide them with news and features on the hobby. Free sample copies of the following are available upon request:

Numismatic News (Weekly)
Iola, Wis., 54945

Coins Magazine (Monthly)
Iola, Wis., 54945

The more advanced collector will also find it beneficial to become a member of the American Numismatic Association, which in addition to providing its members a scholarly monthly journal, also offers a lending library and other services of value to the individual who wants to learn more about his hobby. Full information on the Association may be obtained by writing to:

Executive Director
American Numismatic Association
P.O. Box 2366
Colorado Springs, Colo., 80901

TWENTY CENTS

This shortest lived of U.S. coins - it was actually issued in circulation quantities only in 1875 - was launched at the instigation of Western interests as the answer for change making problems in the West where cents and nickels did not circulate. Authorized by a law dated March 3, 1875, its close similarity in size and design to the quarter contributed to its demise. The coin was proportionate in weight to other silver coins being issued at the time. Congress revoked the authority for the issue on May 2, 1878.

Mintmark

Date	Mintage	G-4	VG-8	F-12	VF-20	XF-40	MS-60	ABP
☐ 1875	39,700	50.00	60.00	100.	150.	295.	2100.	30.00
☐ 1875S	1,155,000	45.00	55.00	70.00	125.	225.	1135.	27.00
☐ 1875CC	133,290	50.00	55.00	100.	150.	275.	1700.	30.00
☐ 1876	15,900	75.00	100.	150.	200.	375.	2100.	45.00
☐ 1876CC	10,000				Auction 80, 1980 A.U. 85,000.			—
☐ 1877	510	—	Proof Only		—	—	—	1500.
☐ Impaired Proof			—	—	500.	850.	—	—
☐ 1878	600	—	Proof Only		—	—	—	1500.
☐ Impaired Proof			—	—	475.	800.	—	—

QUARTERS

If the production of dimes was minimal during the early years of U.S. coinage, the issue of quarters was infinitesimal. Introduced in 1796, as was the dime, the quarter was issued in only six years up to 1818, and in quantity only in 1805-07, to a combined total of some 650,000 pieces. The 1796 draped bust-small eagle type did not carry an indication of value, a trait the quarter shared with the draped bust half dime and dime issues, but the designation "25 C" was added at the base of the reverse with the introduction of the heraldic eagle design when the denomination was next minted in 1804.

Draped Bust Quarters

Date	Mintage	G-4	VG-8	F-12	VF-20	XF-40	MS-60	ABP
☐ 1796	6,146	3500.	4200.	6500.	10,000.	18,000.	35,000.	2100.

HERALDIC EAGLE INTRODUCED

Date	Mintage	G-4	VG-8	F-12	VF-20	XF-40	MS-60	ABP
☐ 1804	6,738	675.	950.	1850.	4250.	10,000.	22,000.	400.
☐ 1805	121,394	275.	375.	700.	1300.	2600.	8800.	165.
☐ 1806	206,124	275.	350.	675.	1300.	2400.	8800.	165.
☐ 1806/5	Inc. Ab.	275.	375.	700.	1600.	2600.	8800.	165.
☐ 1807	220,643	275.	365.	675.	1300.	2400.	8800.	165.

Liberty Cap Quarters

Date	Mintage	G-4	VG-8	F-12	VF-20	XF-40	MS-60	ABP
☐ 1815	89,235	65.00	80.00	100.	300.	600.	3900.	37.50
☐ 1818	361,174	65.00	80.00	100.	300.	600.	3800.	37.50
☐ 1818/15	Inc. Ab.	65.00	80.00	100.	300.	600.	3900.	37.50
☐ 1819 Sm.9	144,000	65.00	80.00	90.00	275.	600.	3800.	37.50
☐ 1819 Lg.9	Inc. Ab.	65.00	80.00	90.00	275.	600.	3800.	37.50
☐ 1820 Sm.O	127,444	65.00	80.00	100.	210.	550.	3800.	37.50
☐ 1820 Lg.O	Inc. Ab.	65.00	80.00	100.	210.	550.	3800.	37.50
☐ 1821	216,851	65.00	80.00	100.	210.	550.	3800.	37.50
☐ 1822	64,080	65.00	80.00	100.	210.	550.	3800.	37.50
☐ 1822 25/50C.	I.A.	175.	350.	450.	800.	1400.	3800	110.
☐ 1823/22	17,800	1500.	6000.	13,500.	16,000.	20,000.	—	900.
			Stack's Auction, Mar. 1977		32,000.		Proof	—
☐ 1824	Unrecorded	65.00	80.00	100.	210.	550.	3800.	37.50
☐ 1825/22	168,000	65.00	80.00	100.	250.	575.	3800.	37.50
☐ 1825/23	Inc. Ab.	65.00	80.00	100.	250.	575.	3800.	37.50
☐ 1825/24	Inc. Ab.	65.00	80.00	100.	250.	575.	3800.	37.50

Date	Mintage	G-4	VG-8	F-12	VF-20	XF-40	MS-60	ABP
☐ 1827 Original	4,000			Garrett Sale 1980		Proof 90,000.		—
☐ 1827 Restrike	I.A.			Stack's Auction 1977		Proof 12,500.		—
☐ 1828	102,000	65.00	80.00	100.	250.	550.	3800.	37.50
☐ 1828 25/50C.	I.A.	70.00	125.	200.	450.	750.	3900.	40.00

MOTTO REMOVED FROM REVERSE

Date	Mintage	G-4	VG-8	F-12	VF-20	XF-40	MS-60	ABP
☐ 1831 Small Letters	398,000	40.00	47.00	55.00	140.	275.	2200.	24.00
☐ 1831 Lg.Let.	Inc. Ab.	40.00	47.00	55.00	140.	275.	2200.	24.00
☐ 1832	320,000	40.00	46.00	55.00	140.	275.	2200.	24.00
☐ 1833	156,000	42.00	50.00	65.00	150.	350.	2200.	24.00
☐ 1834	286,000	40.00	46.00	55.00	140.	275.	2200.	24.00
☐ 1835	1,952,000	40.00	46.00	55.00	140.	275.	2200.	24.00
☐ 1836	472,000	40.00	45.00	55.00	140.	275.	2200.	24.00
☐ 1837	252,400	40.00	45.00	55.00	140.	275.	2200.	24.00
☐ 1838	832,000	40.00	47.00	55.00	140.	275.	2200.	24.00

LIBERTY SEATED QUARTERS

This design was adapted to the quarter in 1838, the year after it was adopted for the lesser fractional silver issues, following the enactment of the January 18, 1837, law which reduced the weight of the coin from 104 grains to 103-1/8. The weight was again lowered to 96 grains in 1853, then increased slightly to 96.45 in 1873. Rays were added in the field around the eagle on the reverse, in addition to the arrows at the date, on the reduced weight 1853 issues. Although the arrows were retained for 1854-55, the rays were dropped. Arrows were again added at the dates in 1873-74 to mark that change.

Mintmark

WITHOUT DRAPERY ON LIBERTY

Date	Mintage	G-4	VG-8	F-12	VF-20	XF-40	MS-60	ABP
☐ 1838	Inc. Ab.	9.50	12.50	17.00	50.00	250.	3150.	5.75
☐ 1839	491,146	9.50	12.50	17.00	50.00	250.	3150.	5.75
☐ 1840O	425,200	9.50	12.50	17.00	50.00	150.	3350.	5.75

DRAPERY ADDED TO LIBERTY

Date	Mintage	G-4	VG-8	F-12	VF-20	XF-40	MS-60	ABP
☐ 1840	188,127	30.00	50.00	85.00	175.	350.	2500.	18.00
☐ 1840O	Inc. Ab.	30.00	50.00	85.00	125.	225.	1600.	18.00
☐ 1841	120,000	75.00	100.	150.	200.	400.	1000.	45.00
☐ 1841O	452,000	25.00	50.00	75.00	100.	200.	1000.	15.00
☐ 1842 Sm Dt	88,000	Bowers & Ruddy Sale, Aug., 1978, Proof					32,500.	—
☐ 1842 Lg Dt	Inc. Ab.	100.	150.	200.	250.	425.	2700.	60.00
☐ 1842O Sm Dt	769,000	400.	500.	700.	1000.	2000.	—	240.
☐ 1842O Lg Dt	Inc. Ab.	25.00	35.00	50.00	85.00	185.	—	15.00
☐ 1843	645,600	8.00	10.00	12.50	21.00	54.00	845.	4.50
☐ 1843O	968,000	25.00	50.00	75.00	100.00	275.	—	15.00
☐ 1844	421,200	8.00	10.00	12.50	21.00	54.00	845.	4.50
☐ 1844O	740,000	8.00	10.00	12.50	21.00	54.00	1200.	4.50
☐ 1845	922,000	8.00	10.00	12.50	21.00	54.00	845.	4.50
☐ 1846	510,000	8.00	10.00	12.50	21.00	54.00	845.	4.50
☐ 1847	734,000	8.00	10.00	12.50	21.00	54.00	845.	4.50
☐ 1847O	368,000	30.00	50.00	75.00	175.	300.	845.	18.00
☐ 1848	146,000	50.00	80.00	125.	200.	375.	845.	30.00
☐ 1849	340,000	25.00	40.00	65.00	100.	175.	845.	15.00
☐ 1849O	Unrecorded	425.	600.	900.	2000.	4000.	—	250.
☐ 1850	190,800	40.00	60.00	90.00	100.	200.	1000.	24.00
☐ 1850O	412,000	25.00	50.00	75.00	100.	200.	1100.	15.00
☐ 1851	160,000	50.00	75.00	100.	125.	250.	1000.	30.00
☐ 1851O	88,000	175.	225.	400.	600.	1200.	—	100.
☐ 1852	177,060	50.00	75.00	100.	125.	250.	900.	30.00
☐ 1852O	96,000	250.	375.	475.	700.	1300.	—	150.
☐ 1853 Recut Date	44,200	200.	300.	400.	500.	700.	4500.	120.

Arrows at Date,

With Rays, 1853 Only

ARROWS AT DATE

Date	Mintage	G-4	VG-8	F-12	VF-20	XF-40	MS-60	ABP
☐ 1853 Rays								
	15,210,020	8.50	12.50	16.00	37.00	125.	1400.	5.00
☐ 1853/4	Inc. Ab.	85.00	150.	350.	500.	1000.	4000.	90.00
☐ 1853O Rays								
	1,332,000	20.00	35.00	50.00	85.00	200.	3000.	12.00
☐ 1854	12,380,000	7.50	10.00	13.50	25.00	115.	1075.	4.25
☐ 1854O	1,484,000	15.00	25.00	40.00	60.00	130.	2500.	9.00
☐ 1854O Huge O								
	Inc. Ab.	150.	250.	350.	700.	1200.	—	90.00
☐ 1855	2,857,000	7.50	10.00	13.50	25.00	115.	1075.	4.25
☐ 1855O	176,000	40.00	55.00	80.00	150.	350.	1850.	24.00
☐ 1855S	396,400	35.00	50.00	75.00	125.	300.	1750.	21.00

ARROWS AT DATE REMOVED

Date	Mintage	G-4	VG-8	F-12	VF-20	XF-40	MS-60	ABP
☐ 1856	7,264,000	8.00	10.00	12.50	21.00	54.00	845.	4.50
☐ 1856O	968,000	20.00	30.00	45.00	65.00	140.	850.	12.00
☐ 1856S	286,000	35.00	55.00	75.00	160.	300.	—	21.00
☐ 1856S/S	Inc. Ab.	100.	150.	400.	700.	1500.	—	60.00
☐ 1857	9,644,000	8.00	10.00	12.50	21.00	54.00	845.	4.50
☐ 1857O	1,180,000	8.00	10.00	12.50	21.00	60.00	900.	4.50
☐ 1857S	82,000	50.00	75.00	175.	260.	500.	—	30.00
☐ 1858	7,368,000	8.00	10.00	12.50	21.00	54.00	845.	4.50
☐ 1858O	520,000	20.00	30.00	45.00	65.00	140.	900.	12.00
☐ 1858S	121,000	30.00	35.00	150.	225.	425.	—	18.00
☐ 1859	1,344,000	8.00	10.00	12.50	21.00	54.00	900.	4.50
☐ 1859O	260,000	35.00	55.00	80.00	115.	225.	900.	21.00
☐ 1859S	80,000	50.00	85.00	165.	250.	475.	—	30.00
☐ 1860	805,400	8.00	10.00	12.50	21.00	54.00	900.	4.50
☐ 1860O	388,000	25.00	35.00	50.00	75.00	160.	925.	15.00
☐ 1860S	56,000	75.00	125.	225.	400.	600.	—	45.00
☐ 1861	4,854,600	8.00	10.00	12.50	21.00	54.00	850.	4.50
☐ 1861S	96,000	30.00	50.00	150.	225.	300.	2600.	18.00
☐ 1862	932,550	8.00	10.00	12.50	65.00	125.	845.	4.50
☐ 1862S	67,000	50.00	75.00	175.	275.	375.	—	30.00
☐ 1863	192,060	25.00	30.00	40.00	75.00	150.	1200.	15.00
☐ 1864	94,070	60.00	75.00	100.	175.	300.	1200.	36.00
☐ 1864S	20,000	150.	200.	350.	500.	1200.	—	90.00
☐ 1865	59,300	60.00	75.00	100.	175.	300.	1250.	36.00
☐ 1865S	41,000	70.00	95.00	160.	250.	400.	2000.	42.00
☐ 1866	—		Unique	—	—	—	—	—

MOTTO ABOVE EAGLE

Date	Mintage	G-4	VG-8	F-12	VF-20	XF-40	MS-60	ABP
☐ 1866	17,525	200.	275.	350.	475.	750.	1400.	120.
☐ 1866S	28,000	150.	200.	350.	500.	800.	—	90.00
☐ 1867	20,625	125.	150.	225.	285.	500.	1300.	75.00
☐ 1867S	48,000	70.00	95.00	185.	285.	450.	3000.	42.00
☐ 1868	30,000	100.	135.	200.	275.	400.	1200.	60.00
☐ 1868S	96,000	25.00	35.00	70.00	140.	225.	2300.	15.00
☐ 1869	16,600	175.	225.	300.	400.	750.	1400.	100.
☐ 1869S	76,000	125.	175.	250.	375.	500.	—	75.00
☐ 1870	87,400	50.00	75.00	115.	185.	275.	1000.	30.00
☐ 1870CC	8,340	900.	1500.	2500.	3000.	4000.	—	525.
☐ 1871	119,160	15.00	25.00	35.00	65.00	125.	1000.	9.00
☐ 1871CC	10,890	500.	700.	1100.	1700.	2600.	—	300.
☐ 1871S	30,900	150.	270.	450.	550.	900.	3000.	90.00
☐ 1872	182,950	11.00	13.00	30.00	65.00	125.	1000.	6.50
☐ 1872CC	22,850	250.	350.	500.	750.	2000.	—	150.
☐ 1872S	83,000	150.	270.	385.	475.	750.	4700.	90.00

Date	Mintage	G-4	VG-8	F-12	VF-20	XF-40	MS-60	ABP
☐ 1873 Clsd.3	212,600	65.00	85.00	175.	215.	350.	—	37.50
☐ 1873 Open 3 Inc. Ab.		30.00	40.00	60.00	115.	200.	630.	18.00
☐ 1873CC	4,000	New England Sale, April, 1980				MS-65 205,000.		—

CLOSED "3", NO ARROWS OPEN "3", ARROWS

ARROWS AT DATE

Date	Mintage	G-4	VG-8	F-12	VF-20	XF-40	MS-60	ABP
☐ 1873	1,271,700	12.00	25.00	30.00	60.00	190.	1325.	7.00
☐ 1873CC	12,462	400.	550.	800.	1500.	2500.	—	240.
☐ 1873S	156,000	12.00	30.00	40.00	65.00	225.	1325.	7.00
☐ 1874	471,900	12.00	25.00	30.00	60.00	190.	1325.	7.00
☐ 1874S	392,000	24.00	30.00	40.00	65.00	225.	1325.	14.00

ARROWS AT DATE REMOVED

Date	Mintage	G-4	VG-8	F-12	VF-20	XF-40	MS-60	ABP
☐ 1875	4,293,500	7.50	9.00	11.00	20.00	75.00	630.	4.25
☐ 1875CC	140,000	50.00	65.00	125.	225.	400.	1400.	30.00
☐ 1875S	680,000	15.00	25.00	40.00	65.00	100.	630.	9.00
☐ 1876	17,817,150	7.50	9.00	11.00	20.00	75.00	630.	4.25
☐ 1876CC	4,944,000	7.50	9.00	11.00	20.00	90.00	630.	4.25
☐ 1876CC (Fine Reeding)								
Inc. Ab.		35.00	50.00	90.00	140.	275.	630.	20.00
☐ 1876S	8,596,000	7.50	9.00	11.00	20.00	75.00	630.	4.25
☐ 1877	10,911,710	7.50	9.00	11.00	20.00	75.00	630.	4.25
☐ 1877CC	4,192,000	10.00	15.00	25.00	50.00	100.	825.	6.00
☐ 1877S	8,996,000	10.00	15.00	25.00	45.00	80.00	630.	6.00
☐ 1877S Over Horizontal S								
Inc. Ab.		45.00	70.00	100.	225.	425.	1400.	27.00
☐ 1878	2,260,800	15.00	18.00	25.00	40.00	75.00	630.	9.00
☐ 1878CC	996,000	25.00	40.00	65.00	85.00	150.	630.	15.00
☐ 1878S	140,000	35.00	50.00	90.00	125.	225.	1500.	20.00
☐ 1879	14,700	90.00	110.	150.	225.	400.	630.	50.00
☐ 1880	14,955	90.00	110.	150.	225.	250.	630.	50.00
☐ 1881	12,975	125.	150.	175.	250.	450.	630.	75.00
☐ 1882	16,300	125.	150.	175.	250.	450.	630.	75.00
☐ 1883	15,439	125.	150.	175.	250.	400.	630.	75.00
☐ 1884	8,875	150.	200.	250.	325.	525.	630.	90.00
☐ 1885	14,530	125.	150.	175.	250.	400.	630.	75.00
☐ 1886	5,886	225.	275.	325.	400.	700.	900.	135.
☐ 1887	10,710	125.	150.	175.	250.	400.	630.	75.00
☐ 1888	10,833	125.	150.	175.	250.	400.	630.	75.00
☐ 1888S	1,216,000	15.00	18.00	25.00	40.00	80.00	630.	9.00
☐ 1889	12,711	125.	150.	175.	250.	400.	630.	75.00
☐ 1890	80,590	50.00	65.00	80.00	100.	200.	630.	30.00
☐ 1891	3,920,600	10.00	18.00	25.00	40.00	80.00	630.	6.00
☐ 1891O	68,000	125.	140.	220.	400.	600.	—	75.00
☐ 1891S	2,216,000	15.00	20.00	25.00	45.00	90.00	630.	9.00

BARBER QUARTERS

Sticking with the tradition of the previous 100 years, during which time the same basic design was carried on all silver units, Barber's Liberty head design was also offered on the quarter in 1892. The larger size of this coin, coupled with the lawful requirement that an eagle be represented on all denominations above the dime, enabled the placement of an eagle on the reverse in substitution for the wreath on the new dime.

Mintmark

Date	Mintage	G-4	VG-8	F-12	VF-20	XF-40	MS-60	MS-65	ABP
☐ 1892	8,237,245	3.75	8.00	16.00	34.00	68.00	475.	2200.	2.25
☐ 1892O	2,640,000	8.00	11.00	22.00	40.00	80.00	575.	3000.	4.50
☐ 1892S	964,079	16.50	25.00	40.00	64.00	130.	700.	4200.	9.50
☐ 1893	5,484,838	3.75	9.00	18.00	36.00	72.00	535.	2200.	2.25
☐ 1893O	3,396,000	5.75	11.50	20.00	39.00	78.00	630.	3150.	2.25
☐ 1893S	1,454,535	9.00	15.00	30.00	49.00	100.00	630.	3150.	5.25
☐ 1894	3,432,972	3.75	8.50	16.00	35.00	70.00	535.	2300.	2.25
☐ 1894O	2,852,000	6.50	13.00	26.00	44.00	89.00	630.	3600.	3.75
☐ 1894S	2,648,821	6.50	12.00	20.00	40.00	80.00	630.	3350.	3.75
☐ 1895	4,440,880	3.75	8.50	16.00	34.00	68.00	535.	2600.	2.25
☐ 1895O	2,816,000	6.50	12.00	22.00	44.00	88.00	700.	4300.	3.75
☐ 1895S	1,764,681	8.00	13.50	28.00	56.00	110.	630.	3150.	4.50
☐ 1896	3,874,762	3.75	10.00	16.00	34.00	68.00	535.	2200.	2.25
☐ 1896O	1,484,000	7.50	15.00	27.00	54.00	125.	2400.	6300.	4.50
☐ 1896S	188,039	300.	350.	775.	950.	1850.	6500.	14,000.	180.
☐ 1897	8,140,731	3.75	7.00	13.00	31.00	66.00	460.	2050.	2.25
☐ 1897O	1,414,800	8.50	17.00	27.00	54.00	115.	1900.	6600.	5.00
☐ 1897S	542,229	13.00	25.00	40.00	70.00	135.	880.	3800.	7.75
☐ 1898	11,100,735	3.75	6.50	13.00	30.00	66.00	460.	2050.	2.25
☐ 1898O	1,868,000	6.50	10.00	23.00	42.00	84.00	880.	6500.	3.75
☐ 1898S	1,020,592	7.00	9.00	19.00	37.00	74.00	585.	4100.	4.00
☐ 1899	12,624,846	3.75	6.75	13.00	30.00	66.00	460.	2050.	3.25
☐ 1899O	2,644,000	6.75	10.00	21.00	42.00	85.00	880.	5700.	3.35
☐ 1899S	708,000	10.00	17.50	30.00	48.00	97.00	750.	3800.	6.00
☐ 1900	10,016,912	3.75	6.75	14.00	33.00	67.00	460.	2050.	2.25
☐ 1900O	3,416,000	8.00	17.00	28.00	55.00	110.	800.	6300.	4.50
☐ 1900S	1,858,585	3.75	9.00	19.00	34.00	69.00	630.	3150.	2.25
☐ 1901	8,892,813	3.75	8.00	14.00	33.00	69.00	460.	2050.	2.25
☐ 1901O	1,612,000	13.00	25.00	45.00	90.00	175.	1575.	8800.	7.75
☐ 1901S	72,664	1350.	1550.	2150.	3000.	4350.	20,000.	50,000.	800.
☐ 1902	12,197,744	3.75	6.75	14.00	31.00	67.00	460.	2050.	2.25
☐ 1902O	4,748,000	6.75	10.00	19.00	40.00	80.00	875.	5000.	2.35
☐ 1902S	1,524,612	10.00	18.00	25.00	50.00	100.	750.	3800.	6.00
☐ 1903	9,670,064	3.75	9.00	14.00	32.00	68.00	460.	2050.	2.25
☐ 1903O	3,500,000	6.75	11.00	18.00	39.00	78.00	630.	4100.	4.00
☐ 1903S	1,036,000	11.00	18.00	28.00	55.00	110.	800.	4400.	6.50

Date	Mintage	G-4	VG-8	F-12	VF-20	XF-40	MS-60	MS-65	ABP
☐ 1904	9,588,813	3.75	9.00	14.00	31.00	67.00	460.	2050.	2.25
☐ 1904O	2,456,000	6.50	11.00	25.00	50.00	110.	1900.	7500.	3.75
☐ 1905	4,968,250	5.50	9.00	15.00	32.00	68.00	460.	2050.	3.25
☐ 1905O	1,230,000	8.00	15.00	29.00	58.00	118.	660.	3300.	4.25
☐ 1905S	1,884,000	7.50	11.00	20.00	40.00	80.00	630.	3100.	3.75
☐ 1906	3,656,435	6.00	10.00	18.00	37.00	75.00	460.	2050.	3.50
☐ 1906D	3,280,000	6.25	10.00	20.00	42.00	84.00	535.	2300.	3.60
☐ 1906O	2,056,000	6.50	12.00	23.00	46.00	90.00	600.	2650.	3.75
☐ 1907	7,192,575	3.75	6.50	13.00	30.00	66.00	460.	2050.	2.25
☐ 1907D	2,484,000	6.75	10.00	21.00	44.00	87.00	600.	2800.	4.00
☐ 1907O	4,560,000	3.75	10.00	18.00	37.00	75.00	535.	2500.	2.25
☐ 1907S	1,360,000	6.00	11.00	20.00	42.00	85.00	700.	3800.	3.50
☐ 1908	4,232,545	3.75	7.00	14.00	32.00	67.00	460.	2250.	2.25
☐ 1908D	5,788,000	3.75	6.50	13.00	30.00	66.00	535.	2400.	2.25
☐ 1908O	6,244,000	3.75	6.50	13.00	30.00	66.00	535.	2400.	2.25
☐ 1908S	784,000	9.00	13.00	26.00	50.00	100.	800.	4100.	5.00
☐ 1909	9,268,650	3.75	6.50	13.00	30.00	66.00	460.	2050.	2.25
☐ 1909D	5,114,000	3.75	6.50	13.00	30.00	66.00	535.	2500.	2.25
☐ 1909O	712,000	10.75	22.00	40.00	80.00	165.	1500.	6300	6.25
☐ 1909S	1,348,000	3.75	8.00	16.00	35.00	72.00	700.	3800.	2.25
☐ 1910	2,244,551	3.75	9.00	17.00	36.00	75.00	460.	2050	2.25
☐ 1910D	1,500,000	6.00	12.00	20.00	42.00	84.00	700.	3800.	3.50
☐ 1911	3,720,543	3.75	9.00	17.00	36.00	72.00	460.	2050.	2.25
☐ 1911D	933,600	6.50	13.00	26.00	53.00	108.	535.	2250.	3.75
☐ 1911S	988,000	6.50	12.00	22.00	45.00	90.00	630.	2800.	3.75
☐ 1912	4,400,700	5.75	8.50	15.00	37.00	74.00	460.	2050.	3.25
☐ 1912S	708,000	6.50	11.00	21.00	43.00	89.00	660.	3000.	3.75
☐ 1913	484,613	11.50	19.00	42.00	130.	375.	3800	10,000.	6.75
☐ 1913D	1,450,800	8.50	14.00	21.00	44.00	95.00	535.	2500.	5.00
☐ 1913S	40,000	385.	465.	775.	1175.	1875.	5000	14,000.	230.
☐ 1914	6,244,610	3.75	6.00	12.00	29.00	65.00	460.	2050.	2.25
☐ 1914D	3,046,000	3.75	6.00	12.00	29.00	65.00	500.	2150.	2.25
☐ 1914S	264,000	14.50	19.50	40.00	95.00	240.	1500.	5000.	8.50
☐ 1915	3,480,450	3.75	6.00	12.00	29.00	65.00	460.	2050.	2.25
☐ 1915D	3,694,000	3.75	6.00	12.00	29.00	65.00	475.	2150.	2.25
☐ 1915S	704,000	6.75	10.00	21.00	45.00	93.00	535.	2500.	4.00
☐ 1916	1,788,000	5.75	7.00	14.00	32.00	68.00	460.	2050.	3.25
☐ 1916D	6,540,800	3.75	6.00	12.00	29.00	65.00	475.	2050.	2.25

STANDING LIBERTY QUARTERS

In 1916 Hermon A. MacNeil's beautiful standing Liberty design for the quarter, which was unfortunately extremely susceptible to wear, was introduced. The devices for this coin were reworked several times in an effort to provide better wearing qualities. The first version, minted in 1916 and early 1917, offers the date atop a raised pedestal below Liberty's feet and presents the eagle low in the field on the reverse. In 1917 the design was reworked for the first time, the most obvious change being in the positioning of the eagle with three stars beneath. This style was continued through 1924, then in 1925 a third version was created by recessing the date in the pedestal beneath Liberty's feet so that it would not wear so easily.

Full Head Detail

Bare Breast
1916-1917

VARIETY I

Date	Mintage	G-4	VG-8	F-12	VF-20	XF-40	MS-60	MS-65	ABP
☐ 1916	52,000	1600.	2000.	2500.	2900.	3250.	5000.	7500.	950.
☐ 1917	8,792,000	12.50	14.00	20.00	35.00	70.00	200.	975.	7.50
☐ 1917D	1,509,200	17.50	21.50	28.00	65.00	140.	315.	975.	10.50
☐ 1917S	1,952,000	16.00	19.00	25.00	55.00	130.	300.	975.	10.00

Normal Head Detail

Mintmark

Chain Mail Clad
1917-1930

Overdate — 18/17S

High Date, 1916-1924

Recessed Date, 1925-1930

VARIETY II

Date	Mintage	G-4	VG-8	F-12	VF-20	XF-40	MS-60	MS-65	ABP
☐ 1917	13,880,000	17.50	20.00	25.00	35.00	70.00	190.	950.	10.50
☐ 1917D	6,224,400	20.00	35.00	45.00	65.00	115.	250.	1500.	12.00
☐ 1917S	5,522,000	21.00	26.50	42.00	60.00	115.	250.	1500.	12.50
☐ 1918	14,240,000	17.50	20.00	27.00	35.00	70.00	190.	975.	10.50
☐ 1918D	7,380,000	24.00	30.00	42.00	65.00	110.	235.	1800.	14.00
☐ 1918S	11,072,000	16.50	19.00	24.00	33.00	74.00	225.	1100.	9.75
☐ 1918S/17	Inc. Ab.	1800.	2600.	3750.	4600.	6000.	12,500.	26,000.	1000.
☐ 1919	11,324,000	30.00	35.00	45.00	55.00	80.00	210.	1100.	18.00
☐ 1919D	1,944,000	50.00	75.00	110.	150.	250.	600.	3000.	30.00
☐ 1919S	1,836,000	48.00	70.00	105.	145.	240.	550.	2650.	28.00
☐ 1920	27,860,000	16.00	18.00	20.00	26.00	52.00	190.	850.	9.50
☐ 1920D	3,586,400	30.00	42.00	60.00	85.00	130.	300.	1900.	18.00
☐ 1920S	6,380,000	17.00	20.00	27.00	35.00	75.00	200.	1075.	10.00
☐ 1921	1,916,000	65.00	95.00	140.	175.	250.	600.	2150.	39.00

Date	Mintage	G-4	VG-8	F-12	VF-20	XF-40	MS-60	MS-65	ABP
☐ 1923	9,716,000	17.00	19.00	21.00	27.00	54.00	225.	900.	10.00
☐ 1923S	1,360,000	165.	225.	295.	350.	465.	950.	2500.	100.
☐ 1924	10,920,000	16.00	18.00	20.00	26.00	50.00	225.	875.	9.00
☐ 1924D	3,112,000	29.00	38.00	54.00	82.00	130.	225.	850.	17.00
☐ 1924S	2,860,000	17.50	20.00	28.00	36.00	62.00	250.	1350.	10.50
☐ 1925	12,280,000	3.50	4.50	10.00	17.50	40.00	190.	625.	2.10
☐ 1926	11,316,000	3.50	4.50	10.00	16.50	40.00	190.	625.	2.10
☐ 1926D	1,716,000	7.50	9.50	15.00	34.00	75.00	190.	650.	4.50
☐ 1926S	2,700,000	5.75	7.00	12.00	25.00	85.00	325.	1650.	3.50
☐ 1927	11,912,000	3.50	4.50	10.00	16.50	40.00	190.	625.	2.10
☐ 1927D	976,400	10.00	13.00	20.00	39.00	97.00	275.	1200.	6.00
☐ 1927S	396,000	18.00	30.00	110.	225.	800.	2500.	7500.	11.00
☐ 1928	6,336,000	3.50	4.50	9.50	16.50	40.00	190.	625.	2.10
☐ 1928D	1,627,600	7.00	8.50	12.00	20.00	52.00	195.	650.	4.25
☐ 1928S	2,644,000	5.75	6.75	11.00	18.00	50.00	250.	650.	3.50
☐ 1929	11,140,000	3.50	4.50	9.50	16.50	40.00	46.00	575.	2.10
☐ 1929D	1,358,000	6.75	8.50	13.00	21.00	54.00	195.	650.	4.00
☐ 1929S	1,764,000	5.75	6.00	12.00	20.00	52.00	250.	650.	3.50
☐ 1930	5,632,000	3.50	4.50	9.50	16.50	40.00	190.	650.	2.10
☐ 1930S	1,556,000	5.75	6.00	12.00	20.00	52.00	250.	650.	4.00

WASHINGTON QUARTERS

Offered in 1932 as a commemorative of the 200th anniversary of Washington's birth, this John Flanagan design was perpetuated as a regular issue in 1934. Flanagan, whose initials appear on the base of the bust to the right of the date, holds the distinction of being the last private artist to author a design for a regular issue U.S. coin with a precious metal content. His work survives on the cupronickel-clad copper quarter introduced in 1965 which had the dual distinction of being the first clad metal issue to be placed in production - August 23 - and in circulation - November 1.

Mintmark
1932-64
Reverse

Since
1968
Obverse

Date	Mintage	G-4	VG-8	F-12	VF-20	XF-40	MS-60	MS-65	ABP
☐ 1932	5,404,000	2.20	2.50	7.50	10.00	11.50	46.00	250.	1.90
☐ 1932D	436,800	46.00	62.00	90.00	125.	190.	1050.	3500.	27.50
☐ 1932S	408,000	45.00	60.00	75.00	100.	140.	650.	2250.	27.00
☐ 1934	31,912,052	2.20	2.50	7.00	8.50	11.00	57.00	60.00	1.90
☐ 1934D	3,527,200	2.20	2.50	8.50	14.00	22.00	190.	580.	1.90
☐ 1935	32,484,000	2.20	2.50	7.00	8.50	11.50	25.00	72.50	1.90
☐ 1935D	5,780,000	2.20	2.50	8.00	14.00	21.00	190.	600.	1.90

Date	Mintage	G-4	VG-8	F-12	VF-20	XF-40	MS-60	MS-65	ABP
☐ 1935S	5,660,000	2.20	2.50	7.50	10.00	13.00	160.	440.	1.90
☐ 1936	41,303,837	2.20	2.50	7.00	8.50	11.50	21.00	72.50	1.90
☐ 1936D	5,374,000	2.20	2.50	8.00	15.00	35.00	380.	1250.	1.90
☐ 1936S	3,828,000	2.20	2.50	7.50	9.50	11.50	80.00	175.	1.90
☐ 1937	19,701,542	2.20	2.50	6.75	8.00	10.00	28.00	50.00	1.90
☐ 1937D	7,189,600	2.20	2.50	3.50	9.50	12.00	65.00	190.	1.90
☐ 1937S	1,652,000	7.25	8.50	10.00	15.00	20.00	190.	440.	3.75
☐ 1938	9,480,045	2.20	2.50	4.00	12.00	17.00	95.00	250.	1.90
☐ 1938S	2,832,000	6.00	6.50	7.50	10.50	13.00	95.00	190.	3.50
☐ 1939	33,548,795	2.20	2.50	3.00	8.00	10.00	20.00	42.00	1.90
☐ 1939D	7,092,000	2.20	2.50	3.00	9.50	11.00	60.00	140.	1.90
☐ 1939S	2,628,000	6.00	6.50	7.50	10.00	13.00	80.00	210.	3.50
☐ 1940	35,715,246	2.20	2.50	3.00	8.00	10.00	16.00	28.00	1.90
☐ 1940D	2,797,600	2.20	2.50	7.50	10.00	15.00	90.00	220.	1.90
☐ 1940S	8,244,000	2.20	2.50	3.00	8.50	11.00	14.00	46.00	1.90
☐ 1941	79,047,287	—	—	2.20	2.50	4.00	8.25	10.50	1.90
☐ 1941D	16,714,800	—	—	2.20	2.50	4.00	25.00	44.00	1.90
☐ 1941S	16,080,000	—	—	2.20	2.50	4.00	25.00	41.00	1.90
☐ 1942	102,117,123	—	—	2.20	2.50	4.00	8.25	11.00	1.90
☐ 1942D	17,487,200	—	—	2.20	2.50	4.00	15.00	23.00	1.90
☐ 1942S	19,384,000	—	—	2.20	2.50	4.00	70.00	95.00	1.90
☐ 1943	99,700,000	—	—	2.20	2.50	4.00	8.25	12.00	1.90
☐ 1943D	16,095,600	—	—	2.20	2.50	4.00	18.00	26.00	1.90
☐ 1943S	21,700,000	—	—	2.20	2.50	4.00	35.00	75.00	1.90
☐ 1944	104,956,000	—	—	2.20	2.50	4.00	6.50	7.50	1.90
☐ 1944D	14,600,800	—	—	2.20	2.50	4.00	8.50	23.00	1.90
☐ 1944S	12,560,000	—	—	2.20	2.50	4.00	9.00	25.00	1.90
☐ 1945	74,372,000	—	—	2.20	2.50	4.00	6.50	12.50	1.90
☐ 1945D	12,341,600	—	—	2.20	2.50	4.00	6.50	17.00	1.90
☐ 1945S	17,004,001	—	—	2.20	2.50	4.00	6.50	13.50	1.90
☐ 1946	53,436,000	—	—	2.20	2.50	4.00	6.50	7.00	1.90
☐ 1946D	9,072,800	—	—	2.20	2.50	4.00	6.50	7.75	1.90
☐ 1946S	4,204,000	—	—	2.20	2.50	4.00	6.50	8.00	1.90
☐ 1947	22,556,000	—	—	2.20	2.50	4.00	6.50	7.25	1.90
☐ 1947D	15,338,400	—	—	2.20	2.50	4.00	6.50	11.50	1.90
☐ 1947S	5,532,000	—	—	2.20	2.50	4.00	6.50	8.00	1.90
☐ 1948	35,196,000	—	—	2.20	2.50	4.00	6.50	6.75	1.90
☐ 1948D	16,766,800	—	—	2.20	2.50	4.00	5.50	6.60	1.90
☐ 1948S	15,960,000	—	—	2.20	2.50	4.00	6.50	11.00	1.90
☐ 1949	9,312,000	—	—	2.20	2.50	4.00	20.00	47.50	1.90
☐ 1949D	10,068,400	—	—	2.20	2.50	4.00	8.00	19.00	1.90
☐ 1950	24,971,512	—	—	2.20	2.50	4.00	6.50	8.00	1.90
☐ 1950D	21,075,600	—	—	2.20	2.50	4.00	6.50	7.25	1.90
☐ 1950 D/S	Inc. Ab.	8.00	15.00	30.00	45.00	125.	280.	—	4.25
☐ 1950S	10,284,004	—	—	2.20	2.50	4.00	8.00	19.00	1.90
☐ 1950S S/D	Inc. Ab.	8.00	15.00	30.00	45.00	140.	440.	—	4.25
☐ 1951	43,505,602	—	—	2.20	2.50	4.00	5.50	7.00	1.90
☐ 1951D	35,354,800	—	—	2.20	2.50	4.00	6.00	7.50	1.90
☐ 1951S	9,048,000	—	—	2.20	2.50	4.00	8.50	17.50	1.90
☐ 1952	38,862,073	—	—	2.20	2.50	4.00	5.50	7.00	1.90
☐ 1952D	49,795,200	—	—	2.20	2.50	4.00	5.50	7.00	1.90
☐ 1952S	13,707,800	—	—	2.20	2.50	4.00	6.50	13.50	1.90
☐ 1953	18,664,920	—	—	2.20	2.50	4.00	5.00	7.00	1.90
☐ 1953D	56,112,400	—	—	2.20	2.50	4.00	5.00	5.25	1.90
☐ 1953S	14,016,000	—	—	2.20	2.50	4.00	5.25	6.25	1.90
☐ 1954	54,645,503	—	—	2.20	2.50	3.00	3.75	4.00	1.90
☐ 1954D	42,305,500	—	—	2.20	2.50	3.50	4.00	4.25	1.90

Date	Mintage	G-4	VG-8	F-12	VF-20	XF-40	MS-60	MS-65	ABP
☐ 1954S	11,834,722	—	—	2.20	2.50	4.00	5.00	5.60	1.90
☐ 1955	18,558,381	—	—	2.20	2.50	3.00	3.25	3.90	1.90
☐ 1955D	3,182,400	—	—	2.20	2.50	4.00	4.50	5.00	1.90
☐ 1956	44,813,384	—	—	2.20	2.50	3.00	3.25	3.65	1.90
☐ 1956D	32,334,500	—	—	2.20	2.50	3.00	3.25	3.65	1.90
☐ 1957	47,779,952	—	—	2.20	2.50	2.75	3.00	3.45	1.90
☐ 1957D	77,924,160	—	—	2.20	2.50	2.75	3.00	3.45	1.90
☐ 1958	7,235,652	—	—	2.20	2.50	3.50	3.75	4.00	1.90
☐ 1958D	78,124,900	—	—	2.20	2.50	2.75	3.00	3.45	1.90
☐ 1959	25,533,291	—	—	2.20	2.50	2.75	2.95	3.15	1.90
☐ 1959D	62,054,232	—	—	2.20	2.40	2.50	2.95	3.15	1.90
☐ 1960	30,855,602	—	—	2.20	2.40	2.50	2.75	3.00	1.90
☐ 1960D	63,000,324	—	—	2.20	2.40	2.50	2.75	3.00	1.90
☐ 1961	40,064,244	—	—	2.20	2.40	2.50	2.75	3.00	1.90
☐ 1961D	83,656,928	—	—	2.20	2.40	2.50	2.75	3.00	1.90
☐ 1962	39,374,019	—	—	2.20	2.40	2.50	2.75	3.00	1.90
☐ 1962D	127,554,756	—	—	2.20	2.40	2.50	2.75	3.00	1.90
☐ 1963	77,391,645	—	—	2.20	2.40	2.50	2.75	3.00	1.90
☐ 1963D	135,288,184	—	—	2.20	2.40	2.50	2.75	3.00	1.90
☐ 1964	564,341,347	—	—	2.20	2.40	2.50	2.75	3.00	1.90
☐ 1964D	704,135,528	—	—	2.20	2.40	2.50	2.75	3.00	1.90

Commencing 1965 - See Modern Singles — Page 117

GRADING STUDIES

Collectors who wish to study the grading or coins in more detail are referred to the *Official A.N.A. Grading Standards for United States Coins,* which provides detailed description and illustrative analysis, through the use of line drawing illustrations, of all coin types of regular issue, in all grades from about good through perfect uncirculated (MS-70) specimens. Two other handy references are *A Guide to the Grading of United States Coins* by Martin R. Brown and John W. Dunn, and *Photograde* by James F. Ruddy.

COINS FROM CIRCULATION

Don't overlook your pocket change when searching for valuable coins. Although most of today's circulating coins are silverless "clad" pieces minted since 1965, along with cents and nickels dating to the late 1950s, which have no premium value and are generally collected by beginners; many valuable coins are still being salvaged from pocket change every day. The bullion content of silver coins makes all of them worth a premium, and many of these issues are even more desirable as collector pieces. Most coins of the World War II era and earlier are worth premiums as collector pieces, particularly those in exceptionally nice condition. Both silver and collector coins can still be frequently encountered by individuals who have an opportunity to search through substantial quantities of change, including rolls of coins obtained at banks or other sources.

HALF DOLLARS

The half dollar was an important product of the mint during its early years, primarily because during a period of more than thirty years beginning in 1805 it was the only coin which was available for large transactions. Aside from sporadic issues of $2.50 and $5 gold pieces during the period, no other large silver or gold coins were produced from 1804 to 1838. Half dollars were issued annually during this period, excepting 1816 when a disasterous fire at the Philadelphia Mint caused a suspension of all precious metal coinage, but most were used only to transfer funds from one bank to another.

The Liberty cap design first engraved by John Reich was introduced to U.S. coinage on the 1807 half. During the period of these issues, 1807-39, the annual production of halves was so substantial that the totals generally exceeded those of the next 35 years by a significant margin. As this was the day of hand engraved dies, the die varieties for most dates are quite numerous, and the series has been extensively collected according to these varieties. In the listing which follows we have enumerated only the most popular of the over 600 known varieties.

The closing years of this type were rather historic ones. First, in 1836 the coin was converted from a lettered edge type to one with reeded edges, at the time the mint was converting to steam power, with new obverse and reverse devices being adopted, with "50 CENTS" placed beneath the eagle in place of "50 C". Second, in 1837 the weight of the coin was lawfully reduced from 208 grains to 206-1/4 and the fineness raised from .8924 to .900. Third, in 1838 the designation of value on the reverse was changed to "HALF DOL". The latter year also marked the inauguration of half dollar production at New Orleans, although the 20 specimens said to have been struck do not appear in the official mint report.

Flowing Hair Half Dollars

Date	Mintage	G-4	VG-8	F-12	VF-20	XF-40	ABP
☐ 1794	23,464	1650.	2500.	3850.	6500.	7900.	975.
☐ 1795	299,680	1150.	1350.	2000.	3275.	5250.	675.
☐ 1795 Recut Date							
	Inc. Ab.	1150.	1350.	2000.	3275.	5350.	675.
☐ 1795 3 Leaves	Inc. Ab.	1350.	1575.	2750.	4500.	7000.	800.

Draped Bust Half Dollars

Date	Mintage	G-4	VG-8	F-12	VF-20	XF-40	ABP
☐ 1796 15 Stars	3,918	13,500.	15,500.	24,500.	40,000.	50,000.	8000.
☐ 1796 16 Stars	Inc. Ab.	13,500.	15,500.	24,500.	40,000.	50,000.	8000.
☐ 1797	Inc. Ab.	13,500.	15,500.	24,500.	42,000.	53,000.	8000.

HERALDIC EAGLE INTRODUCED

Date	Mintage	G-4	VG-8	F-12	VF-20	XF-40	MS-60	ABP
☐ 1801	30,289	150.	325.	800.	1075.	1500.	9500.	90.00
☐ 1802	29,890	175.	375.	800.	1075.	1650.	9200.	100.
☐ 1803 Sm. 3	188,234	100.	175.	275.	695.	1000.	9000.	60.00
☐ 1803 Lg. 3	Inc. Ab.	85.00	125.	200.	500.	950.	9000.	50.00
☐ 1805	211,722	75.00	115.	165.	450.	850.	8900.	45.00
☐ 1805/4	Inc. Ab.	100.	150.	250.	575.	1000.	8900.	60.00
☐ 1806 Round Top 6, Large Stars								
	839,576	75.00	110.	165.	450.	850.	8800.	45.00
☐ 1806 Round Top 6, Small Stars								
	Inc. Ab.	75.00	110.	165.	450.	850.	8800.	45.00
☐ 1806 Pointed Top 6, Stem Not Through Claw								
	Inc. Ab.	75.00	110.	165.	400.	900.	8800.	45.00
☐ 1806 Pointed Top 6, Stem Through Claw								
	Inc. Ab.	75.00	110.	165.	450.	850.	8800.	45.00
☐ 1806/5	Inc. Ab.	80.00	120.	200.	500.	950.	8800.	48.00
☐ 1806 Over Inverted 6								
	Inc. Ab.	100.	140.	250.	550.	975.	8800.	60.00
☐ 1807	301,076	80.00	110.	165.	450.	850.	8800.	48.00

Liberty Cap Half Dollars

Date	Mintage	G-4	VG-8	F-12	VF-20	XF-40	MS-60	ABP
☐ 1807 Sm. Stars	750,500	40.00	50.00	65.00	110.	300.	950.	35.00
☐ 1807 Lg. Stars	Inc. Ab.	37.50	42.50	50.00	85.00	200.	800.	22.00
☐ 1807 50/20 C.	Inc. Ab.	37.50	42.50	50.00	85.00	200.	950.	22.00
☐ 1808	1,368,600	37.50	42.50	53.00	70.00	145.	700.	22.00
☐ 1808/7	Inc. Ab.	37.50	42.50	60.00	80.00	175.	725.	22.00
☐ 1809	1,405,810	36.00	42.50	55.00	75.00	145.	700.	21.00
☐ 1810	1,276,276	34.50	38.00	46.00	65.00	135.	700.	20.00
☐ 1811 Sm. 8	1,203,644	32.00	37.50	45.00	60.00	135.	700.	19.00
☐ 1811 Lg. 8	Inc. Ab.	32.50	37.00	45.00	60.00	135.	700.	16.00
☐ 1811 Dt. 18.11	Inc. Ab.	33.00	38.00	41.00	87.50	135.	735.	19.50
☐ 1812	1,628,059	32.50	37.50	45.00	60.00	135.	700.	19.00
☐ 1812/11	Inc. Ab.	37.50	42.50	55.00	75.00	135.	725.	22.00
☐ 1813	1,241,903	32.50	37.50	45.00	60.00	135.	700.	19.00
☐ 1814	1,039,075	34.50	38.00	41.00	65.00	135.	700.	20.00
☐ 1814/13	Inc. Ab.	37.50	42.50	50.00	70.00	200.	750.	22.00
☐ 1815/12	47,150	450.	650.	900.	1150.	1500.	3600.	270.
☐ 1817	1,215,567	31.50	33.00	40.00	60.00	135.00	665.	18.50
☐ 1817/13	Inc. Ab.	37.50	46.00	70.00	80.00	250.	900.	22.00
☐ 1817/14				5 Pieces Known - Rare				—
☐ 1817 Dt. 181.7	Inc. Ab.	32.00	37.50	45.00	60.00	125.	800.	19.00
☐ 1818	1,960,322	31.50	33.00	40.00	60.00	135.	700.	18.50
☐ 1818/17.	Inc. Ab.	31.50	33.00	40.00	60.00	135.	735.	18.50
☐ 1819	2,208,000	31.50	33.00	40.00	60.00	135.	700.	18.50
☐ 1819/18 Sm. 9	Inc. Ab.	31.50	33.00	40.00	60.00	135.	735.	18.50
☐ 1819/18 Lg. 9	Inc. Ab.	31.50	33.00	40.00	60.00	135.	735.	18.50
☐ 1820 Sm. Dt.	751,122	35.00	47.00	57.00	70.00	140.	800.	21.00
☐ 1820 Lg. Dt.	Inc. Ab.	35.00	47.00	57.00	70.00	160.	750.	21.00
☐ 1820/19	Inc. Ab.	35.00	45.00	55.00	65.00	135.	750.	21.00
☐ 1821	1,305,797	33.00	35.00	40.00	60.00	135.	665.	19.50
☐ 1822	1,559,573	32.00	34.00	40.00	60.00	135.	700.	19.00
☐ 1822/1	Inc. Ab.	45.00	55.00	80.00	115.	225.	800.	27.00
☐ 1823	1,694,200	31.50	33.00	40.00	60.00	135.	735.	18.50
☐ 1823 Broken 3	Inc. Ab.	35.00	50.00	80.00	100.	200.	850.	21.00
☐ 1823 Patched 3	Inc. Ab.	35.00	50.00	75.00	95.00	150.	850.	21.00
☐ 1823 Ugly 3	Inc. Ab.	32.00	35.00	40.00	65.00	135.	800.	19.00
☐ 1824	3,504,954	31.00	33.00	40.00	60.00	135.	700.	18.00
☐ 1824/21	Inc. Ab.	33.00	37.00	42.00	65.00	135.	800.	19.50
☐ 1824/Over Various Dates								
	Inc. Ab.	31.50	33.00	40.00	60.00	135.	800.	18.50
☐ 1825	2,943,166	31.50	33.00	40.00	60.00	135.	685.	18.50
☐ 1826	4,004,180	31.50	33.00	40.00	60.00	125.	685.	18.50

Date	Mintage	G-4	VG-8	F-12	VF-20	XF-40	MS-60	ABP
☐ 1827 Curled 2	5,493,400	33.00	36.00	42.50	65.00	125.	700.	19.50
☐ 1827 Square 2	Inc. Ab.	31.50	33.00	40.00	60.00	125.	685.	18.50
☐ 1827/6	Inc. Ab.	33.50	35.00	40.00	65.00	125.	700.	19.50
☐ 1828 Curled Base 2, No Knob								
	3,075,200	30.00	32.50	37.50	60.00	125.	700.	18.00
☐ 1828 Curled Base 2, Knobbed 2								
	Inc. Ab.	35.00	45.00	60.00	85.00	150.	735.	21.00
☐ 1828 Small 8's, Square Base 2, Large Letters								
	Inc. Ab.	30.00	32.50	37.50	60.00	125.	685.	18.00
☐ 1828 Small 8's, Square Base 2, Small Letters								
	Inc. Ab.	30.00	32.50	45.00	65.00	150.	735.	18.00
☐ 1828 Large 8's, Square Base 2								
	Inc. Ab.	30.00	32.50	37.50	60.00	125.	685.	18.00
☐ 1829	3,712,156	30.00	32.50	37.50	60.00	125.	685.	18.00
☐ 1829/27	Inc. Ab.	31.50	33.00	40.00	65.00	135.	725.	18.50
☐ 1830 Small 0 In Date								
	4,764,800	30.00	32.50	37.00	60.00	125.	665.	18.00
☐ 1830 Large 0 In Date								
	Inc. Ab.	30.00	32.50	37.50	60.00	125.	665.	18.00
☐ 1831	5,873,660	30.00	32.50	37.00	60.00	125.	665.	18.00
☐ 1832 Sm. Lt.	4,797,000	30.00	32.50	37.50	60.00	125.	665.	18.00
☐ 1832 Lg. Let.	Inc. Ab.	30.00	32.50	37.50	60.00	125.	665.	18.00
☐ 1833	5,206,000	30.00	32.50	37.50	60.00	125.	665.	18.00
☐ 1834 Small Date, Large Stars, Small Letters								
	6,412,004	30.00	32.50	37.50	60.00	125.	665.	18.00
☐ 1834 Small Date, Small Stars, Small Letters								
	Inc. Ab.	30.00	32.50	37.50	60.00	125.	665.	18.00
☐ 1834 Large Date, Small Letters								
	Inc. Ab.	30.00	32.50	37.50	60.00	125.	665.	18.00
☐ 1834 Large Date, Large Letters								
	Inc. Ab.	30.00	32.50	37.50	60.00	125.	665.	18.00
☐ 1835	5,352,006	30.00	32.50	37.50	60.00	125.	665.	18.00
☐ 1836	6,545,000	30.00	32.50	37.50	60.00	125.	665.	18.00
☐ 1836 50/00	Inc. Ab.	37.50	45.00	60.00	85.00	175.	700.	22.00

REEDED EDGE - 50 CENTS ON REVERSE

Date	Mintage	G-4	VG-8	F-12	VF-20	XF-40	MS-60	ABP
☐ 1836	1,200	250.	350.	750.	1075.	1875.	4100.	150.
☐ 1837	3,629,820	35.00	42.50	50.00	80.00	185.	2000.	21.00

Mintmark

HALF DOL. ON REVERSE

Date	Mintage	G-4	VG-8	F-12	VF-20	XF-40	MS-60	ABP
☐ 1838	3,546,000	35.00	42.50	50.00	80.00	185.	2100.	21.00
☐ 1838O	Est. 20	—	Stack's Sale, March, 1975, Proof 50,000.					—
☐ 1839	3,334,560	35.00	43.00	50.00	80.00	190.	2000.	21.00
☐ 1839O	178,976	85.00	125.	185.	325.	450.	3250.	50.00

LIBERTY SEATED HALVES

The Liberty seated half dollar series followed the same course as did the quarter series of this type. The reduction of its weight from 206-1/4 grains to 192 in 1853 was marked by the placing of arrows at the date on the 1853-55 issues, while rays were also present on the reverse in 1853, then arrows were again used at the date in 1873-74 to mark a weight increase to 192.9 grains.

Although the 1861-O half has a total recorded mintage of 2,532,633, only a small fraction of that quantity actually constitute U.S. issues. The mint was seized by the government of secessionist Louisiana on January 31, after 330,000 halves had been struck under the U.S. government. From then until the mint was transferred to the Confederacy in April, another 1,240,000 halves are recorded as having been struck. Before the mint's operations were closed out on May 31, another 962,633 pieces were produced, plus four trial strikings of a distinctive Confederate half dollar design which was never placed in production.

Mintmark

Date	Mintage	G-4	VG-8	F-12	VF-20	XF-40	MS-60	ABP
☐ 1839 No Drapery From Elbow								
	Inc. Ab.	32.00	40.00	100.	145.	400.	11,000.	18.00
☐ 1839 Drapery	Inc. Ab.	22.50	27.50	33.50	75.00	150.	800.	13.00
☐ 1840 Sm. Let.	1,435,008	15.00	17.50	38.00	90.00	125.	800.	9.00
☐ 1840 Rev. 1838	Inc. Ab.	60.00	85.00	115.	225.	350.	1500.	35.00
☐ 1840O	855,100	15.00	17.50	38.00	90.00	150.	850.	9.00
☐ 1841	310,000	50.00	75.00	100.	145.	275.	900.	35.00
☐ 1841O	401,000	15.00	17.50	38.00	90.00	175.	900.	9.00
☐ 1842 Sm. Date	2,012,764	15.00	50.00	75.00	125.	225.	850.	9.00
☐ 1842 Lg. Date	Inc. Ab.	15.00	17.50	38.00	90.00	125.	850.	9.00
☐ 1842O Sm. Date	957,000	400.	500.	700.	1000.	2000.	—	240.
☐ 1842O Lg. Date	Inc. Ab.	15.00	17.50	38.00	90.00	150.	800.	9.00
☐ 1843	3,844,000	15.00	17.50	38.00	90.00	125.	800.	9.00
☐ 1843O	2,268,000	15.00	17.50	38.00	90.00	150.	850.	9.00
☐ 1844	1,766,000	15.00	17.50	38.00	90.00	125.	800.	9.00
☐ 1844O	2,005,000	15.00	17.50	38.00	90.00	150.	850.	9.00

Date	Mintage	G-4	VG-8	F-12	VF-20	XF-40	MS-60	ABP
☐ 1845	589,000	40.00	60.00	90.00	140.	235.	950.	24.00
☐ 1845O	2,094,000	15.00	17.50	38.00	110.	175.	1100.	9.00
☐ 1845O No Drapery								
	Inc. Ab.	40.00	60.00	80.00	110.	175.	875.	24.00
☐ 1846 Med Dt	2,210,000	15.00	17.50	38.00	90.00	125.	800.	9.00
☐ 1846 Tall Dt	Inc. Ab.	15.00	17.50	38.00	90.00	125.	800.	9.00
☐ 1846 Over Horizontal 6								
	Inc. Ab.	70.00	100.	150.	200.	350.	875.	40.00
☐ 1846O Med Dt	2,304,000	15.00	17.50	38.00	90.00	125.	800.	9.00
☐ 1846O Tall Dt	Inc. Ab.	80.00	95.00	140.	270.	380.	1200.	45.00
☐ 1847/46	1,156,000	350.	500.	750.	1250.	2000.	—	210.
☐ 1847	Inc. Ab.	15.00	17.50	38.00	90.00	125.	800.	9.00
☐ 1847O	2,584,000	15.00	17.50	38.00	90.00	125.	800.	9.00
☐ 1848	580,000	40.00	55.00	80.00	140.	225.	900.	24.00
☐ 1848O	3,180,000	15.00	17.50	38.00	90.00	125.	800.	9.00
☐ 1849	1,252,000	15.00	17.50	38.00	90.00	180.	800.	9.00
☐ 1849O	2,310,000	15.00	17.50	38.00	90.00	125.	800.	9.00
☐ 1850	227,000	45.00	75.00	130.	200.	400.	800.	27.00
☐ 1850O	2,456,000	15.00	17.50	38.00	90.00	150.	800.	9.00
☐ 1851	200,750	50.00	80.00	115.	225.	350.	950.	30.00
☐ 1851O	402,000	50.00	65.00	85.00	110.	180.	800.	30.00
☐ 1852	77,130	100.	200.	300.	425.	700.	2500.	60.00
☐ 1852O	144,000	75.00	125.	175.	225.	425.	1500.	45.00
☐ 1853O	Unrecorded		Garrett Sale, 1979, VF 40,000.					

ARROWS AT DATE

Date	Mintage	G-4	VG-8	F-12	VF-20	XF-40	MS-60	ABP
☐ 1853 Rays On Reverse								
	3,532,708	16.50	22.50	30.00	80.00	210.	2850.	10.00
☐ 1853O Rays On Reverse								
	1,328,000	22.50	40.00	50.00	150.	275.	2850.	13.00
☐ 1854	2,982,000	15.00	17.50	22.00	38.00	90.00	1200.	9.00
☐ 1854O	5,240,000	15.00	17.50	22.00	38.00	90.00	1200.	9.00
☐ 1855	759,500	15.00	17.50	22.00	38.00	90.00	1400.	9.00
☐ 1855O	3,688,000	15.00	17.50	22.00	38.00	90.00	1200.	9.00
☐ 1855S	129,950	125.	175.	325.	575.	1000.	2750.	75.00

ARROWS AT DATE REMOVED

Date	Mintage	G-4	VG-8	F-12	VF-20	XF-40	MS-60	ABP
☐ 1856	938,000	15.00	17.50	20.00	30.00	60.00	850.	9.00
☐ 1856O	2,658,000	15.00	17.50	20.00	30.00	60.00	850.	9.00
☐ 1856S	211,000	40.00	60.00	80.00	200.	300.	1200.	24.00

Date	Mintage	G-4	VG-8	F-12	VF-20	XF-40	MS-60	ABP
☐ 1857	1,988,000	15.00	17.50	20.00	30.00	60.00	800.	9.00
☐ 1857O	818,000	15.00	17.50	20.00	30.00	60.00	900.	9.00
☐ 1857S	158,000	35.00	55.00	75.00	190.	350.	1200.	21.00
☐ 1858	4,226,000	15.00	17.50	20.00	30.00	60.00	800.	9.00
☐ 1858O	7,294,000	15.00	17.50	20.00	30.00	60.00	800.	9.00
☐ 1858S	476,000	30.00	40.00	50.00	125.	180.	950.	18.00
☐ 1859	748,000	15.00	17.50	20.00	30.00	60.00	800.	9.00
☐ 1859O	2,834,000	15.00	17.50	20.00	30.00	60.00	825.	9.00
☐ 1859S	566,000	30.00	40.00	50.00	125.	150.	900.	18.00
☐ 1860	303,700	50.00	75.00	125.	140.	285.	850.	30.00
☐ 1860O	1,290,000	15.00	17.50	20.00	30.00	60.00	825.	9.00
☐ 1860S	472,000	30.00	40.00	50.00	80.00	150.	850.	18.00
☐ 1861	2,888,400	15.00	17.50	20.00	30.00	60.00	800.	9.00
☐ 1861O	2,532,633	30.00	40.00	50.00	80.00	110.	800.	18.00
☐ 1861S	939,500	15.00	17.50	20.00	30.00	60.00	825.	9.00
☐ 1862	253,550	50.00	75.00	125.	185.	250.	900.	30.00
☐ 1862S	1,352,000	15.00	17.50	20.00	30.00	60.00	800.	9.00
☐ 1863	503,660	24.00	30.00	50.00	85.00	185.	900.	14.00
☐ 1863S	916,000	15.00	17.50	20.00	30.00	60.00	800.	9.00
☐ 1864	379,570	24.00	30.00	50.00	85.00	185.	900.	14.00
☐ 1864S	658,000	15.00	17.50	20.00	30.00	60.00	800.	9.00
☐ 1865	511,900	28.00	35.00	60.00	110.	195.	900.	16.00
☐ 1865S	675,000	15.00	17.50	20.00	30.00	60.00	750.	9.00
☐ 1866	—	—	—	—	Proof, Unique		—	
☐ 1866S	1,054,000	40.00	65.00	100.	190.	275.	850.	24.00

MOTTO ABOVE EAGLE

Date	Mintage	G-4	VG-8	F-12	VF-20	XF-40	MS-60	ABP
☐ 1866	745,625	20.00	25.00	50.00	85.00	170.	900.	12.00
☐ 1866S	Inc. Ab.	20.00	25.00	30.00	60.00	125.	725.	12.00
☐ 1867	449,925	30.00	38.00	70.00	120.	175.	1100.	18.00
☐ 1867S	1,196,000	14.00	17.00	19.00	26.00	50.00	725.	8.50
☐ 1868	418,200	60.00	70.00	90.00	125.	275.	1000.	35.00
☐ 1868S	1,160,000	14.00	17.00	19.00	26.00	50.00	725.	8.50
☐ 1869	795,900	14.00	17.00	19.00	26.00	50.00	725.	8.50
☐ 1869S	656,000	25.00	30.00	40.00	70.00	140.	800.	15.00
☐ 1870	634,900	25.00	30.00	40.00	70.00	115.	800.	15.00
☐ 1870CC	54,617	300.	500.	1000.	1500.	2000.	—	180.
☐ 1870S	1,004,000	30.00	35.00	45.00	80.00	150.	850.	18.00
☐ 1871	1,204,560	14.00	17.00	19.00	26.00	50.00	725.	8.50
☐ 1871CC	153,950	85.00	125.	200.	300.	600.	3500.	50.00
☐ 1871S	2,178,000	14.00	17.00	19.00	26.00	50.00	725.	8.50

Date	Mintage	G-4	VG-8	F-12	VF-20	XF-40	MS-60	ABP
☐ 1872	881,550	14.00	17.00	19.00	26.00	50.00	725.	8.50
☐ 1872CC	272,000	75.00	100.	150.	200.	325.	1500.	45.00
☐ 1872S	580,000	40.00	50.00	85.00	185.	285.	725.	24.00
☐ 1873 Closed 3								
	801,800	25.00	40.00	65.00	125.	225.	800.	15.00
☐ 1873 Open 3								
	Inc. Ab.	100.	200.	500.	1500.	3000.	—	60.00
☐ 1873CC	122,500	75.00	100.	200.	300.	400.	1750.	45.00
☐ 1873S No Arrows		5,000 Minted			No Specimens Known To Survive			

ARROWS AT DATE

Date	Mintage	G-4	VG-8	F-12	VF-20	XF-40	MS-60	ABP
☐ 1873	1,815,700	20.00	30.00	40.00	90.00	200.	2100.	12.00
☐ 1873CC	214,560	75.00	100.	200.	300.	400.	2300.	45.00
☐ 1873S	233,000	27.50	32.50	45.00	95.00	225.	2100.	16.00
☐ 1874	2,360,300	25.00	30.00	40.00	90.00	200.	2250.	15.00
☐ 1874CC	59,000	185.	300.	425.	600.	1000.	2500.	110.
☐ 1874S	394,000	28.00	34.00	50.00	110.	235.	2100.	16.00

ARROWS AT DATE REMOVED

Date	Mintage	G-4	VG-8	F-12	VF-20	XF-40	MS-60	ABP
☐ 1875	6,027,500	14.00	17.00	19.00	26.00	50.00	725.	8.50
☐ 1875CC	1,008,000	20.00	25.00	50.00	65.00	100.	725.	12.00
☐ 1875S	3,200,000	14.00	17.00	19.00	26.00	50.00	725.	8.50
☐ 1876	8,419,150	14.00	17.00	19.00	26.00	50.00	725.	8.50
☐ 1876CC	1,956,000	22.00	30.00	35.00	55.00	100.	725.	13.00
☐ 1876S	4,528,000	14.00	17.00	19.00	26.00	50.00	725.	8.50
☐ 1877	8,304,510	14.00	17.00	19.00	26.00	50.00	725.	8.50
☐ 1877CC	1,420,000	14.00	17.00	19.00	26.00	50.00	725.	8.50
☐ 1877S	5,356,000	14.00	17.00	19.00	26.00	50.00	725.	8.50
☐ 1878	1,378,400	30.00	50.00	65.00	85.00	125.	725.	18.00
☐ 1878CC	62,000	250.	350.	525.	875.	1500.	3000.	150.
☐ 1878S	12,000	3000.	3500.	4500.	5500.	7000.	14,000.	1800.
☐ 1879	5,900	275.	300.	375.	425.	650.	1450.	165.
☐ 1880	9,755	200.	225.	300.	325.	550.	1400.	120.
☐ 1881	10,975	200.	225.	300.	325.	500.	1350.	120.
☐ 1882	5,500	300.	325.	400.	450.	675.	1450.	180.
☐ 1883	9,039	200.	225.	300.	325.	550.	1350.	120.
☐ 1884	5,275	300.	325.	400.	450.	675.	1450.	180.
☐ 1885	6,130	275.	300.	375.	425.	600.	1350.	165.
☐ 1886	5,886	275.	300.	375.	425.	625.	1350.	165.
☐ 1887	5,710	275.	300.	375.	425.	625.	1375.	165.
☐ 1888	12,833	165.	225.	300.	350.	500.	1150.	100.
☐ 1889	12,711	175.	225.	300.	350.	500.	1150.	105.
☐ 1890	12,590	185.	200.	265.	350.	550.	1175.	110.
☐ 1891	200,600	20.00	25.00	35.00	60.00	115.	800.	12.00

BARBER HALVES

The Barber half is identical in design to the quarter, and was issued over the same period of time as it and the dime, excepting that none were minted in 1916.

Mintmark

Date	Mintage	G-4	VG-8	F-12	VF-20	XF-40	MS-60	MS-65	ABP
☐ 1892	935,245	15.00	26.00	40.00	80.00	180.	950.	3600.	9.00
☐ 1892O	390,000	105.	150.	200.	300.	450.	2200.	6300.	60.00
☐ 1892S	1,029,028	115.	140.	180.	275.	375.	1700.	6800.	65.00
☐ 1893	1,826,792	14.50	25.00	44.00	88.00	190.	900.	3600.	8.50
☐ 1893O	1,389,000	21.50	35.00	53.00	120.	260.	1400.	6600.	12.50
☐ 1893S	740,000	65.00	115.	160.	240.	340.	1600.	7250.	39.00
☐ 1894	1,148,972	13.00	25.00	48.00	90.00	210.	1000.	3600.	7.50
☐ 1894O	2,138,000	13.50	27.00	48.00	98.00	230.	1200.	6300.	8.00
☐ 1894S	4,048,690	12.00	20.00	26.00	68.00	180.	1075.	5500.	7.25
☐ 1895	1,835,218	12.00	21.00	31.00	77.00	185.	1075.	4850.	7.25
☐ 1895O	1,766,000	13.00	26.00	45.00	90.00	200.	1400.	6600.	7.50
☐ 1895S	1,108,086	20.00	32.00	58.00	115.	250.	1000.	5000.	11.00
☐ 1896	950,762	15.00	24.00	48.00	100.	220.	1100.	3600.	9.00
☐ 1896O	924,000	18.50	26.00	55.00	125.	300.	2900.	8500.	11.00
☐ 1896S	1,140,948	55.00	80.00	110.	180.	350.	2900.	8500.	33.00
☐ 1897	2,480,731	8.50	17.00	26.50	70.00	165.	850.	3600.	5.00
☐ 1897O	632,000	50.00	70.00	105.	190.	375.	3500.	10,750.	30.00
☐ 1897S	933,900	100.	125.	125.	200.	400.	2500.	9500.	60.00
☐ 1898	2,956,735	8.50	10.00	25.00	65.00	155.	900.	3600.	5.00
☐ 1898O	874,000	19.00	30.00	75.00	160.	350.	1700.	8500.	11.00
☐ 1898S	2,358,550	13.00	22.00	30.00	80.00	165.	1400.	6600.	7.50
☐ 1899	5,538,846	8.50	10.00	25.00	64.00	155.	850.	3600.	5.00
☐ 1899O	1,724,000	8.50	18.00	38.00	90.00	200.	1575.	8800.	5.00
☐ 1899S	1,686,411	13.00	22.00	34.00	70.00	160.	1150.	5500.	7.50
☐ 1900	4,762,912	7.50	15.00	26.50	66.00	155.	850.	3600.	5.00
☐ 1900O	2,744,000	7.50	10.00	28.50	75.00	170.	1900.	10,750.	5.00
☐ 1900S	2,560,322	7.50	18.00	27.50	70.00	155.	1300.	6000.	5.00
☐ 1901	4,268,813	7.50	10.00	20.00	67.00	155.	850.	3600.	5.00
☐ 1901O	1,124,000	7.50	12.00	35.00	110.	275.	2200.	10,000.	5.00
☐ 1901S	847,044	17.00	26.00	60.00	165.	400.	2800.	10,000.	10.00
☐ 1902	4,922,777	7.50	10.00	20.00	65.00	155.	850.	3600.	5.00
☐ 1902O	2,526,000	7.50	12.00	22.00	72.00	160.	1600.	8500.	5.00
☐ 1902S	1,460,670	12.00	21.00	33.00	95.00	190.	1600.	6300.	7.50
☐ 1903	2,278,755	7.50	13.00	30.00	80.00	175.	850.	3600.	5.00
☐ 1903O	2,100,000	7.50	20.00	32.00	90.00	185.	1600.	6600.	5.00
☐ 1903S	1,920,772	7.50	12.00	28.00	75.00	175.	1450.	5700.	5.00

Date	Mintage	G-4	VG-8	F-12	VF-20	XF-40	MS-60	MS-65	ABP
☐ 1904	2,992,670	7.50	10.00	20.00	70.00	156.	900.	3600.	5.00
☐ 1904O	1,117,600	12.00	20.00	42.00	125.	275.	2800.	10,500.	7.50
☐ 1904S	553,038	13.50	25.00	65.00	140.	320.	2300.	8800.	8.00
☐ 1905	662,727	7.50	24.00	53.00	125.	280.	1500.	6300.	5.00
☐ 1905O	505,000	13.50	27.00	60.00	133.	300.	1800.	8000.	8.00
☐ 1905S	2,494,000	7.50	10.00	20.00	70.00	155.	1500.	8200.	7.50
☐ 1906	2,638,675	7.50	10.00	20.00	65.00	155.	850.	3600.	5.00
☐ 1906D	4,028,000	7.50	10.00	20.00	66.00	155.	950.	3600.	5.00
☐ 1906O	2,446,000	7.50	11.00	20.00	68.00	160.	1300.	4200.	5.00
☐ 1906S	1,740,154	7.50	19.00	32.00	80.00	180.	1200.	5000.	5.00
☐ 1907	2,598,575	7.50	10.00	20.00	66.00	155.	850.	3600.	5.00
☐ 1907D	3,856,000	7.50	10.00	20.00	67.00	155.	950.	3600.	5.00
☐ 1907O	3,946,000	7.50	10.00	20.00	67.00	154.	1100.	4200.	5.00
☐ 1907S	1,250,000	7.50	18.00	29.00	77.00	175.	1600.	6300.	5.00
☐ 1908	1,354,545	7.50	12.00	31.00	84.00	200.	900.	3600.	5.00
☐ 1908D	3,280,000	7.50	10.00	20.00	65.00	155.	950.	3600.	5.00
☐ 1908O	5,360,000	7.50	10.00	20.00	65.00	155.	950.	3600.	5.00
☐ 1908S	1,644,828	7.50	11.00	27.00	75.00	170.	1200.	5000.	5.00
☐ 1909	2,368,650	7.50	10.00	20.00	65.00	155.	850.	3600.	5.00
☐ 1909O	925,400	11.00	17.00	28.50	85.00	225.	1850.	8200.	6.50
☐ 1909S	1,764,000	7.50	10.00	20.00	66.00	160.	1300.	5000.	5.00
☐ 1910	418,551	12.50	19.00	45.00	110.	280.	1500.	4600.	7.50
☐ 1910S	1,948,000	7.50	10.00	20.00	66.00	155.	1425.	4400.	5.00
☐ 1911	1,406,543	7.50	10.00	25.00	68.00	160.	850.	3600.	5.00
☐ 1911D	695,080	11.00	17.00	30.00	78.00	195.	950.	3800.	6.50
☐ 1911S	1,272,000	7.50	10.00	26.00	70.00	160.	1075.	4100.	5.00
☐ 1912	1,550,700	7.50	10.00	20.00	65.00	155.	900.	4000.	5.00
☐ 1912D	2,300,800	7.50	10.00	20.00	65.00	155.	850.	3600.	5.00
☐ 1912S	1,370,000	7.50	10.00	20.00	66.00	155.	1100.	5200.	5.00
☐ 1913	188,627	20.00	32.00	75.00	170.	350.	1800.	6800.	12.00
☐ 1913D	534,000	12.00	20.00	32.00	85.00	210.	1100.	4000.	7.50
☐ 1913S	604,000	12.00	19.00	30.00	80.00	200.	1400.	5850.	7.50
☐ 1914	124,610	28.00	42.00	90.00	200.	400.	1850.	6200.	17.00
☐ 1914S	992,000	12.00	16.00	25.00	70.00	175.	1300.	5000.	7.50
☐ 1915	138,450	22.00	36.00	80.00	180.	365.	1650.	8500.	13.00
☐ 1915D	1,170,400	7.50	10.00	20.00	65.00	155.	850.	3600.	5.00
☐ 1915S	1,604,000	7.50	10.00	20.00	65.00	155.	950.	4200.	5.00

WALKING LIBERTY HALVES

Mintmark

Designed, like the new dime introduced in 1916 by A.A. Weinman, whose monogram appears near the rim beneath the eagle's tail feathers on the reverse, this coin expresses the bold character of America in the early 1900s. Its only distinctive aspect is the fact that on the 1916, and some 1917 issues the mintmark appears on the obverse. From 1921 to 1934 its issue was sporadic and restricted to the branch mints.

MINT MARK ON OBVERSE

Date	Mintage	G-4	VG-8	F-12	VF-20	XF-40	MS-60	MS-65	ABP
☐ 1916	608,000	25.00	30.00	55.00	125.	235.	600.	2300.	15.00
☐ 1916D	1,014,400	19.00	22.00	30.00	65.00	145.	550.	2300.	11.00
☐ 1916S	508,000	33.00	43.00	110.	230.	390.	1300.	4500.	20.00
☐ 1917D	765,400	15.00	20.00	32.50	80.00	175.	650.	3150.	9.00
☐ 1917S	952,000	15.00	20.00	40.00	170.	380.	1450.	7000.	9.00

MINT MARK ON REVERSE

Date	Mintage	G-4	VG-8	F-12	VF-20	XF-40	MS-60	MS-65	ABP
☐ 1917	12,292,000	5.50	6.50	8.50	21.00	40.00	225.	1000.	4.00
☐ 1917D	1,940,000	11.00	15.00	19.00	50.00	140.	800.	3750.	6.50
☐ 1917S	5,554,000	11.00	13.50	17.50	25.00	50.00	450.	2950.	6.50
☐ 1918	6,634,000	5.50	6.50	8.50	45.00	135.	550.	2500.	4.00
☐ 1918D	3,853,040	5.50	6.50	8.50	50.00	165.	1200.	7500.	4.00
☐ 1918S	10,282,000	5.50	6.50	8.50	28.00	50.00	475.	2800.	4.00
☐ 1919	962,000	14.00	17.50	30.00	110.	350.	1600.	6500.	8.00
☐ 1919D	1,165,000	12.00	17.50	29.00	135.	410.	3400.	18,000.	7.00
☐ 1919S	1,552,000	11.00	16.00	24.00	95.00	375.	3200.	20,000.	6.50
☐ 1920	6,372,000	5.50	6.50	8.50	25.00	55.00	340.	2650.	4.00
☐ 1920D	1,551,000	5.50	6.50	24.50	100.	250.	2100.	7500.	4.00
☐ 1920S	4,624,000	5.50	6.50	8.50	40.00	115.	1500.	4100.	4.00
☐ 1921	246,000	70.00	95.00	190.	475.	1150.	3500.	8500.	40.00
☐ 1921D	208,000	105.	145.	275.	575.	1425.	3800.	10,250.	65.00
☐ 1921S	548,000	18.00	25.00	40.00	245.	1500.	12,000.	28,500.	12.00
☐ 1923S	2,178,000	5.50	6.50	8.50	40.00	160.	2000.	7000.	4.00
☐ 1927S	2,392,000	5.50	6.50	8.50	28.00	85.00	1450.	6500.	4.00
☐ 1928S	1,940,000	5.50	6.50	8.50	30.00	100.	1700.	8250.	4.00
☐ 1929D	1,001,200	5.50	6.50	8.50	23.00	75.00	575.	2500.	4.00
☐ 1929S	1,902,000	5.50	6.50	8.50	22.00	70.00	585.	2625.	4.00
☐ 1933S	1,786,000	5.50	6.50	8.50	20.00	50.00	575.	2750.	4.00
☐ 1934	6,964,000	5.50	6.50	8.50	11.50	21.00	145.	540.	4.00
☐ 1934D	2,361,400	5.50	6.50	8.50	18.00	45.00	290.	975.	4.00
☐ 1934S	3,652,000	5.50	6.50	8.50	15.00	33.00	480.	2000.	4.00
☐ 1935	9,162,000	5.50	6.50	8.50	11.50	20.00	85.00	230.	4.00
☐ 1935D	3,003,800	5.50	6.50	8.50	16.50	45.00	290.	1025.	4.00
☐ 1935S	3,854,000	5.50	6.50	8.50	15.00	40.00	380.	1235.	4.00
☐ 1936	12,617,901	5.50	6.50	8.50	11.50	20.00	82.00	225.	4.00
☐ 1936D	4,252,400	5.50	6.50	8.50	15.00	33.00	175.	550.	4.00
☐ 1936S	3,884,000	5.50	6.50	8.50	13.50	35.00	250.	800.	4.00
☐ 1937	9,527,728	5.50	6.50	8.50	11.50	19.00	85.00	235.	4.00
☐ 1937D	1,676,000	5.50	6.50	8.50	17.00	50.00	345.	925.	4.00
☐ 1937S	2,090,000	5.50	6.50	8.50	11.50	40.00	280.	820.	4.00
☐ 1938	4,118,152	5.50	6.50	8.50	11.50	22.00	145.	510.	4.00
☐ 1938D	491,600	26.00	27.00	32.50	48.00	100.	800.	2300.	15.00
☐ 1939	6,820,808	5.50	6.50	8.50	11.50	21.00	115.	450.	4.00
☐ 1939D	4,267,800	5.50	6.50	8.50	13.50	21.00	110.	345.	4.00
☐ 1939S	2,552,000	5.50	6.50	8.50	13.00	24.00	165.	500.	4.00

Date	Mintage	G-4	VG-8	F-12	VF-20	XF-40	MS-60	MS-65	ABP
☐ 1940	9,167,279	5.50	6.50	8.50	10.00	19.00	60.00	210.	4.00
☐ 1940S	4,550,000	5.50	6.50	8.50	12.50	21.00	150.	485.	4.00
☐ 1941	24,207,412	5.50	6.50	8.50	10.00	12.50	36.00	95.00	4.00
☐ 1941D	11,248,400	5.50	6.50	8.50	10.00	18.50	65.00	165.	4.00
☐ 1941S	8,098,000	5.50	6.50	8.50	10.00	22.50	225.	500.	4.00
☐ 1942	47,839,120	5.50	6.50	8.50	10.00	12.50	35.00	95.00	4.00
☐ 1942D	10,973,800	5.50	6.50	8.50	10.00	16.50	85.00	200.	4.00
☐ 1942S	12,708,000	5.50	6.50	8.50	10.00	17.50	135.	300.	4.00
☐ 1943	53,190,000	5.50	6.50	8.50	10.00	12.50	35.00	95.00	4.00
☐ 1943D	11,346,000	5.50	6.50	8.50	10.00	18.50	75.00	225.	4.00
☐ 1943S	13,450,000	5.50	6.50	8.50	10.00	20.00	130.	300.	4.00
☐ 1944	28,206,000	5.50	6.50	8.50	10.00	12.50	35.00	95.00	4.00
☐ 1944D	9,769,000	5.50	6.50	8.50	10.00	12.50	60.00	160.	4.00
☐ 1944S	8,904,000	5.50	6.50	8.50	10.00	12.50	100.	235.	4.00
☐ 1945	31,502,000	5.50	6.50	8.50	10.00	12.50	35.00	95.00	4.00
☐ 1945D	9,966,800	5.50	6.50	8.50	10.00	13.50	60.00	160.	4.00
☐ 1945S	10,156,000	5.50	6.50	8.50	10.00	13.50	95.00	200.	4.00
☐ 1946	12,118,000	5.50	6.50	8.50	10.00	13.50	40.00	95.00	4.00
☐ 1946D	2,151,000	5.50	6.50	8.50	10.00	15.00	65.00	110.	4.00
☐ 1946S	3,724,000	5.50	6.50	8.50	10.00	14.50	75.00	200.	4.00
☐ 1947	4,094,000	5.50	6.50	8.50	10.00	12.50	80.00	200.	4.00
☐ 1947D	3,900,600	5.50	6.50	8.50	10.00	12.50	65.00	190.	4.00

FRANKLIN HALVES

The Franklin half, with its Liberty Bell reverse reminscent of the design of the Sesquicentennial commemorative half of 1926, was designed by then chief engraver John R. Sinnock, whose initials appear on the truncation of the bust. The series was ended prematurely in 1963 when Congress called for a switch to an issue honoring President John F. Kennedy, who was assassinated on November 22, 1963.

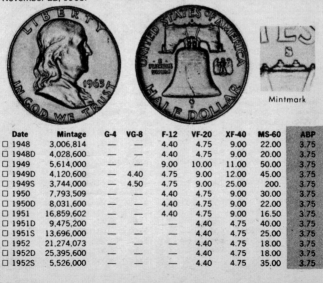

Mintmark

Date	Mintage	G-4	VG-8	F-12	VF-20	XF-40	MS-60	ABP
☐ 1948	3,006,814	—	—	4.40	4.75	9.00	22.00	3.75
☐ 1948D	4,028,600	—	—	4.40	4.75	9.00	20.00	3.75
☐ 1949	5,614,000	—	—	9.00	10.00	11.00	50.00	3.75
☐ 1949D	4,120,600	—	4.40	4.75	9.00	12.00	45.00	3.75
☐ 1949S	3,744,000	—	4.50	4.75	9.00	25.00	200.	3.75
☐ 1950	7,793,509	—	—	4.40	4.75	9.00	30.00	3.75
☐ 1950D	8,031,600	—	—	4.40	4.75	9.00	22.00	3.75
☐ 1951	16,859,602	—	—	4.40	4.75	9.00	16.50	3.75
☐ 1951D	9,475,200	—	—	—	4.40	4.75	40.00	3.75
☐ 1951S	13,696,000	—	—	—	4.40	4.75	25.00	3.75
☐ 1952	21,274,073	—	—	—	4.40	4.75	18.00	3.75
☐ 1952D	25,395,600	—	—	—	4.40	4.75	18.00	3.75
☐ 1952S	5,526,000	—	—	—	4.40	4.75	35.00	3.75

Date	Mintage	G-4	VG-8	F-12	VF-20	XF-40	MS-60	ABP
☐ 1953	2,796,920	—	—	—	4.40	4.75	22.50	3.75
☐ 1953D	20,900,400	—	—	—	4.40	4.75	16.50	3.75
☐ 1953S	4,148,000	—	—	—	4.40	4.75	22.50	3.75
☐ 1954	13,421,503	—	—	—	4.40	4.75	14.00	3.75
☐ 1954D	25,445,580	—	—	—	4.40	4.75	16.50	3.75
☐ 1954S	4,993,400	—	—	—	4.40	4.75	16.50	3.75
☐ 1955	2,876,381	—	—	—	4.40	4.75	20.00	3.75
☐ 1956	4,701,384	—	—	—	4.40	4.75	14.50	3.75
☐ 1957	6,361,952	—	—	—	4.40	4.75	16.50	3.75
☐ 1957D	19,966,850	—	—	—	4.40	4.75	12.00	3.75
☐ 1958	4,917,652	—	—	—	4.40	4.75	14.00	3.75
☐ 1958D	23,962,412	—	—	—	4.40	4.75	10.00	3.75
☐ 1959	7,349,291	—	—	—	4.40	4.75	14.00	3.75
☐ 1959D	13,053,750	—	—	—	4.40	4.75	14.00	3.75
☐ 1960	7,715,602	—	—	—	4.40	4.75	9.50	3.75
☐ 1960D	18,215,812	—	—	—	4.40	4.75	9.50	3.75
☐ 1961	11,318,244	—	—	—	4.40	4.75	8.50	3.75
☐ 1961D	20,276,442	—	—	—	4.40	4.75	8.50	3.75
☐ 1962	12,932,019	—	—	—	4.40	4.75	8.50	3.75
☐ 1962D	35,473,281	—	—	—	4.40	4.75	8.50	3.75
☐ 1963	25,239,645	—	—	—	4.40	4.75	8.50	3.75
☐ 1963D	67,069,292	—	—	—	4.40	4.75	8.50	3.75

KENNEDY HALVES

This young series has already had an interesting history. Thus far it has been issued in three metallic varieties - .900 fine silver in 1964, .400 clad silver from 1965-1970 and 1975-1976, and cuffonickel-clad copper commencing 1971 - and with mintmarks on both the reverse (1964) and the obverse (from 1968).

Mintmark

Date	Mintage	MS-60	ABP	Date	Mintage	MS-60	ABP
☐ 1964	277,254,766	5.50	3.75	☐ 1972D	141,890,000	.75	—
☐ 1964D	156,205,446	5.50	3.75	☐ 1972S	3,267,667	4.50	2.50
☐ 1965	65,879,366	3.00	1.25	☐ 1973	64,964,000	.75	—
☐ 1966	108,984,932	3.00	1.25	☐ 1973D	83,171,400	.75	—
☐ 1967	295,046,978	3.00	1.25	☐ 1973S	2,769,624	5.00	3.00
☐ 1968D	246,951,930	3.00	1.25	☐ 1974	201,596,000	.75	—
☐ 1968S	3,041,506	—	—	☐ 1974D	79,066,300	.75	—
☐ 1969D	129,881,800	3.00	1.25	☐ 1974S	2,617,350	4.50	2.50
☐ 1969S	2,934,631	—	—	☐ 1975 See Bicentennial Coinage			
☐ 1970D	2,150,000	32.50	20.00	☐ 1976 See Bicentennial Coinage			
☐ 1970S	2,632,810	—	—	☐ 1977	43,598,000	.75	—
☐ 1971	155,640,000	1.00	—	☐ 1977D	31,449,106	.75	—
☐ 1971D	302,097,424	1.00	—	☐ 1977S	3,251,152	3.75	2.25
☐ 1971S	3,244,183	4.25	2.50	☐ 1978	14,350,000	.75	—
☐ 1972	153,180,000	.75	—	☐ 1978D	13,765,799	.75	—
				☐ 1978S	3,127,781	2.75	1.65

SILVER DOLLARS

The silver dollar provided the base from which all other coins in the nation's currency system, as established by the act of April 2, 1792, was calculated, with gold coins provided for on a ratio of 15 to 1 from this standard. In name, our dollar's origins can be traced to the late 1400s when the first large silver coins - Joachimsthalers - were produced in Germany, while it was patterned after the Spanish milled dollar which predominated in the Western Hemisphere in the late 1700s.

The pure silver weight of the dollar coin was set at slightly more than 371 grains, with the total weight of the .8924 fine coin being 420 grains, or approximately the same as the prevalent standard for the Spanish milled dollar of the day. There was, however, enough of a differential to provide for a profitable trade in the export of U.S. silver dollars in favor of Spanish dollars, which could be turned into the mint for recoining at a profit.

This situation ultimately led to the suspension of silver dollar mintage in just ten years persuant to an order issued by President Thomas Jefferson on March 28, 1804. Prior to that time a quantity of 19,570 dollars had been struck using 1803 dies, but none dated 1804. The use of dies dated for the previous year early in the following year was a common practice at the time, as all dies were used until they were no longer serviceable.

Dollars dated 1804 do exist, however, there being a total of 15 known in three varieties. The first known specimen to surface was obtained from the mint by Matthew Stickney in 1843 in exchange for a coin needed for the mint cabinet. This was one of eight so-called "originals" produced in 1834-35 to insert in special presentation proof sets which had been requested by the Secretary of State. The seven so-called "restrikes", six of one variety and one of another, were produced around 1859 by mint officials intent on serving the needs of collectors who wanted specimens of the coin.

Flowing Hair Silver Dollars

Date	Mintage	G-4	VG-8	F-12	VF-20	XF-40	ABP
☐ 1794	1,758	9500.	14,500.	23,000.	28,000.	52,000.	5700
			Kreisberg Auction, Oct., 1978				
☐ 1795 2 Leaves	203,033	1950.	2500.	3500.	5300.	9000.	1150.
☐ 1795 3 Leaves	Inc. Ab.	1950.	2500.	3500.	5300.	9000.	1150.

Draped Bust Silver Dollars

SMALL EAGLE

Date	Mintage	G-4	VG-8	F-12	VF-20	XF-40	ABP
☐ 1795	Inc. Ab.	1200.	1600.	1850.	2800.	4800.	725.
☐ 1796 Small Date, Small Letters							
	72,920	1100.	1500.	1700.	2600.	4400.	650.
☐ 1796 Small Date, Large Letters							
	Inc. Ab.	1100.	1500.	1700.	2600.	4400.	650.
☐ 1796 Large Date, Small Letters							
	Inc. Ab.	1100.	1500.	1700.	2600.	4400.	650.
☐ 1797 9 Stars Left, 7 Stars Right, Small Letters							
	7,776	1200.	1600.	1850.	2800.	4500.	725.
☐ 1797 9 Stars Left, 7 Stars Right, Large Letters							
	Inc. Ab.	1150.	1600.	1850.	2800.	4500.	690.
☐ 1797 10 Stars Left, 6 Stars Right							
	Inc. Ab.	1150.	1600.	1700.	2600.	4400.	690.
☐ 1798 13 Stars	327,536	1100.	1500.	1700.	2600.	4400.	650.
☐ 1798 15 Stars	Inc. Ab.	1200.	1700.	1950.	2900.	4600.	725.

Heraldic Eagle

Date	Mintage	G-4	VG-8	F-12	VF-20	XF-40	ABP
☐ 1798 Knob 9	Inc. Ab.	300.	375.	550.	700.	1250.	175.
☐ 1798 10 Arrows	Inc. Ab.	300.	375.	550.	700.	1200.	175.

Date	Mintage	G-4	VG-8	F-12	VF-20	XF-40	ABP
☐ 1798 4 Berries	Inc. Ab.	300.	375.	550.	700.	1250.	175.
☐ 1798 5 Berries, 12 Arrows							
	Inc. Ab.	300.	375.	550.	700.	1250.	175.
☐ 1798 High 8	Inc. Ab.	300.	375.	550.	700.	1250.	175.
☐ 1798 13 Arrows	Inc. Ab.	300.	375.	550.	700.	1250.	175.
☐ 1799/98 13 Star Reverse							
	423,515	300.	375.	550.	700.	1250.	175.
☐ 1799/98 15 Star Reverse							
	Inc. Ab.	300.	375.	550.	700.	1250.	175.
☐ 1799 Irregular Date, 13 Star Reverse							
	Inc. Ab.	300.	375.	550.	700.	1225.	175.
☐ 1799 Irregular Date, 15 Star Reverse							
	Inc. Ab.	300.	375.	550.	700.	1225.	175.
☐ 1799 Perfect Date, 7 And 6 Star Obverse, No Berries							
	Inc. Ab.	300.	375.	550.	700.	1225.	175.
☐ 1799 Perfect Date, 7 And 6 Star Obverse, Small Berries							
	Inc. Ab.	300.	375.	550.	700.	1225.	175.
☐ 1799 Perfect Date, 7 And 6 Star Obverse, Medium Large Berries							
	Inc. Ab.	300.	375.	550.	700.	1225.	175.
☐ 1799 Perfect Date, 7 And 6 Star Obverse, Extra Large Berries							
	Inc. Ab.	300.	375.	550.	700.	1225.	175.
☐ 1799 8 Stars Left, 5 Stars Right On Obverse							
	Inc. Ab.	300.	375.	550.	700.	1225.	175.
☐ 1800 Liberty "R" Double Cut							
	220,920	300.	375.	550.	700.	1225.	175.
☐ 1800 States First "T" Double Cut							
	Inc. Ab.	300.	375.	550.	700.	1225.	175.
☐ 1800 Both Letters Double Cut							
	Inc. Ab.	300.	375.	550.	700.	1225.	175.
☐ 1800 United, "T" Double Cut							
	Inc. Ab.	300.	375.	550.	700.	1225.	175.
☐ 1800 Very Wide Date, Low 8							
	Inc. Ab.	300.	375.	550.	700.	1225.	175.
☐ 1800 Sm. Berries	Inc. Ab.	300.	375.	550.	700.	1225.	175.
☐ 1800 Dot Date	Inc. Ab.	300.	375.	550.	700.	1225.	175.
☐ 1800 12 Arrows	Inc. Ab.	300.	375.	550.	700.	1225.	175.
☐ 1800 10 Arrows	Inc. Ab.	300.	375.	550.	700.	1250.	175.
☐ 1800 "Americai"	Inc. Ab.	300.	375.	550.	700.	1250.	175.
☐ 1801	54,454	300.	375.	550.	700.	1250.	175.
☐ 1801	(Unrecorded)	Proof Restrike - Rare					—
☐ 1802/1 Close	1250.	300.	375.	550.	700.	1200.	175.
☐ 1802/1 Wide	1250.	300.	375.	550.	700.	1200.	175.
☐ 1802 Close, Perfect Date							
	Inc. Ab.	300.	375.	550.	700.	1250.	175.
☐ 1802 Wide, Perfect Date							
	Inc. Ab.	300.	375.	550.	700.	1250.	175.
☐ 1802	(Unrecorded)	Proof Restrike - Rare					—
☐ 1803 Lg. 3	85,634	300.	375.	550.	700.	1250.	175.
☐ 1803 Sm. 3	Inc. Ab.	300.	375.	550.	700.	1250.	175.
☐ 1803	(Unrecorded)	Proof Restrike - Rare					—
☐ 1804	15 Known	3 Varieties. Private Sale, 1979 200,000.					—

GOBRECHT PATTERNS

In anticipation of a reduction in standard for the silver dollar which would allow its reintroduction, as a similar move in 1834 had allowed the Mint to reintroduce the production of gold coins which would circulate, officials sanctioned the development of patterns for the issue. The preparation of the new designs was placed in the hands of Christian Gobrecht, who engraved the work of artists Thomas Sully (obverse) and Titian Peale (reverse).

Several patterns dated 1836 were prepared from Gobrecht's designs. They were struck in silver and copper, with plain and reeded edges, with the engraver's name on and below the base of Liberty, and with the eagle in a field of stars and in a plain field. About 1,000 examples of the 1836 Gobrecht dollar were struck in silver, plain edge, name on base, starred reverse. Several similar patterns were prepared in 1838 and 1839, with an arc of stars added to the obverse and the engraver's name removed. These obverse designs are the same as were adopted for the minor silver coins of 1837, without the stars, and revised with stars added in 1838.

Date	Mintage	VF-20	XF-40	ABP
☐ 1836 No Stars Obverse	Est. 1000	1600.	3000.	950.
☐ 1838 No Stars Reverse	Est. 25 (Proof Only)	2750.	3500.	1650.
☐ 1839 No Stars Reverse	Est. 300 (Proof Only)	2250.	2450.	1350.

LIBERTY SEATED DOLLARS

Minting of the silver dollar was resumed in 1840, with the lawful content of the silver having been reduced to 412-1/2 grains from 416, and its fineness raised to .900 to facilitate striking under terms of the new coinage law of January 18, 1837. Production of the coin remained nominal, however, until its issue was discontinued by the coinage law of February 12, 1873, in part because enactment of the February 21, 1853, law which reduced the relative bullion content of the fractional silver issues, left the dollar at 412-1/2 grains, worth more than its face value.

Mintmark

NO MOTTO

Date	Mintage	G-4	VG-8	F-12	VF-20	XF-40	MS-60	ABP
☐ 1840	61,005	125.	140.	185.	250.	400.	1400.	75.00
☐ 1841	173,000	90.00	110.	165.	200.	325.	1400.	50.00
☐ 1842	184,618	90.00	110.	165.	195.	325.	1400.	50.00
☐ 1843	165,100	90.00	110.	165.	195.	325.	1400.	50.00
☐ 1844	20,000	150.	175.	220.	275.	435.	1800.	90.00
☐ 1845	24,500	140.	165.	210.	250.	450.	1800.	85.00
☐ 1846	110,600	95.00	115.	175.	200.	325.	1400.	55.00
☐ 1846O	59,000	125.	150.	200.	295.	450.	—	75.00
☐ 1847	140,750	90.00	110.	165.	195.	325.	1750.	52.00
☐ 1848	15,000	165.	200.	250.	325.	700.	1925.	100.
☐ 1849	62,600	110.	135.	175.	225.	365.	1750.	65.00
☐ 1850	7,500	225.	275.	325.	450.	800.	3500.	135.
☐ 1850O	40,000	150.	175.	245.	295.	800.	3500.	90.00
☐ 1851	1,300	—	—	—	Rare	—	—	—
☐ 1852	1,100	—	—	—	Rare	—	—	—
☐ 1853	46,110	135.	150.	185.	275.	495.	1400.	80.00
☐ 1854	33,140	175.	200.	295.	475.	1250.	1750.	105.
☐ 1855	26,000	250.	300.	425.	900.	1450.	1900.	150.
☐ 1856	63,500	140.	165.	245.	400.	650.	1800.	85.00
☐ 1857	94,000	125.	150.	200.	335.	525.	1400.	75.00
☐ 1858	Est. 80	—	—	—	Proof	Only	—	—
	Impaired Proof		1850.	2250.	2750.	3500.	—	—
☐ 1859	256,500	90.00	110.	165.	200.	325.	1400.	52.00
☐ 1859O	360,000	85.00	100.	160.	195.	300.	1400.	50.00
☐ 1859S	20,000	130.	160.	235.	375.	600.	—	75.00
☐ 1860	218,930	90.00	110.	165.	195.	325.	1400.	52.00
☐ 1860O	515,000	85.00	100.	160.	195.	300.	1400.	50.00
☐ 1861	78,500	110.	150.	185.	225.	425.	1400.	65.00
☐ 1862	12,090	235.	300.	425.	595.	850.	2200.	140.
☐ 1863	27,660	175.	195.	250.	385.	600.	1900.	105.
☐ 1864	31,170	165.	185.	240.	350.	550.	1400.	100.
☐ 1865	47,000	135.	160.	230.	340.	520.	1400.	80.00
☐ 1866	Only 2 Known Without Motto							

MOTTO ADDED ON REVERSE

Date	Mintage	G-4	VG-8	F-12	VF-20	XF-40	MS-60	ABP
☐ 1866	49,625	140.	165.	225.	325.	550.	1800.	85.00
☐ 1867	47,525	135.	160.	220.	335.	535.	1800.	80.00
☐ 1868	162,700	110.	130.	200.	275.	400.	1500.	65.00
☐ 1869	424,300	95.00	115.	165.	200.	300.	1500.	55.00
☐ 1870	416,000	95.00	115.	155.	195.	300.	1500.	55.00
☐ 1870CC	12,462	140.	175.	295.	425.	750.	2100.	85.00
☐ 1870S	Unrecorded			Aug. 1978 ANA Sale		VF	39,000.	—
☐ 1871	1,074,760	85.00	95.00	160.	190.	350.	1500.	50.00
☐ 1871CC	1,376	450.	550.	875.	1375.	2350.	6000.	270.
☐ 1872	1,106,450	85.00	95.00	160.	190.	310.	1500.	50.00
☐ 1872CC	3,150	325.	425.	575.	850.	1450.	3200.	195.
☐ 1872S	9,000	150.	200.	300.	550.	1200.	2750.	90.00
☐ 1873	293,600	100.	120.	180.	225.	375.	1500.	60.00
☐ 1873CC	2,300	750.	975.	1500.	2000.	3250.	7500.	450.
☐ 1873S	700			Unknown				—

TRADE DOLLARS

The trade dollar is the only U.S. monetary obligation that has ever been, in effect, demonetized. Although this 420 grain, .900 fine silver coin was originally authorized by the act of February 12, 1873, to compete with other

trade coins of the day in the Orient, it was also provided with legal tender status. The legal tender provision was erased by a June 22, 1876, law which restricted future production of the coin to export demand.

Enactment of the coinage act of February 28, 1878, authorizing the restoration of the standard silver dollar brought an end to the production of the trade dollar, except for proofs which were struck through 1885. An act of March 3, 1887, repealed the trade dollar provisions and provided for their redemption. Under the provisions of this law $7,689,036 of the coins were redeemed at face value for recoinage into standard dollars and subsidiary coins, with all that remained outstanding reverting to bullion value.

Mintmark

Date	Mintage	G-4	VG-8	F-12	VF-20	XF-40	MS-60	ABP
☐ 1873	397,500	55.00	60.00	75.00	90.00	175.	1000.	32.00
☐ 1873CC	124,500	55.00	65.00	80.00	95.00	175.	1500.	32.00
☐ 1873S	703,000	50.00	55.00	70.00	85.00	160.	1200.	36.00
☐ 1874	987,800	47.50	50.00	68.00	80.00	155.	850.	28.00
☐ 1874CC	1,373,200	52.50	57.00	68.00	80.00	155.	1200.	31.00
☐ 1874S	2,549,000	50.00	55.00	70.00	80.00	150.	850.	30.00
☐ 1875	218,900	65.00	80.00	125.	190.	350.	950.	40.00
☐ 1875CC	1,573,700	60.00	65.00	75.00	90.00	195.	1100.	35.00
☐ 1875S	4,487,000	50.00	55.00	68.00	80.00	155.	850.	30.00
☐ 1875S/CC	Inc.Ab.	80.00	110.	230.	360.	500.	1500.	50.00
☐ 1876	456,150	50.00	55.00	68.00	80.00	155.	850.	30.00
☐ 1876CC	509,000	60.00	65.00	70.00	85.00	175.	1100.	35.00
☐ 1876S	5,227,000	47.50	55.00	68.00	80.00	150.	850.	28.00
☐ 1877	3,039,710	47.00	55.00	68.00	80.00	150.	1500.	28.00
☐ 1877CC	534,000	60.00	68.00	90.00	125.	195.	950.	35.00
☐ 1877S	9,519,000	47.50	55.00	68.00	80.00	150.	850.	28.00
☐ 1878	900		Proof Only					1800.
	Impaired Proof	425.	465.	500.	550.	—		250.
☐ 1878CC	97,000	100.	150.	200.	265.	500.	2500.	60.00
☐ 1878S	4,162,000	47.50	55.00	68.00	80.00	150.	2500.	28.00
☐ 1879	1,541		Proof	Only				1800.
	Impaired Proof	550.	650.	775.	1000.	—		325.
☐ 1880	1,987		Proof	Only				1800.
	Impaired Proof	500.	600.	750.	1000.	—		300.
☐ 1881	960		Proof	Only				1800.
	Impaired Proof	600.	750.	875.	1150.	—		350.
☐ 1882	1,097		Proof	Only				1800.
	Impaired Proof	575.	675.	800.	1075.	—		325.
☐ 1883	979		Proof	Only				1800.
	Impaired Proof	600.	750.	875.	1150.	—		350.
☐ 1884	10	Proof Only, Ivy Auction Aug. 1980						
☐ 1885	Proof 5	Only, RARCOA	Auction AUG. 1980 110,000.					—

MORGAN DOLLARS

A five year lapse in the minting of standard silver dollars was ended by enactment of a February 28, 1878, coinage law, which held the metallic content of the coin to its former standard. Issue of the standard dollar had been halted in favor of the trade dollar, a slightly heavier coin authorized on a standard designed to allow it to compete with the dollar size coins of other nations in the Orient trade.

The 1878 turn around, achieved by the silver interests who had witnessed a rapid decline in the value of their commodity, ushered in the era of the silver dollar. In the years that followed the Treasury was required to purchase and convert into dollar coins such large quantities of silver that the available supplies far exceeded the demand, even for the Silver Certificate issues which they backed.

The initial mintages were authorized by the Bland-Allison Act, and that measure was followed in 1890 by the Sherman Act, and the War Revenue Act of 1898. With the exhaustion of the government's bullion stock in 1904 production of the silver dollar was again discontinued, to be renewed in 1921 under provisions of the Pittman Act of 1918. Under the provisions of this act over 270 million Morgan dollars were melted down for export and recoinage into subsidiary coins, accounting for the several scarce issues in the Morgan series which have coinage records of a million or more pieces.

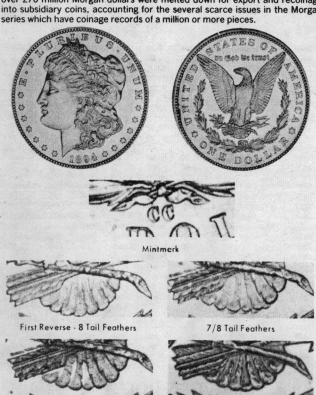

Mintmark

First Reverse - 8 Tail Feathers

7/8 Tail Feathers

Second Reverse - 7 Tail Feathers
Top Arrow Feather Straight
Concave Breast

Third Reverse - 7 Tail Feathers
Top Arrow Feather Slanted
Convex Breast

Date	Mintage	VG-8	F-12	VF-20	XF-40	AU-50	MS-60	MS-65	ABP
☐ 1878 8 Tail Feathers									
	750,000	21.00	23.00	28.00	33.00	40.00	72.00	350.	12.00

Date	Mintage	VG-8	F-12	VF-20	XF-40	AU-50	MS-60	MS-65	ABP
☐ 1878 7 Over 8 Tail Feathers									
	9,759,550	22.00	24.00	33.50	45.00	63.00	88.00	610.	13.00
☐ 1878 7 Tail Feathers									
☐ 1878 7 Tail Feathers, Second Reverse									
	Inc. Ab.	21.00	22.00	24.00	27.00	30.00	63.00	280.	12.00
☐ 1878 7 Tail Feathers, Third Reverse									
	Inc. Ab.	21.00	22.00	24.00	27.00	30.00	63.00	280.	12.00
☐ 1878S	9,744,000	21.00	22.00	23.00	24.00	25.00	54.00	140.	12.00
☐ 1878CC	2,212,000	26.00	30.00	37.00	45.00	57.00	120.	245.	15.00
☐ 1879	14,807,100	15.00	18.00	21.00	22.00	24.00	53.00	430.	10.00
☐ 1879O	2,887,000	15.00	18.00	21.00	22.00	27.00	78.00	1065.	10.00
☐ 1879S Second Reverse									
	9,110,000	15.00	18.00	21.00	22.00	24.00	49.00	105.	10.00
☐ 1879S Third Reverse									
	Inc. Ab.	15.00	18.00	21.00	22.00	24.00	49.00	105.	10.00
☐ 1879S	9,110,000	15.00	18.00	21.00	22.00	24.00	49.00	105.	10.00
☐ 1879CC	756,000	42.00	45.00	85.00	285.	630.	1150.	7550.	25.00
☐ 1880	12,601,335	15.00	18.00	21.00	22.00	24.00	53.00	350.	10.00
☐ 1880 8/7* Inc. Ab.		90.00	110.	175.	250.	400.	—	—	55.00
☐ 1880O	5,305,000	—	15.00	18.00	21.00	24.00	107.	1375.	10.00
☐ 1880O 8/7* I.A.		40.00	50.00	60.00	75.00	95.00	175.	—	24.00
☐ 1880S	8,900,000	—	15.00	21.00	22.00	24.00	50.00	125.	10.00
☐ 1880S 8/7* I.A.		—	—	—	—	—	65.00	—	—
☐ 1880CC Second Reverse									
	591,000	42.00	50.00	73.00	93.00	150.	245.	380.	75.00
☐ 1880/79CC Second Reverse									
	Inc. Ab.	42.00	50.00	73.00	93.00	150.	245.	380.	25.00
☐ 1880CC Third Reverse									
	Inc. Ab.	42.00	50.00	73.00	93.00	150.	245.	380.	25.00
☐ 1880CC	591,000	42.00	50.00	73.00	93.00	150.	245.	380.	25.00
☐ *Die Varieties Exist For These Issues.									
☐ 1880CC 8/7 Third Reverse, High 7*									
	Inc. Ab.	—	—	—	—	—	245.	380.	—
☐ 1880CC 8/7 Third Reverse, Low 7									
	Inc. Ab.	—	—	—	—	—	200.	—	—
☐ 1881	9,163,975	15.00	18.00	21.00	22.00	24.00	50.00	335.	10.00
☐ 1881O	5,708,000	15.00	18.00	21.00	22.00	24.00	69.00	435.	10.00
☐ 1881S	12,760,000	15.00	18.00	21.00	22.00	24.00	47.00	100.	10.00
☐ 1881CC	296,000	70.00	79.00	100.	120.	165.	245.	395.	42.00
☐ 1882	11,101,100	15.00	18.00	21.00	22.00	24.00	50.00	335.	10.00
☐ 1882O	6,090,000	15.00	18.00	21.00	22.00	24.00	69.00	425.	10.00
☐ 1882O/S Inc. Ab.		15.00	18.00	21.00	22.00	24.00	69.00	425.	10.00
☐ 1882S	9,250,000	15.00	18.00	21.00	22.00	24.00	49.00	140.	10.00
☐ 1882CC	1,133,000	26.00	30.00	40.00	49.00	70.00	107.	175.	15.00
☐ 1883	12,291,039	15.00	18.00	21.00	22.00	24.00	50.00	320.	10.00
☐ 1883O	8,725,000	15.00	18.00	21.00	22.00	24.00	45.00	155.	10.00
☐ 1883S	6,250,000	15.00	18.00	28.00	45.00	160.	610.	4025.	10.00
☐ 1883CC	1,204,000	26.00	30.00	40.00	48.00	70.00	95.00	140.	15.00
☐ 1884	14,070,875	15.00	18.00	21.00	22.00	24.00	78.00	380.	10.00
☐ 1884O	9,730,000	15.00	18.00	21.00	22.00	24.00	43.00	155.	10.00
☐ 1884S	3,200,000	15.00	18.00	21.00	42.50	280.	1480.	17,500.	10.00
☐ 1884CC	1,136,000	38.00	43.00	49.00	58.00	75.00	95.00	145.	22.00
☐ 1885	17,787,767	15.00	18.00	21.00	22.00	24.00	38.00	150.	10.00
☐ 1885O	9,185,000	15.00	18.00	21.00	22.00	24.00	43.00	155.	10.00
☐ 1885S	1,497,000	15.00	20.00	25.00	35.00	66.00	215.	1000.	10.00
☐ 1885CC	228,000	195.	215.	225.	235.	240.	280.	380.	115.
☐ 1886	19,963,886	15.00	18.00	21.00	22.00	24.00	38.00	117.	10.00

Date	Mintage	VG-8	F-12	VF-20	XF-40	AU-50	MS-60	MS-65	ABP
☐ 1886O	10,710,000	15.00	18.00	21.00	24.00	60.00	620.	9450.	10.00
☐ 1886S	750,000	28.00	30.00	38.00	50.00	71.00	330.	1060.	17.00
☐ 1887	20,290,710	15.00	18.00	21.00	22.00	24.00	38.00	117.	10.00
☐ 1887O	11,550,000	15.00	18.00	21.00	22.00	33.00	63.00	750.	10.00
☐ 1887S	1,771,000	21.00	22.00	25.00	27.00	35.00	150.	550.	12.00
☐ 1888	19,183,833	15.00	18.00	21.00	22.00	24.00	39.00	280.	10.00
☐ 1888O	12,150,000	15.00	18.00	21.00	24.00	30.00	47.00	325.	10.00
☐ 1888S	657,000	26.00	31.00	47.00	65.00	88.00	330.	1060.	15.00
☐ 1889	21,726,811	15.00	18.00	21.00	22.00	24.00	47.00	315.	10.00
☐ 1889O	11,875,000	15.00	18.00	21.00	25.00	31.00	170.	2200.	10.00
☐ 1889S	700,000	29.00	34.00	50.00	55.00	80.00	200.	640.	17.00
☐ 1889CC	350,000	190.	240.	415.	880.	2250.	8950.	33,000.	115.
☐ 1890	16,802,590	15.00	18.00	21.00	22.00	26.00	47.00	460.	10.00
☐ 1890O	10,701,000	18.00	21.00	22.00	25.00	33.00	100.	945.	11.00
☐ 1890S	8,230,373	22.00	23.00	24.00	29.00	36.00	90.00	280.	13.00
☐ 1890CC	2,309,041	26.00	30.00	38.00	46.00	75.00	240.	725.	15.00
☐ 1890CC Tail Bar Variety									
	Inc. Ab.	—	—	38.00	46.00	75.00	240.	725.	23.00
☐ 1891	8,694,206	21.00	22.00	23.00	26.00	50.00	190.	945.	12.00
☐ 1891O	7,954,529	21.00	22.00	23.00	26.00	50.00	200.	3275.	12.00
☐ 1891S	5,296,000	22.00	23.00	25.00	29.00	40.00	98.00	370.	13.00
☐ 1891CC	1,618,000	26.00	30.00	38.00	46.00	75.00	180.	610.	15.00
☐ 1892	1,037,245	21.00	23.00	27.00	31.00	40.00	220.	2000.	12.00
☐ 1892O	2,744,000	21.00	23.00	27.00	31.00	65.00	300.	3650.	12.00
☐ 1892S	1,200,000	23.00	30.00	70.00	200.	975.	7050.	29,500.	14.00
☐ 1892CC	1,352,000	38.00	43.00	53.00	95.00	235.	410.	1385.	23.00
☐ 1893	378,792	45.00	55.00	70.00	125.	235.	695.	3275.	27.00
☐ 1893O	300,000	50.00	70.00	145.	315.	450.	1500.	25,000.	30.00
☐ 1893S	100,000	1150.	1300.	2700.	4800.	14,500.	29,500.	79,000.	690.
☐ 1893CC	677,000	48.00	75.00	195.	500.	695.	1325.	6750.	29.00
☐ 1894	110,972	345.	410.	535.	750.	1000.	1765.	8600.	200.
☐ 1894O	1,723,000	23.00	26.00	30.00	45.00	110.	695.	10,700.	14.00
☐ 1894S	1,260,000	25.00	31.50	65.00	125.	240.	600.	2650.	15.00
☐ 1895	12,880			Struck Only In Proof				—	10,000.
	Impaired Proof	4000.	5000.	6500.	7500.		—	—	2400.
☐ 1895O	450,000	60.00	70.00	165.	410.	880.	3800.	60,500.	36.00
☐ 1895S	400,000	72.00	95.00	175.	570.	1075.	2000.	7375.	43.00
☐ 1896	9,967,762	15.00	18.00	21.00	22.00	24.00	45.00	240.	10.00
☐ 1896O	4,900,000	15.00	18.00	23.00	26.00	88.00	1060.	16,250.	10.00
☐ 1896S	5,000,000	25.00	31.00	57.00	120.	280.	1050.	3100.	15.00
☐ 1897	2,822,731	15.00	18.00	21.00	22.00	24.00	59.00	340.	10.00
☐ 1897O	4,004,000	15.00	21.00	23.00	30.00	75.00	660.	8250.	10.00
☐ 1897S	5,825,000	22.00	23.00	26.00	30.00	35.00	100.	440.	13.00
☐ 1898	5,884,735	15.00	18.00	21.00	22.00	24.00	53.00	250.	10.00
☐ 1898O	4,440,000	15.00	18.00	21.00	22.00	24.00	50.00	225.	10.00
☐ 1898S	4,102,000	22.00	23.00	26.00	30.00	65.00	390.	1400.	13.00
☐ 1899	330,846	38.00	50.00	65.00	82.00	95.00	140.	540.	22.00
☐ 1899O	12,290,000	15.00	18.00	21.00	22.00	24.00	50.00	245.	10.00
☐ 1899S	2,562,000	23.00	26.00	33.00	40.00	75.00	515.	1170.	14.00
☐ 1900	8,880,938	15.00	18.00	21.00	22.00	24.00	47.00	250.	10.00
☐ 1900O	12,590,000	15.00	18.00	21.00	22.00	24.00	53.00	275.	10.00
☐ 1900O/CC*Inc. Ab.		15.00	18.00	21.00	22.00	24.00	53.00	275.	10.00
☐ 1900S	3,540,000	22.00	23.00	26.00	28.00	65.00	330.	945.	13.00
☐ 1901	6,962,813	30.00	35.00	40.00	58.00	240.	1325.	16,400.	18.00
☐ 1901O	13,320,000	15.00	18.00	21.00	22.00	24.00	54.00	380.	10.00
☐ 1901S	2,284,000	21.00	27.00	30.00	45.00	75.00	515.	2600.	12.00

Date	Mintage	VG-8	F-12	VF-20	XF-40	AU-50	MS-60	MS-65	ABP
☐ 1902	7,994,777	21.00	22.00	24.00	27.00	40.00	90.00	895.	12.00
☐ 1902O	8,636,000	15.00	18.00	21.00	22.00	24.00	45.00	210.	10.00
☐ 1902S	1,530,000	28.00	40.00	75.00	120.	200.	565.	1700.	17.00
☐ 1903	4,652,755	21.00	22.00	24.00	27.00	38.00	100.	570.	12.00
☐ 1903O	4,450,000	245.	280.	350.	380.	395.	500.	725.	145.
☐ 1903S	1,241,000	24.00	29.00	55.00	200.	750.	3400.	10,450.	14.00
☐ 1904	2,788,650	21.00	22.00	25.00	30.00	60.00	425.	2500.	12.00
☐ 1904O	3,720,000	15.00	18.00	21.00	22.00	24.00	42.00	200.	10.00
☐ 1904S	2,304,000	30.00	48.00	63.00	150.	600.	1950.	7300.	18.00
☐ 1921	44,690,000	15.00	18.00	21.00	22.00	24.00	31.00	140.	10.00
☐ 1921D	20,345,000	15.00	18.00	21.00	22.00	24.00	44.00	560.	10.00
☐ 1921S	21,695,000	15.00	18.00	21.00	22.00	24.00	75.00	1135.	10.00

PEACE DOLLARS

The new Peace dollar, featuring the word PEACE on the rocky crag upon which the eagle is perched and dedicated to a world thought to be at permanent peace as a result of the war to end all wars, was designed by Anthony de Francisci, whose signature appears below the truncated bust of Liberty. Credit for the release of this new design rests at least in part with the American Numismatic Association and Farran Zerbe, a veteran numismatist and frequent participant in government numismatic projects.

A last issue of .900 fine silver dollars was authorized on August 3, 1964, but the projected 45 million example edition was never produced. The issue of this coin had been debated by the Treasury and White House for more than a year, before a permanent delay in its production was announced on May 25, 1965. Before that happened, however, dies were prepared (presumably of the Peace dollar design) with the 1964 date, and sample production runs were carried out at the Denver Mint. No examples are known to exist, Mint officials reporting they were all destroyed.

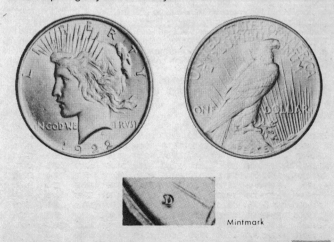

Mintmark

Date	Mintage	VG-8	F-12	VF-20	XF-40	AU-50	MS-60	MS-65	ABP
☐ 1921	1,006,473	38.00	40.00	50.00	70.00	110.	650.	3150.	22.00

Date	Mintage	VG-8	F-12	VF-20	XF-40	AU-50	MS-60	MS-65	ABP
☐ 1922	51,737,000	—	15.00	18.00	21.00	22.00	26.00	112.	10.00
☐ 1922D	15,063,000	—	15.00	18.00	21.00	24.00	63.00	565.	10.00
☐ 1922S	17,475,000	—	15.00	18.00	21.00	24.00	75.00	880.	10.00
☐ 1923	30,800,000	—	15.00	18.00	21.00	22.00	26.00	112.	10.00
☐ 1923D	6,811,000	—	15.00	18.00	22.00	26.00	70.00	870.	10.00
☐ 1923S	19,020,000	—	15.00	18.00	21.00	23.00	110.	1070.	10.00
☐ 1924	11,811,000	—	15.00	18.00	21.00	23.00	40.00	295.	10.00
☐ 1924S	1,728,000	21.00	23.00	25.00	34.00	50.00	320.	2500.	12.00
☐ 1925	10,198,000	—	15.00	18.00	21.00	22.00	45.00	210.	10.00
☐ 1925S	1,610,000	21.00	22.00	24.00	28.00	40.00	350.	2140.	12.00
☐ 1926	1,939,000	15.00	21.00	25.00	27.00	37.00	70.00	530.	10.00
☐ 1926D	2,348,700	21.00	22.00	25.00	29.00	45.00	190.	1100.	12.00
☐ 1926S	6,980,000	21.00	22.00	24.00	27.00	35.00	75.00	465.	12.00
☐ 1927	848,000	22.00	25.00	30.00	33.00	59.00	145.	1100.	13.00
☐ 1927D	1,268,900	15.00	21.00	26.00	35.00	110.	390.	3650.	10.00
☐ 1927S	866,000	23.00	24.00	26.00	34.00	75.00	485.	2000.	14.00
☐ 1928	360,649	160.	170.	185.	215.	265.	450.	2235.	95.00
☐ 1928S	1,632,000	22.00	23.00	25.00	33.00	60.00	360.	2000.	13.00
☐ 1934	954,057	22.00	30.00	32.50	37.00	75.00	170.	1185.	13.00
☐ 1934D	1,569,500	22.00	23.00	25.00	35.00	70.00	235.	2175.	13.00
☐ 1934S	1,011,000	22.00	26.00	55.00	210.	750.	3600.	7600.	13.00
☐ 1935	1,576,000	22.00	23.00	25.00	30.00	47.00	115.	800.	13.00
☐ 1935S	1,964,000	22.00	23.00	24.00	32.50	70.00	295.	2140.	13.00

EISENHOWER DOLLARS

The new Eisenhower dollar was created to serve the immediate needs of the Nevada gaming industry, and the future needs of the vending industry. In addition to being minted for circulation in the cupro-nickel clad copper composition, silver interests were able to give the issue a tie to the dollar's historic past by providing for special limited issue uncirculated and proof editions of the coin to be offered, at premiums, in .400 fine silver. Designed by Frank Gasparro, the Eisenhower obverse is tied to an Apollo reverse which pays tribute to the nation's space program, and particularly the Apollo 11 moon landing of July 20, 1969, which commenced during the administration of President Eisenhower.

The coin exists in both high and low relief varieties. All proofs are of the high relief variety, while the uncirculated silver edition of 1971 is low relief

and that of 1972 high relief. The 1971 clad metal editions and the 1972 Denver Mint issues are all low relief, while the 1972 Philadelphia issue exists in both high and low relief versions.

Mintmark

Date	MS-65	ABP	Date	MS-65	ABP
☐ 1971	2.80	2.00	☐ 1974S Silver Prf.	24.00	17.00
☐ 1971D	3.75	2.70	☐ 1974S Clad Prf.	7.00	4.95
☐ 1971S Silver Unc.	4.50	3.25	☐ 1976 Type I	4.00	2.90
☐ 1971S Silver Prf.	7.25	5.15	☐ 1976 Type II	2.00	1.05
☐ 1972	2.80	2.00	☐ 1976D Type I	2.40	1.35
☐ 1972D	2.15	1.55	☐ 1976D Type II	1.75	1.00
☐ 1972S Silver Unc.	11.65	8.30	☐ 1976S Cld.Prf.,Typ.I	8.25	5.85
☐ 1972S Silver Prf.	16.50	11.75	☐ 1976S Cld.Prf.,Ty.II	4.40	3.15
☐ 1973	15.75	11.25	☐ 1976S Silver Unc.	9.75	7.00
☐ 1973D	15.75	11.25	☐ 1976S Silver Prf.	12.00	8.50
☐ 1973S Silver Unc.	12.00	8.50	☐ 1977	2.35	1.70
☐ 1973S Silver Prf.	82.00	58.00	☐ 1977-D	2.30	1.60
☐ 1973S Clad Prf.	7.00	5.00	☐ 1977-S Clad Prf.	3.80	2.70
☐ 1974	2.00	1.05	☐ 1978	1.70	1.20
☐ 1974D	2.00	1.05	☐ 1978-D	1.75	1.20
☐ 1974S Silver Unc.	11.65	8.30	☐ 1978S Clad Prf.	10.00	7.20

SUSAN B. ANTHONY

Minting of the new Susan B. Anthony mini-dollar began with the 1979 issuance. Original estimates indicated the coin would last 12 times longer than the paper dollar and result in savings of hundreds of millions of dollars in production and related costs.

However, the public shunned the coin and $500 million of the $850 million struck remain in Federal Reserve bank vaults.

SUSAN B. ANTHONY

Date	MS-65	ABP	Date	MS-65	ABP
☐ 1979P	1.25	—	1980D	1.25	—
☐ 1979D	1.25	—	1980S	4.50	3.00
☐ 1979S	1.25	—	1980S Prf.	9.75	7.00
☐ 1979S Prf.	13.25	9.50	1981S Prf.	10.50	7.25
☐ 1980P	1.25				

GOLD DOLLARS

The issue of a gold dollar unit was not authorized in the original national coinage law of 1792, although a legal tender ratio of 15 to 1 between silver and gold was specified therein. It was to materialize in 1849, under an act dated March 3, largely at the instigation of the influential gold lobby spawned by the general opposition to bank money and the California gold rush. During its 41 year life the issue was to be offered in three basic types, all of which were designed by James B. Longacre. The gold standard was .900 fine, with the first type being thicker and 2mm smaller in diameter than the others.

The gold dollar soon became a circulating coin, where the silver dollar had not, as the relative value of gold declined due to the large quantities being mined from California fields. By the mid-1860s the ratio had begun to slide back and the issue of gold dollars abated. During the Civil War the issue was all but halted, as both silver and gold coins disappeared from circulation, a situation which prevailed until the resumption of specie payments in 1876. By that time the silver dollar was the coin of issue and the gold dollar was allowed to linger until its life was legislatively ended by an act of September 26, 1890.

Mintmark

Liberty Head

Date	Mintage	F-12	VF-20	XF-40	MS-60	ABP
☐ 1849 Open Wreath						
	688,567	165.	255.	270.	760.	100.
☐ 1849 Closed Wreath						
	Inc. Ab.	165.	255.	270.	760.	100.
☐ 1849C Closed Wreath						
	11,634	275.	425.	650.	1750.	165.
☐ 1849C Open Wreath						
	Inc. Ab.				Rare	—
☐ 1849D Open Wreath						
	21,588	350.	725.	1000.	3000.	210.
☐ 1849O Open Wreath						
	215,000	165.	255.	270.	760.	100.
☐ 1850	481,953	165.	255.	270.	760.	100.
☐ 1850C	6,966	165.	550.	725.	2400.	100.
☐ 1850D	8,382	375.	800.	1050.	3250.	225.
☐ 1850O	14,000	165.	255.	270.	760.	100.
☐ 1851	3,317,671	165.	255.	270.	760.	100.
☐ 1851C	41,267	165.	425.	550.	1550.	100.
☐ 1851D	9,882	275.	800.	1050.	3250.	165.
☐ 1851O	290,000	275.	255.	270.	760.	165.
☐ 1852	2,045,351	165.	255.	270.	760.	100.
☐ 1852C	9,434	275.	550.	725.	2400.	165.
☐ 1852D	6,360	275.	800.	1050.	3250.	165.
☐ 1852O	140,000	165.	255.	270.	760.	100.
☐ 1853	4,076,051	165.	255.	270.	760.	100.
☐ 1853C	11,515	165.	425.	650.	1750.	100.

Date	Mintage	F-12	VF-20	XF-40	MS-60	ABP
☐ 1853D	6,583	275.	800.	1050.	3250.	165.
☐ 1853O	290,000	165.	255.	270.	900.	100.
☐ 1854	736,709	165.	255.	270.	760.	100.
☐ 1854D	2,935	350.	975.	1500.	4950.	185.
☐ 1854S	14,632	165.	255.	425.	2600.	100.

MINTMARK
BELOW
WREATH TIE

Small Indian Head

Date	Mintage	F-12	VF-20	XF-40	MS-60	ABP
☐ 1854	902,736	250.	480.	730.	3375.	150.
☐ 1855	758,269	250.	480.	730.	3375.	150.
☐ 1855C	9,803	400.	775.	1250.	8750.	250.
☐ 1855D	1,811	1750.	3000.	5250.	10,000.	1100.
☐ 1855O	55,000	350.	575.	1050.	8250.	210.
☐ 1856S	24,600	350.	495.	900.	7500.	210.

MINTMARK
BELOW
WREATH TIE

Large Indian Head

Date	Mintage	F-12	VF-20	XF-40	MS-60	ABP
☐ 1856 Upright 5	1,762,936	150.	210.	225.	675.	100.
☐ 1856 Slant 5	Inc. Ab.	150.	210.	225.	675.	100.
☐ 1856D	1,460	2250.	3750.	5750.	14,500.	1350.
☐ 1857	774,789	150.	210.	225.	675.	100.
☐ 1857C	13,280	150.	475.	650.	2150.	100.
☐ 1857D	3,533	350.	775.	1450.	3750.	210.
☐ 1857S	10,000	150.	325.	-355.	1550.	100.
☐ 1858	117,995	150.	210.	225.	675.	100.
☐ 1858D	3,477	450.	775.	1500.	4250.	300.
☐ 1858S	10,000	150.	210.	225.	1200.	100.
☐ 1859	168,244	150.	210.	225.	675.	100.
☐ 1859C	5,235	150.	475.	750.	2350.	100.
☐ 1859D	4,952	250.	750.	1300.	3500.	150.
☐ 1859S	15,000	150.	210.	375.	2250.	100.
☐ 1860	36,668	150.	210.	225.	675.	100.
☐ 1860D	1,566	2000.	3500.	5750.	11,500.	1250.
☐ 1860S	13,000	150.	325.	375.	1100.	100.
☐ 1861	527,499	150.	210.	225.	675.	100.
☐ 1861D	Unrecorded	3500.	8000.	13,500.	22,500.	2250.
☐ 1862	1,361,390	150.	210.	225.	675.	100.
☐ 1863	6,250	150.	450.	750.	4500.	100.
☐ 1864	5,950	150.	425.	600.	3200.	100.

Date	Mintage	F-12	VF-20	XF-40	MS-60	ABP
☐ 1865	3,725	150.	425.	700.	3500.	100.
☐ 1866	7,130	150.	325.	425.	1750.	100.
☐ 1867	5,250	150.	325.	400.	1750.	100.
☐ 1868	10,525	150.	325.	350.	1500.	100.
☐ 1869	5,925	150.	330.	375.	1600.	100.
☐ 1870	6,335	150.	325.	375.	1400.	100.
☐ 1870S	3,000	350.	500.	1100.	3750.	210.
☐ 1871	3,930	150.	350.	500.	1750.	100.
☐ 1872	3,530	150.	350.	500.	1900.	100.
☐ 1873 Clsd 3	125,125	150.	210.	550.	1550.	100.
☐ 1873 Open 3	Inc. Ab.	150.	210.	225.	675.	100.
☐ 1874	198,820	150.	210.	225.	675.	100.
☐ 1875	420	—	2500.	3500.	9750.	2000.
☐ 1876	3,245	150.	330.	375.	1850.	100.
☐ 1877	3,920	150.	350.	550.	1950.	100.
☐ 1878	3,020	150.	350.	550.	1850.	100.
☐ 1879	3,030	150.	350.	575.	1600.	100.
☐ 1880	1,636	150.	350.	575.	1450.	100.
☐ 1881	7,707	150.	325.	350.	1100.	100.
☐ 1882	5,125	150.	325.	375.	1100.	100.
☐ 1883	11,007	150.	210.	225.	675.	100.
☐ 1884	6,236	150.	300.	350.	1200.	100.
☐ 1885	12,261	150.	210.	225.	675.	100.
☐ 1886	6,016	150.	325.	375.	1100.	100.
☐ 1887	8,543	150.	325.	350.	675.	100.
☐ 1888	16,580	150.	210.	225.	675.	100.
☐ 1889	30,729	150.	210.	225.	675.	100.

HOW TO BUY AND SELL COINS

Neither the authors or Krause Publications are able to serve as a clearing house for coin transactions, so the individual desiring to buy or sell coins must do so through collectors or dealers. Collectors are generally interested only in the purchase of single coins, while dealers purchase singly or in quantity to maintain a stock for their regular customers.

Today most cities with a population of more than a few thousand have at least one coin dealer. You will find him listed in the telephone directory Yellow Pages under the heading of "Coin Dealer," or perhaps "Stamp and Coin Dealers" or "Hobby Shops." Dealers are generally glad to appraise the value of a single coin at no charge, but it is often necessary to pay for the appraisal of a large accumulation.

Coins may also be sold to, or purchased from many dealers who advertise in hobby publications, and daily newspapers. Coins should never be sent to a dealer for purchase, however, without first receiving written confirmation of his interest. All coins sent to a dealer through the mail should be securely packaged and registered or insured. Always enclose and keep a copy of a list of the coins submitted, and enclose sufficient postage for return of the package.

QUARTER EAGLES

The quarter eagle of $2.50 gold piece, along with its sister multiples of $5 and $10, was authorized by the original coinage law of April 2, 1792. Its stipulated weight was 67-1/2 grains of .916-2/3 fine gold, where it remained until the standard was changed to 64-1/2 grains at .899225 fine by the act of June 28, 1834, the latter being subsequently revised to .900 fine by a law of January 18, 1837.

The Liberty cap type, which was designed by Robert Scot, did not carry a designation of value. The Turban head design of John Reich introduced in 1808 carried the designation "2-1/2 D." on the reverse below the eagle and proved to be the last issue for 13 years as the increasing value of gold was driving the coins from circulation as soon as they were released. A small coinage was resumed on a sporadic basis in 1821 with the coin reduced significantly in size, but maintained at the former weight and fineness standards.

The new standard specified by the law of 1834 led to the introduction of a new design featuring the Liberty band holding the hair, but with the turban removed, executed by William Kneass. This coin became a regular issue, with the quantities produced increasingly significant.

Liberty Cap

Date	Mintage	F-12	VF-20	XF-40	MS-60	ABP
☐ 1796 No Stars	963	9000.	17,000.	22,500.	50.000.	5400.
☐ 1796 Stars	432	6000.	9000.	14,000.	32,000.	3600.
☐ 1797	427	4500.	6750.	9500.	22,500.	2700.
☐ 1798	1,094	2500.	4700.	6750.	19,500.	1500.
☐ 1802 Over 1	3,035	2250.	3500.	6000.	18,000.	1350.
☐ 1804 13 Star Reverse	3,327	3400.	6500.	10,000.	19,000.	2400.
☐ 1804 14 Star Reverse	Inc. Ab.	2350.	3500.	6000.	18,000.	1400.
☐ 1805	1,781	2500.	3500.	6000.	18,000.	1500.
☐ 1806 Over 4	1,616	2500.	3500.	6000.	18,000.	1500.
☐ 1806 Over 5	Inc. Ab.	4000.	6500.	10,000.	19,000.	2600.
☐ 1807	6,812	2500.	3500.	6000.	18,000.	1500.

Turban Head

Date	Mintage	F-12	VF-20	XF-40	MS-60	ABP
☐ 1808 (20MM Dia.)	2,710	6500.	13,000.	21,000.	55,000.	3900.

Date	Mintage	F-12	VF-20	XF-40	MS-60	ABP
☐ 1821 (18.5MM Dia.)	6,448	2500.	5000.	8250.	15,000.	1500.
☐ 1824 Over 21	2,600	2500.	4500.	8250.	14,000.	1500.
☐ 1825	4,434	2500.	4500.	8250.	14,000.	1500.
☐ 1826 Over 25	760	3500.	5500.	10,000.	18,000.	2100.
☐ 1827	2,800	2500.	4500.	8250.	13,500.	1500.
☐ 1829	3,403	2500.	4750.	7500.	22,000.	1500.
☐ 1830	4,540	2500.	4750.	7500.	22,000.	1500.
☐ 1831	4,520	2500.	4750.	7500.	22,000.	1500.
☐ 1832	4,400	2500.	4750.	7500.	22,000.	1500.
☐ 1833	4,160	2500.	4750.	7500.	22,000.	1500.
☐ 1834	4,000	3500.	7000.	12,000.	25,000.	2100.

Mintmark

Liberty Without Turban

Date	Mintage	F-12	VF-20	XF-40	MS-60	ABP
☐ 1834	112,234	225.	360.	450.	2800.	135.
☐ 1835	131,402	225.	360.	450.	2800.	135.
☐ 1836	547,986	225.	360.	450.	2800.	135.
☐ 1837	45,080	225.	360.	450.	280.	135.
☐ 1838	47,030	225.	360.	450.	2800.	135.
☐ 1838C	7,880	250.	450.	850.	5000.	150.
☐ 1839	27,021	225.	360.	450.	2800.	135.
☐ 1839C	18,140	225.	425.	750.	5000.	135.
☐ 1839D	13,674	225.	850.	1500.	7500.	135.
☐ 1839O	17,781	225.	360.	750.	4500.	135.

MINTMARK

Coronet Head

Date	Mintage	F-12	VF-20	XF-40	MS-60	ABP
☐ 1840	18,859	200.	350.	450.	—	120.
☐ 1840C	12,822	250.	350.	625.	1500.	150.
☐ 1840D	3,532	250.	650.	1000.	—	150.
☐ 1840O	33,580	200.	250.	375.	1000.	120.
☐ 1841			Stack's Sale, 1976			—
☐ 1841C	10,281	200.	350.	525.	1500.	120.
☐ 1841D	4,164	225.	600.	1300.	3750.	135.
☐ 1842	2,823	250.	450.	800.	—	150.
☐ 1842C	6,729	225.	350.	550.	1350.	135.
☐ 1842D	4,643	225.	1500.	2500.	—	135.
☐ 1842O	19,800	200.	300.	400.	1250.	120.
☐ 1843	100,546	200.	250.	300.	550.	120.
☐ 1843C Sm Dt	26,064	750.	1500.	2500.	7500.	450.
☐ 1843C Lg Dt	Inc. Ab.	200.	375.	600.	1350.	120.

Date	Mintage	F-12	VF-20	XF-40	MS-60	ABP
☐ 1843D	36,209	200.	600.	1050.	2400.	120.
☐ 1843O Sm Dt	288,002	200.	250.	300.	600.	120.
☐ 1843O Lg Dt	76,000	200.	250.	300.	700.	120.
☐ 1844	6,784	200.	350.	600.	2000.	120.
☐ 1844C	11,622	200.	350.	525.	2000.	120.
☐ 1844D	17,332	200.	600.	1000.	2300.	120.
☐ 1845	91,051	200.	250.	300.	600.	120.
☐ 1845D	19,460	200.	600.	1000.	2300.	120.
☐ 1845O	4,000	400.	850.	1250.	—	250.
☐ 1846	21,598	200.	250.	300.	600.	120.
☐ 1846C	4,808	250.	600.	850.	2250.	150.
☐ 1846D	19,303	300.	600.	1000.	2300.	180.
☐ 1846O	66,000	200.	250.	300.	900.	120.
☐ 1847	29,814	200.	250.	300.	600.	120.
☐ 1847C	23,226	250.	350.	525.	1200.	150.
☐ 1847D	15,784	300.	600.	1000.	2300.	180.
☐ 1847O	124,000	200.	250.	300.	600.	120.
☐ 1848	7,497	300.	500.	800.	1750.	180.

Enlarged

Date	Mintage	F-12	VF-20	XF-40	MS-60	ABP
☐ 1848 CAL.	1,389	3500.	4500.	8000.	17,500.	2100.
☐ 1848C	16,788	250.	350.	550.	1300.	150.
☐ 1848D	13,771	300.	600.	1100.	2500.	180.
☐ 1849	23,294	200.	250.	300.	600.	120.
☐ 1849C	10,220	250.	350.	550.	2000.	150.
☐ 1849D	10,945	250.	600.	1000.	2500.	150.
☐ 1850	252,923	200.	250.	300.	600.	120.
☐ 1850C	9,148	250.	350.	550.	1600.	150.
☐ 1850D	12,148	250.	600.	1000.	2400.	150.
☐ 1850O	84,000	200.	250.	300.	900.	120.
☐ 1851	1,372,748	200.	250.	300.	540.	120.
☐ 1851C	14,923	250.	350.	500.	1350.	150.
☐ 1851D	11,264	250.	600.	1000.	2400.	150.
☐ 1851O	148,000	200.	250.	300.	750.	120.
☐ 1852	1,159,681	200.	250.	300.	540.	120.
☐ 1852C	9,772	250.	350.	575.	1350.	150.
☐ 1852D	4,078	250.	700.	1400.	3450.	150.
☐ 1852O	140,000	200.	250.	300.	750.	120.
☐ 1853	1,404,668	200.	250.	300.	540.	120.
☐ 1853D	3,178	250.	700.	1300.	3000.	150.
☐ 1854	596,258	200.	250.	300.	550.	120.
☐ 1854C	7,295	200.	350.	550.	1400.	120.
☐ 1854D	1,760	2250.	3500.	5000.	—	1350.
☐ 1854O	153,000	200.	250.	300.	600.	120.
☐ 1854S	246	10,000.	20,000.	30,000.	—	7500.
☐ 1855	235,480	200.	250.	300.	540.	120.
☐ 1855C	3,677	500.	800.	1250.	—	300.
☐ 1855D	1,123	2500.	3750.	5500.	7500.	1500.

Date	Mintage	F-12	VF-20	XF-40	MS-60	ABP
☐ 1856	384,240	200.	250.	300.	825.	120.
			Stack's Sale, Feb. 1977			—
☐ 1856C	7,913	225.	400.	550.	—	135.
☐ 1856D	874	4500.	7250.	9000.	15,000.	2700.
☐ 1856O	21,100	200.	250.	325.	1200.	120.
☐ 1856S	71,120	200.	250.	325.	1000.	120.
☐ 1857	214,130	200.	250.	300.	540.	120.
☐ 1857D	2,364	250.	900.	1400.	4500.	150.
☐ 1857O	34,000	200.	250.	300.	600.	120.
☐ 1857S	69,200	200.	250.	300.	1500.	120.
☐ 1858	47,377	200.	250.	300.	600.	120.
☐ 1858			Stack's Sale, Feb.,1977			—
☐ 1858C	9,056	250.	350.	500.	1400.	150.
☐ 1859	39,444	200.	250.	300.	600.	120.
☐ 1859D	2,244	250.	900.	1400.	3250.	150.
☐ 1859S	15,200	200.	250.	300.	750.	120.
☐ 1860	22,675	200.	250.	300.	550.	120.
☐ 1860C	7,469	250.	350.	575.	1850.	150.
☐ 1860S	35,600	200.	250.	300.	650.	120.
☐ 1861	1,283,878	150.	185.	230.	540.	100.
☐ 1861S	24,000	200.	250.	300.	700.	120.
☐ 1862	98,543	200.	250.	300.	600.	120.
☐ 1862 Over 1	Inc. Ab.	—	1000.	1500.	3500.	750.
☐ 1862S	8,000	200.	250.	375.	1000.	120.
☐ 1863	30		Bowers & Ruddy, Aug. 1978, Proof Only			—
☐ 1863S	10,800	200.	250.	300.	600.	120.
☐ 1864	2,874	600.	1000.	2000.	3500.	360.
☐ 1865	1,545	450.	900.	1800.	3250.	270.
☐ 1865S	23,376	200.	250.	300.	600.	120.
☐ 1866	3,110	225.	300.	500.	1250.	135.
☐ 1866S	38,960	200.	250.	300.	600.	120.
☐ 1867	3,250	225.	275.	450.	950.	135.
☐ 1867S	28,000	200.	250.	300.	600.	120.
☐ 1868	3,625	250.	300.	400.	1050.	150.
☐ 1868S	34,000	200.	250.	325.	650.	120.
☐ 1869	4,345	200.	250.	325.	750.	120.
☐ 1869S	29,500	200.	250.	300.	750.	120.
☐ 1870	4,555	210.	260.	350.	750.	125.
☐ 1870S	16,000	200.	250.	300.	650.	120.
☐ 1871	5,350	210.	275.	325.	750.	125.
☐ 1871S	22,000	200.	250.	300.	650.	120.
☐ 1872	3,030	225.	275.	400.	900.	135.
☐ 1872S	18,000	200.	250.	300.	600.	120.
☐ 1873 Clsd 3	178,025	150.	185.	230.	535.	100.
☐ 1873 Open 3	Inc. Ab.	200.	250.	300.	535.	120.
☐ 1873S	27,000	200.	250.	300.	535.	120.
☐ 1874	3,940	225.	300.	375.	750.	135.
☐ 1875	420	1500.	3000.	5500.	9000.	900.
☐ 1875S	11,600	200.	250.	300.	600.	120.
☐ 1876	4,221	210.	250.	300.	900.	125.
☐ 1876S	5,000	210.	250.	325.	1050.	125.
☐ 1877	1,652	325.	450.	700.	2000.	195.
☐ 1877S	35,400	150.	185.	230.	535.	100.
☐ 1878	286,260	150.	185.	230.	535.	100.
☐ 1878S	178,000	150.	185.	230.	535.	100.
☐ 1879	88,990	150.	185.	230.	535.	100.
☐ 1879S	43,500	150.	185.	230.	535.	100.

Date	Mintage	F-12	VF-20	XF-40	MS-60	ABP
☐ 1880	2,996	215.	250.	325.	800.	130.
☐ 1881	691	600.	950.	1750.	3500.	360.
☐ 1882	4,067	215.	170.	325.	700.	130.
☐ 1883	2,002	225.	170.	400.	800.	135.
☐ 1884	2,023	225.	170.	400.	800.	135.
☐ 1885	887	500.	850.	1500.	3000.	300.
☐ 1886	4,088	215.	170.	195.	650.	130.
☐ 1887	6,282	140.	170.	195.	600.	100.
☐ 1888	16,098	140.	170.	195.	535.	100.
☐ 1889	17,648	140.	170.	195.	535.	100.
☐ 1890	8,813	140.	170.	195.	535.	100.
☐ 1891	11,040	140.	170.	195.	535.	100.
☐ 1892	2,545	140.	170.	350.	800.	100.
☐ 1893	30,106	140.	170.	195.	540.	100.
☐ 1894	4,122	140.	170.	325.	800.	100.
☐ 1895	6,199	140.	170.	195.	650.	100.
☐ 1896	19,202	140.	170.	195.	535.	100.
☐ 1897	29,904	140.	170.	195.	535.	100.
☐ 1898	24,165	140.	170.	195.	535.	100.
☐ 1899	27,350	140.	170.	195.	535.	100.
☐ 1900	67,205	140.	170.	195.	535.	100.
☐ 1901	91,322	140.	170.	195.	535.	100.
☐ 1902	133,733	140.	170.	195.	535.	100.
☐ 1903	201,257	140.	170.	195.	535.	100.
☐ 1904	160,960	140.	170.	195.	535.	100.
☐ 1905	217,944	140.	170.	195.	535.	100.
☐ 1906	176,490	140.	170.	195.	535.	100.
☐ 1907	336,448	140.	170.	195.	535.	100.

INDIAN HEAD QTR. EAGLES

This $2-1/2 gold piece, and its sister $5 issue, has the distinction of presenting a design on which the relief is recessed below the surface of the field. It is the work of Bela Lyon Pratt.

Mintmark

Date	Mintage	F-12	VF-20	XF-40	MS-60	ABP
☐ 1908	565,057	200.	175.	195.	340.	120.
☐ 1909	441,899	200.	175.	195.	600.	120.
☐ 1910	492,682	200.	175.	195.	600.	120.
☐ 1911	704,191	200.	175.	195.	550.	120.
☐ 1911D	55,680	300.	750.	1800.	6000.	180.
☐ 1912	616,197	200.	175.	195.	340.	120.
☐ 1913	722,165	200.	175.	195.	340.	120.
☐ 1914	240,117	200.	175.	300.	1400.	120.
☐ 1914D	448,000	200.	175.	195.	340.	120.

Date	Mintage	F-12	VF-20	XF-40	MS-60	ABP
☐ 1915	606,100	200.	175.	195.	340.	120.
☐ 1925D	578,000	200.	175.	195.	340.	120.
☐ 1926	446,000	200.	175.	195.	340.	120.
☐ 1927	388,000	200.	175.	195.	340.	120.
☐ 1928	416,000	200.	175.	195.	340.	120.
☐ 1929	532,000	200.	175.	195.	340.	120.

THREE DOLLARS

Authorized on February 21, 1853, this unpopular issue survived 36 years despite the fact that more than 100,000 examples were produced only in the first year. The coin's logical application was to purchase sheets of 3-cent stamps, the adoption of that postal rate having led to the introduction of the silver three cent piece two years earlier. The designs are by James B. Longacre.

MINTMARK
BELOW
WREATH TIE

Date	Mintage	F-12	VF-20	XF-40	MS-60	ABP
☐ 1854	138,618	500.	760.	950.	3800.	350.
☐ 1854D	1,120	—	10,000.	14,000.	—	5000.
☐ 1854O	24,000	500.	760.	1200.	5500.	350.
☐ 1855	50,555	500.	760.	950.	3800.	350.
☐ 1855S	6,600	550.	760.	1400.	—	375.
☐ 1856	26,010	500.	760.	950.	3150.	350.
☐ 1856S	34,500	500.	760.	950.	5500.	350.
☐ 1857	20,891	500.	760.	950.	3150.	350.
☐ 1857S	14,000	510.	760.	1150.	5500.	350.
☐ 1858	2,133	550.	800.	1350.	5000.	375.
☐ 1859	15,638	500.	760.	1100.	3150.	350.
☐ 1860	7,155	550.	760.	1200.	4500.	375.
☐ 1860S	7,000	525.	760.	1200.	5500.	365.
☐ 1861	6,072	550.	760.	1200.	5000.	375.
☐ 1862	5,785	525.	760.	1200.	4500.	365.
☐ 1863	5,039	600.	760.	1350.	6000.	450.
☐ 1864	2,680	600.	760.	1350.	7500.	450.
☐ 1865	1,165	700.	800.	1350.	9000.	500.
☐ 1866	4,030	525.	760.	1250.	4500.	365.
☐ 1867	2,650	575.	800.	1350.	5250.	400.
☐ 1868	4,875	525.	760.	1100.	4500.	365.
☐ 1869	2,525	575.	760.	1200.	3150.	400.
☐ 1870	3,535	525.	760.	950.	4500.	365.
☐ 1870S	2	Only One Specimen Known				
☐ 1871	1,330	550.	880.	1700.	5000.	375.
☐ 1872	2,030	525.	800.	1350.	5500.	365
☐ 1873 Open 3	25	Proof	Only			—
☐ 1873 Closed 3	Inc. Ab.	Restrikes	—		8500.	—

Date	Mintage	F-12	VF-20	XF-40	MS-60	ABP
☐ 1874	41,820	500.	760.	950.	3150.	350.
☐ 1875	20	(Proofs Only)				
		RARCOA Auction July, 1981		125,000.		—
☐ 1876	45	(Proofs Only)				
		RARCOA Auction July, 1981		37,500.		—
☐ 1877	1,488	600.	900.	1600.	6000.	450.
☐ 1878	82,324	500.	760.	950.	3150.	350.
☐ 1879	3,030	550.	800.	1150.	4800.	375.
☐ 1880	1,036	550.	900.	1350.	5000.	375.
☐ 1881	554	900.	1400.	2250.	9000.	540.
☐ 1882	1,576	550.	800.	1150.	4500.	375.
☐ 1883	989	550.	900.	1350.	5000.	375.
☐ 1884	1,106	550.	800.	1250.	4600.	375.
☐ 1885	910	550.	800.	1300.	6500.	375.
☐ 1886	1,142	550.	900.	1250.	4600.	375.
☐ 1887	6,160	525.	760.	950.	4500.	365.
☐ 1888	5,291	525.	760.	950.	4500.	365.
☐ 1889	2,429	525.	760.	950.	4400.	365.

STELLA

This coin - in reality a pattern - is one of the more intriguing products of the U.S. Mint. Its standing is much akin to that accorded the 1856 Flying Eagle cent, which was also nothing more than a pattern, although the cent design ultimately enjoyed a short life of active issue. While the Stella never emerged as a coin-of-the-realm issue, it is actively collected by many who can afford it as an adjunct to the regular U.S. gold coinage series.

Date	Type	Mintage	Proof	ABP
☐ 1879	Flowing Hair	415	60,000.	35,000.
☐ 1879	Coiled Hair	10	130,000.	—
☐ 1880	Flowing Hair	15	85,000.	—
☐ 1880	Coiled Hair	10	125,000.	—

HALF EAGLES

The history of this denomination closely parallels that of the quarter eagle, with the legal specifications always being double those of the lesser value coin. The Turban head design was issued regularly, although in small quantities, from the time of its introduction in 1807 to 1834. The large issues of the 1830s are a direct result of the mining activities in the southeast during this period. Again, the major change in coinage standards instituted in 1834 led to the introduction of a new design featuring the Liberty head without a turban.

Liberty Cap

Date	Mintage	F-12	VF-20	XF-40	MS-60	ABP
☐ 1795 Sm. Eagle	8,707	3500.	6500.	8500.	35,000.	2500.
☐ 1795 Lg. Eagle	Inc. Ab.	4000.	7500.	10,000.	37,000.	3000.
☐ 1796 Over 95 Small Eagle	6,196	3750.	6500.	10,000.	26,000.	2750.
☐ 1797 Over 95 Large Eagle	3,609	4200.	5250.	8500.	15,000.	3200.
☐ 1797 15 Stars, Small Eagle	Inc. Ab.	4750.	6000.	8500.	24,000.	3750.
☐ 1797 16 Stars, Small Eagle	Inc. Ab.	4750.	6250.	9500.	19,000.	3750.
☐ 1798 Sm. Eagle	24,867	—	- Very Rare		—	—
☐ 1798 Large Eagle, Small 8	Inc. Ab.	1000.	2750.	5000.	11,500.	750.
☐ 1798 Large Eagle, Large 8, 13 Star Reverse	Inc. Ab.	1000.	2750.	5000.	11,000.	750.
☐ 1798 Large Eagle, Large 8, 14 Star Reverse	Inc. Ab.	1150.	2750.	5000.	12,500.	850.
☐ 1799	7,451	1000.	2500.	4750.	11,000.	750.
☐ 1800	37,628	1000.	2500.	4250.	10,000.	750.
☐ 1802 Over 1	53,176	1000.	2500.	4250.	10,000.	750.
☐ 1803 Over 2	33,506	1000.	2500.	4250.	10,000.	750.
☐ 1804 Sm. 8	30,475	1000.	2500.	4000.	10,000.	750.
☐ 1804 Lg. 8	Inc. Ab.	1000.	2500.	4000.	10,000.	750.
☐ 1805	33,183	1000.	2500.	4000.	10,000.	750.
☐ 1806 Pointed 6	64,093	1000.	2500.	4000.	10,000.	750.
☐ 1806 Round 6	Inc. Ab.	1000.	2500.	4000.	10,000.	750.
☐ 1807	32,488	1000.	2500.	4000.	10,000.	750.

Turban Head

Date	Mintage	F-12	VF-20	XF-40	MS-60	ABP
☐ 1807	51,605	1100.	2000.	3450.	8750.	825.
☐ 1808	55,578	1100.	2000.	3450.	8250.	825.
☐ 1808 Over 7	Inc. Ab.	1200.	2100.	3700.	9000.	900.
☐ 1809 Over 8	33,875	1100.	2000.	3450.	8250.	825.
☐ 1810 Small Date, Sm 5	100,287	—	Rare	—	—	—
☐ 1810 Small Date, Lg. 5						
	Inc. Ab.	1200.	2000.	3450.	9500.	900.
☐ 1810 Large Date, Sm. 5						
	Inc. Ab.	1100.	2750.	4800.	11,000.	825.
☐ 1810 Large Date, Lg. 5						
	Inc. Ab.	1100.	2000.	3450.	8250.	825.
☐ 1811 Small 5	99,581	1200.	2000.	3450.	8250.	900.
☐ 1811 Large 5	Inc. Ab.	1250.	2200.	3800.	9250.	925.
☐ 1812	58,087	1150.	2000.	3450.	9500.	850.

LARGE HEAD TYPE INTRODUCED

Date	Mintage	F-12	VF-20	XF-40	MS-60	ABP
☐ 1813	95,428	1300.	2500.	3500.	11,000.	800.
☐ 1814 Over 13	15,454	1500.	2800.	4000.	12,500.	900.
☐ 1815	635	- Very Rare				—
☐ 1818	48,588	2000.	3250.	4500.	12,500.	1200.
☐ 1819	51,723	—	Rare	—	—	—
☐ 1820 Curve Base 2, Small Letters						
	263,806	1500.	2500.	3250.	12,500.	900.
☐ 1820 Curve Base 2, Large Letters						
	Inc. Ab.	1500.	2500.	3250.	12,500.	900.
☐ 1820 Square Base 2	Inc. Ab.	1350.	2500.	3000.	12,500.	800.
☐ 1821	34,641	3000.	4500.	7500.	15,000.	1800.
☐ 1822	17,796	3 Known - Very Rare		—	—	—
☐ 1823	14,485	1800.	2800.	4000.	14,500.	1000.
☐ 1824	17,340	—	Rare	—	—	—
☐ 1825 Over 21	29,060	3250.	5000.	7500.	15,000.	2000.

Date	Mintage	F-12	VF-20	XF-40	MS-60	ABP
☐ 1825 Over 24	Inc. Ab.	-	Very Rare	—		
☐ 1826	18,069	2750.	6000.	8500.	15,000.	1650.
☐ 1827	24,913	—	Rare	—	60,000.	—
☐ 1828 8 Over 7	28,029	—	Rare	—	—	—
☐ 1828	Inc. Ab.	—	Auction '79; MS-65 110,000.			—
☐ 1829 Lg. Dt.	57,442		Stack's Auction 1976, 65,000.			—
☐ 1829 Sm. Dt.	Inc. Ab.		Stack's Sale, Aug. 1976, 65,000.			
☐ 1830 Sm. 5D.	126,351	1750.	5500.	7750.	17,000.	1050.
☐ 1830 Lg. 5D.	Inc. Ab.	1750.	5500.	7750.	17,000.	1050.
☐ 1831	140,594	1500.	5500.	7750.	17,000.	900.
☐ 1832 Curve Base 2, 12 Stars	157,487	—	Rare	—	—	—
☐ 1832 Square Base 2, 13 Stars	Inc. Ab.	2500.	6500.	8750.	21,000.	1500.
☐ 1833	193,630	1750.	5500.	7750.	17,000.	1050.
☐ 1834 Plain 4	50,141	1750.	6000.	8000.	19,000.	1050.
☐ 1834 Crosslet 4	Inc. Ab.	1750.	6000.	8000.	19,000.	1050.

MINTMARK
ABOVE
DATE

Liberty Without Turban

Date	Mintage	F-12	VF-20	XF-40	MS-60	ABP
☐ 1834 Plain 4	658,028	225.	325.	535.	3900.	135.
☐ 1834 Crosslet 4	Inc. Ab.	250.	450.	750.	6500.	150.
☐ 1835	371,534	225.	325.	535.	3900.	135.
☐ 1836	553,147	225.	325.	535.	3900.	135.
☐ 1837	207,121	225.	325.	535.	3900.	135.
☐ 1838	286,588	225.	325.	535.	3900.	135.
☐ 1838C	17,179	500.	800.	1750.	6000.	300.
☐ 1838D	20,583	500.	1000.	1900.	8000.	300.

CORONET HALF EAGLES

When this new design by Christian Gobrecht was introduced in 1839 the diameter of the coin was reduced by slightly less than 1mm. The basic design was to survive until 1908, with the motto "In God We Trust" being added above the eagle on the reverse in 1866.

MINTMARKS:
ABOVE DATE 1839

BELOW EAGLE FROM 1840

Date	Mintage	F-12	VF-20	XF-40	MS-60	ABP
☐ 1839	118,143	200.	230.	350.	1800.	150.
☐ 1839 Over 8 Curved Date						
	Inc. Ab.	200.	300.	600.	1800.	150.
☐ 1839C	17,205	250.	450.	750.	2500.	160.
☐ 1839D	18,939	250.	800.	1300.	5000.	160.
☐ 1840	137,382	150.	170.	270.	1800.	125.
☐ 1840C	18,992	225.	350.	550.	1950.	175.
☐ 1840D	22,896	225.	700.	1100.	5000.	175.
☐ 1840O	40,120	200.	230.	300.	—	150.
☐ 1841	15,833	200.	230.	275.	1800.	150.
☐ 1841C	21,467	225.	350.	550.	1950.	175.
☐ 1841D	30,495	225.	650.	1000.	4500.	175.
☐ 1841O	50	Only 2 Known		—		—
☐ 1842 Sm Let	27,578	200.	230.	300.	1800.	150.
☐ 1842 Lg Let	Inc. Ab.	200.	230.	275.	1800.	150.
☐ 1842C Sm Dt	28,184	350.	800.	1500.	4000.	250.
☐ 1842C Lg Dt	Inc. Ab.	225.	350.	600.	2200.	175.
☐ 1842D Sm Dt	59,608	225.	650.	1000.	4500.	175.
☐ 1842D Lg Dt	Inc. Ab.	250.	750.	1300.	—	200.
☐ 1842O	16,400	225.	400.	550.	1800.	175.
☐ 1843	611,205	150.	170.	270.	1800.	125.
☐ 1843C	44,201	200.	325.	500.	1850.	150.
☐ 1843D	98,452	200.	650.	1000.	4500.	150.
☐ 1843O Sm Let	19,075	200.	230.	350.	1800.	150.
☐ 1843O Lg Let	82,000	200.	230.	300.	1800.	150.
☐ 1844	340,330	150.	170.	270.	1800.	125.
☐ 1844C	23,631	200.	325.	550.	2200.	150.
☐ 1844D	88,982	200.	650.	1000.	4500.	150.
☐ 1844O	364,600	200.	230.	300.	1800.	150.
☐ 1845	417,099	200.	230.	270.	1800.	150.
☐ 1845D	90,629	200.	650.	1000.	4500.	150.
☐ 1845O	41,000	200.	230.	300.	1800.	150.
☐ 1846	395,942	150.	170.	270.	1800.	125.
☐ 1846C	12,995	300.	500.	700.	2200.	225.
☐ 1846D	80,294	225.	650.	1000.	4500.	175.
☐ 1847	915,981	150.	170.	270.	1800.	125.
☐ 1847C	84,151	275.	355.	600.	1950.	210.
☐ 1847D	64,405	200.	650.	1000.	4500.	150.
☐ 1847O	12,000	250.	400.	750.	2000.	200.
☐ 1848	260,775	150.	170.	270.	1800.	125.
☐ 1848C	64,472	225.	325.	550.	2000.	175.
☐ 1848D	47,465	250.	650.	1000.	5000.	200.
☐ 1849	133,070	150.	170.	270.	1800.	125.
☐ 1849C	64,823	225.	325.	550.	1850.	175.
☐ 1849D	39,036	250.	650.	1000.	4500.	200.
☐ 1850	64,491	150.	170.	270.	1800.	125.
☐ 1850C	63,591	200.	325.	550.	1850.	150.
☐ 1850D	43,984	200.	650.	1000.	4750.	150.
☐ 1851	377,505	150.	170.	270.	1800.	125.
☐ 1851C	49,176	225.	325.	550.	1850.	175.
☐ 1851D	62,710	200.	650.	1000.	4500.	150.
☐ 1851O	41,000	200.	230.	275.	1800.	150.
☐ 1852	573,901	150.	170.	270.	1800.	125.
☐ 1852C	72,574	225.	325.	600.	1800.	175.
☐ 1852D	91,584	225.	600.	1000.	4500.	175.
☐ 1853	305,770	150.	170.	270.	1800.	125.
☐ 1853C	65,571	225.	350.	600.	1800.	175.

Date	Mintage	F-12	VF-20	XF-40	MS-60	ABP
☐ 1853D	89,678	200.	650.	1000.	4500.	150.
☐ 1854	160,675	150.	170.	270.	1800.	125.
☐ 1854C	39,283	200.	325.	550.	1900.	150.
☐ 1854D	56,413	200.	650.	1000.	4500.	150.
☐ 1854O	46,000	200.	250.	325.	1800.	150.
☐ 1854S	268	—		Very Rare		—
☐ 1855	117,098	150.	170.	270.	1800.	125.
☐ 1855C	39,788	200.	325.	600.	1850.	150.
☐ 1855D	22,432	200.	700.	1150.	5500.	150.
☐ 1855O	11,100	250.	400.	650.	1850.	200.
☐ 1855S	61,000	200.	250.	375.	1800.	150.
☐ 1856	197,990	150.	170.	270.	1800.	125.
☐ 1856C	28,457	250.	400.	600.	2250.	200.
☐ 1856D	19,786	225.	650.	1100.	5500.	175.
☐ 1856O	10,000	275.	400.	800.	1900.	210.
☐ 1856S	105,100	150.	170.	270.	1800.	125.
☐ 1857	98,188	150.	170.	270.	1800.	125.
☐ 1857C	31,360	275.	400.	600.	1850.	210.
☐ 1857D	17,046	225.	650.	1100.	6000.	175.
☐ 1857O	13,000	200.	300.	450.	1950.	150.
☐ 1857S	87,000	150.	170.	270.	1800.	125.
☐ 1858	15,136	200.	230.	350.	1800.	150.
☐ 1858C	38,856	200.	350.	600.	1950.	150.
☐ 1858D	15,362	275.	650.	1100.	6000.	210.
☐ 1858S	18,600	200.	230.	350.	1800.	150.
☐ 1859	16,814	200.	230.	275.	1800.	150.
☐ 1859C	31,847	200.	325.	600.	2000.	150.
☐ 1859D	10,366	250.	700.	1200.	6000.	200.
☐ 1859S	13,220	250.	350.	550.	1800.	200.
☐ 1860	19,825	200.	230.	275.	1800.	150.
☐ 1860C	14,813	225.	400.	650.	2250.	175.
☐ 1860D	14,635	225.	700.	1200.	6000.	175.
☐ 1860S	21,200	200.	250.	350.	1800.	150.
☐ 1861	688,150	150.	170.	270.	1800.	125.
☐ 1861C	6,879	500.	800.	1500.	3000.	300.
☐ 1861D	1,597	2500.	5250.	7500.	15,000.	1500.
☐ 1861S	18,000	200.	350.	600.	—	150.
☐ 1862	4,465	250.	450.	650.	1800.	200.
☐ 1862S	9,500	200.	275.	500.	—	150.
☐ 1863	2,472	600.	900.	1500.	3000.	375.
☐ 1863S	17,000	200.	350.	600.	—	150.
☐ 1864	4,220	400.	600.	950.	3500.	250.
☐ 1864S	3,888	1000.	1500.	2000.	5000.	650.
☐ 1865	1,295	600.	900.	1500.	3000.	375.
☐ 1865S	27,612	200.	300.	600.	—	150.
☐ 1866S	9,000	200.	325.	650.	—	150.

MOTTO ADDED OVER EAGLE

Date	Mintage	F-12	VF-20	XF-40	MS-60	ABP
☐ 1866	6,730	225.	375.	700.	—	175.
☐ 1866S	34,920	200.	300.	500.	1250.	150.
☐ 1867	6,920	225.	350.	700.	1250.	175.
☐ 1867S	29,000	200.	225.	400.	—	150.
☐ 1868	5,725	200.	325.	600.	—	150.
☐ 1868S	52,000	200.	225.	300.	—	150.
☐ 1869	1,785	500.	750.	1250.	—	300.
☐ 1869S	31,000	200.	225.	400.	—	150.
☐ 1870	4,035	200.	350.	750.	—	150.
☐ 1870CC	7,675	1500.	2500.	3800.	—	900.
☐ 1870S	17,000	200.	250.	350.	800.	150.
☐ 1871	3,230	250.	400.	600.	1000.	200.
☐ 1871CC	20,770	400.	600.	850.	—	250.
☐ 1871S	25,000	200.	250.	350.	800.	150.
☐ 1872	1,690	500.	750.	1250.	2500.	300.
☐ 1872CC	16,980	500.	750.	1250.	—	300.
☐ 1872S	36,400	200.	225.	275.	550.	150.
☐ 1873 Clsd 3	49,305	200.	225.	235.	395.	150.
☐ 1873 Open 3	63,200	200.	225.	235.	395.	150.
☐ 1873CC	7,416	500.	950.	1350.	2500.	300.
☐ 1873S	31,000	200.	225.	300.	650.	150.
☐ 1874	3,508	250.	400.	600.	1000.	200.
☐ 1874CC	21,198	250.	450.	900.	3500.	200.
☐ 1874S	16,000	200.	250.	325.	—	150.
☐ 1875	220	—	—	Rare	—	—
☐ 1875CC	11,828	450.	775.	1250.	—	275.
☐ 1875S	9,000	250.	350.	750.	2000.	200.
☐ 1876	1,477	400.	650.	1100.	2250.	250.
☐ 1876CC	6,887	400.	850.	1200.	2250.	250.
☐ 1876S	4,000	1250.	2000.	2500.	—	750.
☐ 1877	1,152	500.	800.	1250.	2500.	300.
☐ 1877CC	8,680	400.	800.	1500.	2750.	250.
☐ 1877S	26,700	200.	225.	235.	450.	150.
☐ 1878	131,740	200.	225.	235.	395.	150.
☐ 1878CC	9,054	750.	1750.	2700.	—	450.
☐ 1878S	144,700	200.	225.	235.	395.	150.
☐ 1879	301,950	200.	225.	235.	395.	150.
☐ 1879CC	17,281	200.	300.	550.	950.	150.
☐ 1879S	426,200	200.	225.	235.	395.	150.
☐ 1880	3,166,436	130.	140.	160.	395.	110.
☐ 1880CC	51,017	130.	140.	550.	950.	110.
☐ 1880S	1,348,900	130.	140.	160.	395.	110.
☐ 1881	5,708,802	130.	140.	160.	395.	110.
☐ 1881/80	(Inc. Ab.)			Only 2 Known		—
☐ 1881CC	13,886	130.	350.	550.	950.	110.
☐ 1881S	969,000	130.	140.	160.	395.	110.
☐ 1882	2,514,568	130.	140.	160.	395.	110.
☐ 1882CC	82,817	130.	140.	500.	950.	110.
☐ 1882S	969,000	130.	140.	160.	395.	110.
☐ 1883	233,461	130.	140.	160.	395.	110.
☐ 1883CC	12,958	130.	140.	400.	950.	110.
☐ 1883S	83,200	130.	140.	160.	395.	110.
☐ 1884	191,078	130.	140.	160.	395.	110.
☐ 1884CC	16,402	130.	140.	500.	850.	110.
☐ 1884S	177,000	130.	140.	160.	250.	110.

Date	Mintage	F-12	VF-20	XF-40	MS-60	ABP
☐ 1885	601,506	130.	140.	160.	250.	110.
☐ 1885S	1,211,500	130.	140.	160.	250.	110.
☐ 1886	388,432	130.	140.	160.	250.	110.
☐ 1886S	3,268,000	130.	140.	160.	250.	110.
☐ 1887	87	—	Proofs Only		—	—
☐ 1887S	1,912,000	130.	140.	160.	250.	110.
☐ 1888	18,296	130.	140.	160.	250.	110.
☐ 1888S	293,900	130.	140.	160.	250.	110.
☐ 1889	7,565	130.	300.	400.	800.	110.
☐ 1890	4,328	225.	250.	400.	800.	175.
☐ 1890CC	53,800	130.	140.	550.	900.	110.
☐ 1891	61,413	130.	140.	160.	280.	110.
☐ 1891CC	208,000	130.	140.	500.	900.	110.
☐ 1892	753,572	130.	140.	160.	250.	110.
☐ 1892CC	82,968	130.	140.	600.	900.	110.
☐ 1892O	10,000	500.	750.	1000.	2250.	300.
☐ 1892S	298,400	130.	140.	160.	250.	110.
☐ 1893	1,528,197	130.	140.	160.	250.	110.
☐ 1893CC	60,000	130.	140.	600.	900.	110.
☐ 1893O	110,000	130.	140.	300.	700.	110.
☐ 1893S	224,000	130.	140.	160.	250.	110.
☐ 1894	957,955	130.	140.	160.	250.	110.
☐ 1894O	16,600	130.	140.	300.	750.	110.
☐ 1894S	55,900	130.	140.	160.	250.	110.
☐ 1895	1,345,936	130.	140.	160.	250.	110.
☐ 1895S	112,000	130.	140.	160.	250.	110.
☐ 1896	59,063	130.	140.	160.	250.	110.
☐ 1896S	155,400	130.	140.	160.	250.	110.
☐ 1897	867,883	130.	140.	160.	250.	110.
☐ 1897S	354,000	130.	140.	160.	250.	110.
☐ 1898	633,495	130.	140.	160.	250.	110.
☐ 1898S	1,397,400	130.	140.	160.	250.	110.
☐ 1899	1,710,729	130.	140.	160.	250.	110.
☐ 1899S	1,545,000	130.	140.	160.	250.	110.
☐ 1900	1,405,730	130.	140.	160.	250.	110.
☐ 1900S	329,000	130.	140.	160.	250.	110.
☐ 1901	616,040	130.	140.	160.	250.	110.
☐ 1901S	3,648,000	130.	140.	160.	250.	110.
☐ 1902	172,562	130.	140.	160.	250.	110.
☐ 1902S	939,000	130.	140.	160.	250.	110.
☐ 1903	227,024	130.	140.	160.	250.	110.
☐ 1903S	1,855,000	130.	140.	160.	250.	110.
☐ 1904	392,136	130.	140.	160.	250.	110.
☐ 1904S	97,000	130.	140.	160.	250.	110.
☐ 1905	302,308	130.	140.	160.	250.	110.
☐ 1905S	880,700	130.	140.	160.	250.	110.
☐ 1906	348,820	130.	140.	160.	250.	110.
☐ 1906D	320,000	130.	140.	160.	250.	110.
☐ 1906S	598,000	130.	140.	160.	250.	110.
☐ 1907	626,192	130.	140.	160.	250.	110.
☐ 1907D	888,000	130.	140.	160.	250.	110.
☐ 1908	421,874	130.	140.	160.	250.	110.

INDIAN HEAD HALF EAGLES

This design by Bela L. Pratt, as was the case with the like design for the $2.50 gold piece, materialized as a direct result of President Theodore Roosevelt's interest in fathering the development of a more artistic coinage.

MINTMARK
AT POINT
OF FASCES

Date	Mintage	F-12	VF-20	XF-40	MS-60	ABP
☐ 1908	578,012	150.	170.	190.	950.	125.
☐ 1908D	148,000	150.	170.	190.	950.	125.
☐ 1908S	82,000	150.	325.	550.	4200.	125.
☐ 1909	627,138	150.	170.	190.	950.	125.
☐ 1909D	3,423,560	150.	170.	190.	790.	125.
☐ 1909O	34,200	275.	500.	1150.	13,500.	225.
☐ 1909S	297,200	150.	170.	350.	3000.	125.
☐ 1910	604,250	150.	170.	190.	950.	125.
☐ 1910D	193,600	150.	170.	190.	2500.	125.
☐ 1910S	770,200	150.	170.	350.	3250.	125.
☐ 1911	915,139	150.	170.	190.	790.	125.
☐ 1911D	72,500	225.	350.	600.	6600.	175.
☐ 1911S	1,416,000	150.	170.	325.	2200.	125.
☐ 1912	790,144	150.	170.	190.	790.	125.
☐ 1912S	392,000	150.	170.	350.	2600.	125.
☐ 1913	916,099	150.	170.	190.	790.	125.
☐ 1913S	408,000	200.	300.	425.	6500.	150.
☐ 1914	247,125	150.	170.	190.	950.	125.
☐ 1914D	247,000	150.	170.	190.	950.	125.
☐ 1914S	263,000	150.	170.	350.	2200.	125.
☐ 1915	588,075	150.	170.	190.	790.	125.
☐ 1915S	164,000	150.	300.	400.	4250.	125.
☐ 1916S	240,000	200.	240.	325.	2000.	150.
☐ 1929	662,000	—	2000.	4000.	12,000.	1250.

CLEANING COINS

Coin cleaning is a very touchy subject, especially among advanced collectors. It is generally acknowledged, however, that a dirty or heavily tarnished coin is better cleaned than not, but only if the coin is properly cleaned, not polished.

There are several good coin cleaners available, some multi-purpose, others specifically suited for bronze, nickel or silver coins. Properly used, they can beautify dirty or tarnished coins, but a cleaner should never be used on a collector coin until the user has first experimented with the product on a common coin.

Rubbing or polishing a coin with any cleaner will remove the natural surface luster of the metal, and should be avoided, as should the application of any abrasive cleaning element. Valuable coins should never be cleaned except by someone experienced in using the agent, as their values can be greatly diminished through improper cleaning.

EAGLES

This highest denomination ($10) coin authorized by the original coinage act, this unit was not minted during the years 1805 through 1837 because it could not be maintained in circulation. The legal 15 to 1 silver to gold ratio at which it was minted had been exceeded in the world markets, meaning the nation's gold coins were undervalued in terms of silver, causing them to flow out of the country.

Liberty Cap

Date	Mintage	F-12	VF-20	XF-40	MS-60	ABP
☐ 1795	5,583	—	11,000.	17,000.	40,000.	6500.
☐ 1796	4,146	—	11,000.	17,000.	40,000.	6500.
☐ 1797 Sm. Eagle	3,615	—	11,000.	17,000.	40,000.	6500.

Heraldic Eagle Introduced

Date	Mintage	F-12	VF-20	XF-40	MS-60	ABP
☐ 1797 Lg. Eagle	10,940	1950.	3000.	7500.	17,500.	1450.
☐ 1798 Over 97, 9 Stars Left, 4 Right	900		Auction '79, XF 17,500.			—
☐ 1798 Over 97, 7 Stars Left, 6 Right	842		Auction '79, AU 60,000.			—
☐ 1799	37,449	2000.	3750.	6500.	17,000.	1500.
☐ 1800	5,999	2250.	3750.	6500.	18,500.	1750.
☐ 1801	44,344	2000.	3750.	6500.	17,000.	1500.
☐ 1803	15,017	2250.	3750.	6500.	18,500.	1750.
☐ 1804	3,757	2750.	4500.	7750.	20,000.	2200.

CORONET EAGLES

Enactment of the 1834 law, which significantly reduced the fine gold content of all U.S. gold coins enabled a resumption of eagle coinage in 1838. This signalled the first introduction of the Coronet design by Christian Gobrecht, which except for the addition of the motto "In God We Trust" over the eagle on the reverse survived until 1907.

Mintmark

Date	Mintage	F-12	VF-20	XF-40	MS-60	ABP
☐ 1838	7,200	600.	1250.	2700.	10,500.	450.
☐ 1839 Lg. Lts.	38,248	400.	700.	2300.	8000.	300.

OLD STYLE   (ENLARGED)   **NEW STYLE**

NEW TYPE LIBERTY HEAD INTRODUCED

Date	Mintage	F-12	VF-20	XF-40	MS-60	ABP
☐ 1839 Sm. Lts.	Inc. Ab.	500.	1000.	1500.	5000.	400.
☐ 1840	47,338	350.	375.	450.	4700.	275.
☐ 1841	63,131	350.	375.	450.	4700.	275.
☐ 1841O	2,500	400.	650.	1200.	6500.	325.
☐ 1842 Sm. Dt.	81,507	350.	375.	450.	4700.	275.
☐ 1842 Lg. Dt.	Inc. Ab.	350.	375.	450.	4700.	275.

Date	Mintage	F-12	VF-20	XF-40	MS-60	ABP
☐ 1842O	27,400	350.	375.	450.	4700.	275.
☐ 1843	75,462	350.	375.	450.	4700.	275.
☐ 1843O	175,162	350.	375.	450.	4700.	275.
☐ 1844	6,361	350.	500.	450.	5500.	275.
☐ 1844O	118,700	350.	375.	450.	5500.	275.
☐ 1845	26,153	350.	400.	460.	5500.	275.
☐ 1845O	47,500	350.	400.	460.	5500.	275.
☐ 1846	20,095	350.	400.	460.	5500.	275.
☐ 1846O	81,780	350.	400.	460.	5500.	275.
☐ 1847	862,258	350.	400.	460.	5500.	275.
☐ 1847O	571,500	350.	400.	460.	5500.	275.
☐ 1848	145,484	350.	400.	460.	5500.	275.
☐ 1848O	38,850	350.	400.	460.	3600.	275.
☐ 1849	653,618	350.	400.	460.	3600.	275.
☐ 1849O	23,900	350.	400.	460.	3600.	275.
☐ 1850	291,451	350.	400.	460.	3600.	275.
☐ 1850O	57,500	350.	400.	460.	3600.	275.
☐ 1851	176,328	350.	400.	460.	3600.	275.
☐ 1851O	263,000	350.	400.	460.	3600.	275.
☐ 1852	263,106	350.	400.	460.	3600.	275.
☐ 1852O	18,000	350.	400.	460.	3600.	275.
☐ 1853	201,253	350.	400.	460.	3600.	275.
☐ 1853O	51,000	350.	400.	460.	3600.	275.
☐ 1854	54,250	350.	400.	460.	3600.	275.
☐ 1854O	52,500	350.	400.	460.	3600.	275.
☐ 1854S	123,826	350.	400.	460.	3600.	275.
☐ 1855	121,701	350.	400.	460.	3600.	275.
☐ 1855O	18,000	350.	400.	460.	3600.	275.
☐ 1855S	9,000	400.	750.	1100.	5250.	350.
☐ 1856	60,490	350.	400.	460.	3600.	275.
☐ 1856O	14,500	350.	400.	460.	3600.	275.
☐ 1856S	68,000	350.	400.	460.	3600.	275.
☐ 1857	16,606	350.	400.	460.	3600.	275.
☐ 1857O	5,500	550.	1000.	1750.	—	400.
☐ 1857S	26,000	350.	400.	460.	3600.	275.
☐ 1858	2,521	3000.	4500.	6000.	—	2250.
☐ 1858O	20,000	350.	400.	460.	3600.	275.
☐ 1858S	11,800	350.	400.	460.	3850.	275.
☐ 1859	16,093	350.	400.	460.	3600.	275.
☐ 1859O	2,300	1275.	2350.	3500.	—	800.
☐ 1859S	7,000	500.	800.	1150.	3600.	400.
☐ 1860	15,105	350.	400.	460.	3600.	275.
☐ 1860O	11,100	350.	400.	700.	3600.	275.
☐ 1860S	5,000	550.	900.	1250.	6000.	400.
☐ 1861	113,233	350.	400.	460.	3600.	275.
☐ 1861S	15,500	350.	400.	500.	3600.	275.
☐ 1862	10,995	350.	400.	460.	3600.	275.
☐ 1862S	12,500	350.	400.	825.	3600.	275.
☐ 1863	1,248	2000.	3500.	5000.	9000.	1500.
☐ 1863S	10,000	350.	450.	950.	—	275.
☐ 1864	3,580	600.	1000.	1500.	5500.	450.
☐ 1864S	2,500	1250.	1650.	2000.	—	800.
☐ 1865	4,005	550.	900.	1250.	5750.	400.
☐ 1865S	16,700	400.	825.	1200.	4750.	325.
☐ 1865S Over Inverted 186						
	Inc. Ab.	New England Sale, May 1978		VF 600.		—
☐ 1866S	8,500	950.	1450.	2000.	—	700.

MOTTO ADDED OVER EAGLE

Date	Mintage	F-12	VF-20	XF-40	MS-60	ABP
☐ 1866	3,780	—	375.	500.	1200.	300.
☐ 1866S	11,500	—	400.	600.	1400.	325.
☐ 1867	3,140	—	375.	500.	1100.	300.
☐ 1867S	9,000	—	450.	650.	1250.	350.
☐ 1868	10,655	—	375.	400.	800.	300.
☐ 1868S	13,500	—	400.	550.	1000.	325.
☐ 1869	1,855	—	1500.	2500.	4000.	1000.
☐ 1869S	6,430	—	450.	650.	1350.	350.
☐ 1870	4,025	—	450.	850.	1250.	350.
☐ 1870CC	5,908	—	1700.	3600.	—	1300.
☐ 1870S	8,000	—	450.	600.	1200.	350.
☐ 1871	1,820	—	1500.	2250.	3500.	1000.
☐ 1871CC	8,085	—	700.	1500.	2500.	600.
☐ 1871S	16,500	—	400.	550.	950.	325.
☐ 1872	1,650	—	1250.	2000.	3500.	900.
☐ 1872CC	4,600	—	750.	1000.	—	600.
☐ 1872S	17,300	—	375.	500.	950.	300.
☐ 1873	825	—	2000.	2500.	5000.	1400.
☐ 1873CC	4,543	—	1400.	1750.	—	900.
☐ 1873S	12,000	—	375.	550.	1000.	300.
☐ 1874	53,160	—	375.	385.	650.	300.
☐ 1874CC	16,767	—	400.	900.	1600.	325.
☐ 1874S	10,000	—	400.	650.	1250.	325.
☐ 1875	120		Garrett Sale, 1976			—
☐ 1875CC	7,715	—	750.	1300.	2500.	550.
☐ 1876	732	—	2250.	4000.	8500.	1500.
☐ 1876CC	4,696	—	1200.	1750.	3500.	800.
☐ 1876S	5,000	—	700.	1000.	2000.	550.
☐ 1877	817	—	2500.	4500.	7500.	1850.
☐ 1877CC	3,332	—	1700.	2250.	4000.	1100.
☐ 1877S	17,000	—	375.	400.	650.	300.
☐ 1878	73,800	—	230.	260.	320.	210.
☐ 1878CC	3,244	—	1700.	2250.	4000.	1100.
☐ 1878S	26,100	—	310.	350.	575.	275.
☐ 1879	384,770	—	230.	260.	320.	210.
☐ 1879CC	1,762	—	5250.	7500.	—	4000.
☐ 1879O	1,500	—	2500.	3500.	6000.	1800.
☐ 1879S	224,000	—	230.	260.	320.	210.
☐ 1880	1,644,876	—	230.	260.	320.	210.
☐ 1880CC	11,190	—	230.	700.	1400.	210.
☐ 1880O	9,200	—	400.	600.	1100.	350.
☐ 1880S	506,250	—	230.	260.	320.	210.
☐ 1881	3,877,260	—	230.	260.	320.	210.
☐ 1881CC	24,015	—	230.	450.	1150.	210.
☐ 1881O	8,350	—	230.	500.	900.	210.
☐ 1881S	970,000	—	230.	260.	320.	210.

Date	Mintage	F-12	VF-20	XF-40	MS-60	ABP
☐ 1882	2,324,480	—	230.	260.	320.	210.
☐ 1882CC	6,764	—	230.	550.	1600.	210.
☐ 1882O	10,820	—	230.	350.	650.	210.
☐ 1882S	132,000	—	230.	260.	320.	210.
☐ 1883	208,740	—	230.	260.	320.	210.
☐ 1883CC	12,000	—	230.	700.	1400.	210.
☐ 1883O	800	—	3500.	5000.	9000.	2800.
☐ 1883S	38,000	—	230.	260.	320.	210.
☐ 1884	76,905	—	230.	260.	320.	210.
☐ 1884CC	9,925	—	230.	550.	1400.	210.
☐ 1884S	124,250	—	230.	260.	320.	210.
☐ 1885	253,527	—	230.	260.	320.	210.
☐ 1885S	228,000	—	230.	260.	320.	210.
☐ 1886	236,160	—	230.	260.	320.	210.
☐ 1886S	826,000	—	230.	260.	320.	210.
☐ 1887	53,680	—	230.	260.	320.	210.
☐ 1887S	817,000	—	230.	260.	320.	210.
☐ 1888	132,996	—	230.	260.	320.	210.
☐ 1888O	21,335	—	230.	350.	850.	210.
☐ 1888S	648,700	—	230.	260.	320.	210.
☐ 1889	4,485	—	400.	650.	1500.	350.
☐ 1889S	425,400	—	230.	260.	320.	210.
☐ 1890	58,043	—	230.	260.	320.	210.
☐ 1890CC	17,500	—	230.	450.	950.	210.
☐ 1891	91,868	—	230.	260.	320.	210.
☐ 1891CC	103,732	—	230.	450.	950.	210.
☐ 1892	797,552	—	230.	260.	320.	210.
☐ 1892CC	40,000	—	230.	600.	950.	210.
☐ 1892O	28,688	—	230.	260.	650.	210.
☐ 1892S	115,500	—	230.	260.	320.	210.
☐ 1893	1,840,895	—	230.	260.	320.	210.
☐ 1893CC	14,000	—	230.	450.	950.	210.
☐ 1893O	17,000	—	230.	350.	750.	210.
☐ 1893S	141,350	—	230.	260.	320.	210.
☐ 1894	2,470,778	—	230.	260.	320.	210.
☐ 1894O	107,500	—	230.	260.	320.	210.
☐ 1894S	25,000	—	230.	260.	320.	210.
☐ 1895	567,826	—	230.	260.	320.	210.
☐ 1895O	98,000	—	230.	260.	320.	210.
☐ 1895S	49,000	—	230.	260.	320.	210.
☐ 1896	76,348	—	230.	260.	320.	210.
☐ 1896O	123,750	—	230.	260.	320.	210.
☐ 1897	1,000,159	—	230.	260.	320.	210.
☐ 1897O	42,500	—	230.	260.	320.	210.
☐ 1897S	234,750	—	230.	260.	320.	210.
☐ 1898	812,197	—	230.	260.	320.	210.
☐ 1898S	473,600	—	230.	260.	320.	210.
☐ 1899	1,262,305	—	230.	260.	320.	210.
☐ 1899O	37,047	—	230.	260.	320.	210.
☐ 1899S	841,000	—	230.	260.	320.	210.
☐ 1900	293,960	—	230.	260.	320.	210.
☐ 1900S	81,000	—	230.	260.	320.	210.
☐ 1901	1,718,825	—	230.	260.	320.	210.
☐ 1901O	72,041	—	230.	260.	320.	210.
☐ 1901S	2,812,750	—	230.	260.	320.	210.
☐ 1902	82,513	—	230.	260.	320.	210.

Date	Mintage	F-12	VF-20	XF-40	MS-60	ABP
☐ 1902S	469,500	—	230.	260.	320.	210.
☐ 1903	125,926	—	230.	260.	320.	210.
☐ 1903O	112,771	—	230.	260.	320.	210.
☐ 1903S	538,000	—	230.	260.	320.	210.
☐ 1904	162,038	—	230.	260.	320.	210.
☐ 1904O	108,950	—	230.	260.	320.	210.
☐ 1905	201,078	—	230.	260.	320.	210.
☐ 1905S	369,250	—	230.	260.	320.	210.
☐ 1906	165,497	—	230.	260.	320.	210.
☐ 1906D	981,000	—	230.	260.	320.	210.
☐ 1906O	86,895	—	230.	260.	320.	210.
☐ 1906S	457,000	—	230.	260.	320.	210.
☐ 1907	1,203,973	—	230.	260.	320.	210.
☐ 1907D	1,030,000	—	230.	260.	320.	210.
☐ 1907S	210,500	—	230.	260.	320.	210.

INDIAN HEAD EAGLES

Another of the coin designs directly attributable to President Theodore Roosevelt's instigation, this issue was designed by Augustus Saint-Gaudens, America's leading sculptor of his day. The initial issues did not carry the motto "In God We Trust" because the President personally objected to its use on coins, but it was restored through Congressional pressure in 1908. Unlike the reeded edges carried on all other gold coins, excepting the Saint-Gaudens double eagle, this coin carries raised stars; 46 from 1907-11, then with the admission of Arizona and New Mexico to statehood, 48 commencing in 1912.

MINTMARK

AT POINT OF FASCES

Date	Mintage	F-12	VF-20	XF-40	MS-60	ABP
☐ 1907 Wire Edge, Periods Before And After Legends						
	500	—	—	3000.	9500.	2100.
☐ 1907 Same, Without Stars On Edge						
		—	—	Unique	—	—
☐ 1907 Rolled Edge, Periods						
	42	—	—	—	50,000.	—
☐ 1907 Without Periods						
	239,406	—	—	490.	525.	1300.	375.
☐ 1908 Without Motto						
	33,500	—	—	500.	600.	3600.	400.
☐ 1908D Without Motto						
	210,000	—	—	490.	525.	2100.	375.

IN GOD WE TRUST MOTTO ADDED

Date	Mintage	F-12	VF-20	XF-40	MS-60	ABP
☐ 1908	341,486	—	380.	450.	1100.	300.
☐ 1908D	836,500	—	380.	450.	1700.	300.
☐ 1908S	59,850	—	550.	800.	5250.	450.
☐ 1909	184,863	—	380.	450.	1200.	300.
☐ 1909D	121,540	—	380.	450.	2050.	300.
☐ 1909S	292,350	—	380.	450.	2900.	300.
☐ 1910	318,704	—	380.	450.	1050.	300.
☐ 1910D	2,356,640	—	380.	450.	1050.	300.
☐ 1910S	811,000	—	380.	450.	3000.	300.
☐ 1911	505,595	—	380.	450.	1000.	300.
☐ 1911D	30,100	—	700.	1200.	9500.	575.
☐ 1911S	51,000	—	550.	750.	5500.	450.
☐ 1912	405,083	—	380.	450.	1050.	300.
☐ 1912S	300,000	—	380.	550.	3750.	300.
☐ 1913	442,071	—	380.	450.	1000.	300.
☐ 1913S	66,000	—	600.	900.	22,500.	450.
☐ 1914	151,050	—	380.	450.	1300.	300.
☐ 1914D	343,500	—	380.	450.	1250.	300.
☐ 1914S	208,000	—	380.	450.	3250.	300.
☐ 1915	351,075	—	380.	450.	790.	300.
☐ 1915S	59,000	—	380.	450.	6000.	300.
☐ 1916S	138,500	—	380.	450.	3250.	300.
☐ 1920S	126,500	—	10,000.	16,000.	47,500.	7000.
☐ 1926	1,014,000	—	380.	450.	790.	300.
☐ 1930S	96,000	—	3500.	5000.	16,000.	2750.
☐ 1932	4,463,000	—	380.	450.	790.	300.
☐ 1933	312,500	—	—	15,000.	50,000.	10,000.

CORONET DOUBLE EAGLES

The largest regular issue U.S. coin, the $20 gold piece was born as a direct result of the economic realities of the development of the California gold fields. Its standard is exactly double that of the eagle, at 516 grains .900 fine, and was authorized by the act of March 3, 1849.

Like the other Coronet designs, this one is the work of Longacre, with the motto again being added in 1866, then a switch to a fully spelled out denomination being made in 1877. The only issue of particular note in the series is the 1861 and 1861S offering with a distinctively different reverse, distinguished by its tall, slim letters, executed by A.C. Paquet but quickly withdrawn from production.

Mintmark

Date	Mintage	F-12	VF-20	XF-40	MS-60	ABP
☐ 1849	1	Unique, In U. S. Mint Collection				—
☐ 1850	1,170,261	—	540.	675.	2200.	435.
☐ 1850O	141,000	—	540.	850.	3750.	435.
☐ 1851	2,087,155	—	540.	675.	1900.	435.
☐ 1851O	315,000	—	540.	675.	3300.	435.
☐ 1852	2,053,026	—	540.	675.	1900.	435.
☐ 1852O	190,000	—	540.	675.	3250.	435.
☐ 1853	1,261,326	—	540.	675.	1900.	435.
☐ 1853O	71,000	—	540.	950.	3750.	435.
☐ 1854	757,899	—	540.	675.	1900.	435.
☐ 1854O	3,250		Auction '79, XF 45,000.			—
☐ 1854S	141,468	—	540.	675.	2800.	435.
☐ 1855	364,666	—	540.	675.	1900.	435.
☐ 1855O	8,000	—	1750.	3200.	10,000.	1200.
☐ 1855S	879,675	—	540.	675.	1900.	435.
☐ 1856	329,878	—	540.	675.	1900.	435.
☐ 1856O	2,250					—
☐ 1856S	1,189,750	—	540.	675.	1900.	435.
☐ 1857	439,375	—	540.	675.	1900.	435.
☐ 1857O	30,000	—	540.	900.	4000.	435.
☐ 1857S	970,500	—	540.	675.	1900.	435.
☐ 1858	211,714	—	540.	675.	1900.	435.
☐ 1858O	35,250	—	540.	1400.	4000.	435.
☐ 1858S	846,710	—	540.	675.	1900.	435.
☐ 1859	43,597	—	540.	950.	3500.	435.
☐ 1859O	9,100	—	1750.	3000.	7250.	1200.
☐ 1859S	636,445	—	540.	675.	1900.	435.
☐ 1860	577,670	—	540.	675.	1900.	435.
☐ 1860O	6,600	—	3000.	4000.	8000.	2100.
☐ 1860S	544,950	—	540.	675.	1900.	435.
☐ 1861	2,976,453	—	540.	675.	1900.	435.
☐ 1861 Paquet Rev.	Inc. Ab.			Extremely Rare		—
☐ 1861O	17,741	—	1500.	2250.	7500.	1100.
☐ 1861S	768,000	—	540.	675.	1900.	435.
☐ 1861S Paquet Rev.	Inc. Ab.		Auction '79, AU 20,000.			—
☐ 1862	92,133	—	540.	675.	3500.	435.
☐ 1862S	854,173	—	540.	675.	1900.	435.
☐ 1863	142,790	—	540.	675.	3300.	435.
☐ 1863S	966,570	—	540.	675.	1900.	435.
☐ 1864	204,285	—	540.	675.	3300.	435.
☐ 1864S	793,660	—	540.	675.	1900.	435.
☐ 1865	351,200	—	540.	675.	3200.	435.
☐ 1865S	1,042,500	—	540.	675.	1900.	435.
☐ 1866S	Inc. Below	—	540.	1200.	4000.	435.

1861
PAQUET
REVERSE

MOTTO ADDED OVER EAGLE

Date	Mintage	F-12	VF-20	XF-40	MS-60	ABP
☐ 1866	698,775	—	535.	795.	1500.	425.
☐ 1866S	842,250	—	535.	795.	1500.	425.
☐ 1867	251,065	—	535.	795.	950.	425.
☐ 1867S	920,750	—	535.	630.	1300.	425.
☐ 1868	98,600	—	535.	630.	1750.	425.
☐ 1868S	837,500	—	535.	630.	1350.	425.
☐ 1869	175,155	—	535.	630.	1100.	425.
☐ 1869S	686,750	—	535.	630.	1100.	425.
☐ 1870	155,185	—	535.	630.	1050.	425.
☐ 1870CC	3,789					—
☐ 1870S	982,000	—	535.	630.	1050.	425.
☐ 1871	80,150	—	535.	630.	1500.	425.
☐ 1871CC	17,387	—	1850.	2750.	4000.	1250.
☐ 1871S	928,000	—	535.	630.	900.	425.
☐ 1872	251,880	—	535.	630.	900.	425.
☐ 1872CC	26,900	—	535.	900.	2400.	425.
☐ 1872S	780,000	—	535.	630.	900.	425.
☐ 1873 Closed 3						
	Est. 208,925	—	535.	630.	1750.	425.

NOTE: Specimens of common date gold coins from the period 1873 through 1928 free of surface blemishes often command substantial premiums above the prices quoted in the uncirculated column.

Date	Mintage	F-12	VF-20	XF-40	MS-60	ABP
☐ 1873 Open 3						
	Est. 1,500,900	—	535.	630.	900.	425.
☐ 1873CC	22,410	—	535.	1300.	2800.	425.
☐ 1873S	1,040,600	—	535.	630.	900.	425.
☐ 1874	366,800	—	535.	630.	900.	425.
☐ 1874CC	115,085	—	535.	850.	1750.	425.
☐ 1874S	1,214,000	—	535.	630.	900.	425.
☐ 1875	295,740	—	535.	630.	900.	425.
☐ 1875CC	111,151	—	535.	800.	1800.	425.
☐ 1875S	1,230,000	—	535.	630.	900.	425.
☐ 1876	583,905	—	535.	630.	900.	425.
☐ 1876CC	138,441	—	535.	800.	1250.	425.
☐ 1876S	1,597,000	—	535.	630.	900.	425.

TWENTY DOLLARS SPELLED OUT

Date	Mintage	F-12	VF-20	XF-40	MS-60	ABP
☐ 1877	397,670	—	510.	525.	585.	400.
☐ 1877CC	42,565	—	800.	850.	2500.	600.
☐ 1877S	1,735,000	—	510.	525.	585.	400.
☐ 1878	543,645	—	510.	525.	585.	400.
☐ 1878CC	13,180	—	800.	850.	2750.	600.
☐ 1878S	1,739,000	—	510.	525.	585.	400.
☐ 1879	207,630	—	510.	525.	585.	400.
☐ 1879CC	10,708	—	850.	1500.	3750.	650.
☐ 1879O	2,325	—	1750.	2500.	8000.	1100.
☐ 1879S	1,223,800	—	510.	525.	585.	400.
☐ 1880	51,456	—	510.	525.	585.	400.
☐ 1880S	836,000	—	510.	525.	585.	400.
☐ 1881	2,260	—	2500.	4500.	14,000.	—
☐ 1881S	727,000	—	510.	525.	585.	400.
☐ 1882	630	—	8000.	15,000.	35,000.	6000.
☐ 1882CC	39,140	—	750.	800.	1450.	550.
☐ 1882S	1,125,000	—	510.	525.	585.	400.
☐ 1883	92					
☐ 1883CC	59,962	—	750.	765.	1500.	550.
☐ 1883S	1,189,000	—	510.	525.	585.	400.
☐ 1884	71					—
☐ 1884CC	81,139	—	750.	765.	1400.	550.
☐ 1884S	916,000	—	510.	525.	585.	400.
☐ 1885	828	—	4500.	7500.	25,000.	3000.
☐ 1885CC	9,450	—	850.	1250.	3000.	650.
☐ 1885S	683,500	—	510.	525.	585.	400.
☐ 1886	1,106	—	5000.	10,000.	22,000.	3500.
☐ 1887	121					—
☐ 1887S	283,000	—	510.	525.	585.	400.
☐ 1888	226,266	—	510.	525.	585.	400.
☐ 1888S	859,600	—	510.	525.	585.	400.
☐ 1889	44,111	—	510.	525.	585.	400.
☐ 1889CC	30,945	—	850.	900.	1450.	600.
☐ 1889S	774,700	—	510.	525.	585.	400.
☐ 1890	75,995	—	510.	525.	585.	400.
☐ 1890CC	91,209	—	850.	900.	1400.	600.
☐ 1890S	802,750	—	510.	525.	585.	400.
☐ 1891	1,442	—	2000.	3000.	7500.	1350.
☐ 1891CC	5,000	—	1200.	1750.	5500.	750.
☐ 1891S	1,288,125	—	510.	525.	585.	400.

Date	Mintage	F-12	VF-20	XF-40	MS-60	ABP
☐ 1892	4,523	—	1200.	1750.	5000.	750.
☐ 1892CC	27,265	—	750.	900.	2150.	550.
☐ 1892S	930,150	—	510.	525.	585.	400.
☐ 1893	344,339	—	510.	525.	585.	400.
☐ 1893CC	18,402	—	750.	950.	2800.	550.
☐ 1893S	996,175	—	510.	525.	585.	400.
☐ 1894	1,368,990	—	510.	525.	585.	400.
☐ 1894S	1,048,550	—	510.	525.	585.	400.
☐ 1895	1,114,656	—	510.	525.	585.	400.
☐ 1895S	1,143,500	—	510.	525.	585.	400.
☐ 1896	792,663	—	510.	525.	585.	400.
☐ 1896S	1,403,925	—	510.	525.	585.	400.
☐ 1897	1,383,261	—	510.	525.	585.	400.
☐ 1897S	1,470,250	—	510.	525.	585.	400.
☐ 1898	170,470	—	510.	525.	585.	400.
☐ 1898S	2,575,175	—	510.	525.	585.	400.
☐ 1899	1,669,384	—	510.	525.	585.	400.
☐ 1899S	2,010,300	—	510.	525.	585.	400.
☐ 1900	1,874,584	—	510.	525.	585.	400.
☐ 1900S	2,459,500	—	510.	525.	585.	400.
☐ 1901	111,526	—	510.	525.	585.	400.
☐ 1901S	1,596,000	—	510.	525.	585.	400.
☐ 1902	31,254	—	510.	525.	585.	400.
☐ 1902S	1,753,625	—	510.	525.	585.	400.
☐ 1903	287,428	—	510.	525.	585.	400.
☐ 1903S	954,000	—	510.	525.	585.	400.
☐ 1904	6,256,797	—	510.	525.	585.	400.
☐ 1904S	5,134,175	—	510.	525.	585.	400.
☐ 1905	59,011	—	510.	525.	585.	400.
☐ 1905S	1,813,000	—	510.	525.	585.	400.
☐ 1906	69,690	—	510.	525.	585.	400.
☐ 1906D	620,250	—	510.	525.	585.	400.
☐ 1906S	2,065,750	—	510.	525.	585.	400.
☐ 1907	1,451,864	—	510.	525.	585.	400.
☐ 1907D	842,250	—	510.	525.	585.	400.
☐ 1907S	2,165,800	—	510.	525.	585.	400.

SAINT-GAUDENS $20

ROMAN NUMERAL DATE — HIGH RELIEF

Perhaps America's most beautiful coin, the production issues of the Augustus Saint-Gaudens double eagle pale in comparison with his original models and the rare 1907 high relief strikes. The 1907 issue also includes varieties with Roman numeral dating. The 1907 and some 1908 issues do not bear the motto "In God We Trust". The motto, "E Pluribus Unum", is carried on the coin's edge. Although specimens dated 1933 were struck, none were released prior to President Franklin D. Roosevelt's move in 1934 to prohibit American citizens from holding gold, so none may be legally held. This series includes one of four 20th century overdates.

ARABIC DATE TYPE

Mintmark   Roman Numerals

Date	Mintage	VF-20	XF-40	MS-60	ABP
☐ 1907 Extremely High Relief, Plain Edge					
	Unique				—
☐ 1907 Extremely High Relief, Lettered Edge					
	Unrecorded	Stack's Sale, May 23-24 1974			—
☐ 1907 High Relief, Roman Numerals, Plain Edge					
		Currently offered at 180,000.			—
☐ 1907 High Relief, Roman Numerals, Wire Rim					
	11,250	3200.	5750.	14,500.	2400.
☐ 1907 High Relief, Roman Numerals, Flat Rim					
	Inc. Ab.	3200.	5750.	14,500.	2400.
☐ 1907 Large Letters On Edge				Unique	—
☐ 1907 Small Letters On Edge					
	361,667	765.	785.	1050.	575.
☐ 1908	4,271,551	765.	785.	950.	575.
☐ 1908D	663,750	765.	785.	1050.	575.

IN GOD WE TRUST
MOTTO ADDED BELOW EAGLE

Date	Mintage	VF-20	XF-40	MS-60	ABP
☐ 1908	156,359	545.	585.	950.	445.
☐ 1908D	349,500	545.	585.	625.	445.
☐ 1908S	22,000	800.	1200.	4500.	650.
☐ 1909 Over 8	161,282	545.	585.	2300.	445.
☐ 1909	Inc. Ab.	545.	585.	1400.	445.
☐ 1909D	52,500	545.	585.	3500.	445.
☐ 1909S	2,774,925	785.	800.	950.	600.
☐ 1910	482,167	545.	585.	625.	445.
☐ 1910D	429,000	545.	585.	625.	445.
☐ 1910S	2,128,250	545.	585.	625.	445.
☐ 1911	197,350	545.	585.	625.	445.
☐ 1911D	846,500	545.	585.	625.	445.
☐ 1911S	775,750	545.	585.	625.	445.
☐ 1912	149,824	545.	585.	1150.	445.
☐ 1913	168,838	545.	585.	1050.	445.
☐ 1913D	393,500	545.	585.	625.	445.
☐ 1913S	34,000	545.	900.	1900.	445.
☐ 1914	95,320	545.	585.	1050.	445.
☐ 1914D	453,000	545.	585.	625.	445.
☐ 1914S	1,498,000	545.	585.	625.	445.
☐ 1915	152,050	545.	585.	1100.	445.
☐ 1915S	567,500	545.	585.	625.	445.
☐ 1916S	796,000	545.	585.	1050.	445.
☐ 1920	228,250	545.	585.	1100.	445.
☐ 1920S	558,000	5000.	9000.	24,000.	3500.
☐ 1921	528,500	12,500.	20,000.	34,500.	8500.
☐ 1922	1,375,500	545.	585.	620.	445.
☐ 1922S	2,658,000	545.	900.	1450.	445.
☐ 1923	566,000	545.	585.	625.	445.
☐ 1923D	1,702,250	545.	900.	1350.	445.
☐ 1924	4,323,500	545.	585.	625.	445.
☐ 1924D	3,049,500	545.	900.	2200.	445.
☐ 1924S	2,927,500	545.	900.	1900.	445.
☐ 1925	2,831,750	545.	585.	625.	445.
☐ 1925D	2,938,500	875.	1150.	3100.	675.
☐ 1925S	3,776,500	875.	1150.	3000.	675.
☐ 1926	816,750	545.	585.	625.	445.
☐ 1926D	481,000	1000.	1200.	3300.	750.
☐ 1926S	2,041,500	875.	1100.	2200.	675.
☐ 1927	2,946,750	545.	585.	625.	445.
☐ 1927D	180,000				—
☐ 1927S	3,107,000	2750.	4500.	13,000.	2000.
☐ 1928	8,816,000	545.	585.	625.	445.
☐ 1929	1,779,750	1750.	3500.	10,250.	1100.
☐ 1930S	74,000	6000.	10,000.	22,000.	4500.
☐ 1931	2,938,250	4250.	7500.	18,500.	3500.
☐ 1931D	106,500	3750.	7250.	21,000.	2500.
☐ 1932	1,101,750	5000.	9000.	23,000.	3500.
☐ 1933	445,500	None placed in circulation			—

PROOF SETS

Proof sets are composed of specially minted coins representing the ultimate in the minter's art. Proof coins - the term relates to the method of manufacture, not the condition of the coin - are characterized by a sharpness of detail, a bold, squared-off edge and, generally, a mirror-like surface. This result is achieved through the utilization of specially selected and polished coinage blanks and dies, in combination with multiple striking (usually double) on special presses.

The scope of the listing which follows is limited to proof set issues of the modern era (i.e., commencing in 1936), although the U.S. Mint has annually offered proof sets and individual coins to the public since 1858. Those issues of the pre-1936 era are seldom encountered in sets, and when sold the individual coins are generally scaled from $100 sharply upward. Valuations for these individual coins (the regular issue of proof coins was suspended from 1916 to 1936) are incorporated in the regular date listings of this guide.

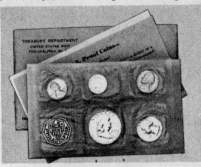

Date	Value	ABP	Date	Value	ABP
☐ 1936	5900.	4700.	☐ 1964	14.50	10.25
☐ 1937	3850.	2750.	☐ 1965 SMS*	5.70	4.05
☐ 1938	1800.	1395.	☐ 1966 SMS*	6.75	4.50
☐ 1939	1550.	1200.	☐ 1967 SMS*	14.00	9.90
☐ 1940	1300.	1000.	☐ 1968S	5.00	3.60
☐ 1941	1100.	850.	☐ 1968 S No S 10 C	11,500.	8850.
☐ 1942 both 5C	1450.	1125.	☐ 1969S	5.00	3.60
☐ 1942 5 coins	1100.	850.	☐ 1970S lg. date	12.50	9.00
☐ 1950	615.	440.	☐ 1970S sm. date	135.	90.00
☐ 1951	430.	300.	☐ 1970S No S 10 C	1675.	1200.
☐ 1952	245.	175.	☐ 1971S	5.00	3.60
☐ 1953	150.	110.	☐ 1971S No S 5C	2300.	1665.
☐ 1954	90.00	65.00	☐ 1972S	5.00	3.60
☐ 1955 box	78.00	55.00	☐ 1973S	10.75	7.65
☐ 1955 flat pack	82.00	58.00	☐ 1974S	10.00	7.20
☐ 1956	42.00	30.00	☐ 1975S	17.95	12.75
☐ 1957	25.00	17.75	☐ 1976S 3pc.	23.00	16.50
☐ 1958	30.00	21.50	☐ 1976S	7.50	5.40
☐ 1959	23.00	16.00	☐ 1977S	7.25	5.25
☐ 1960 lg. date	20.00	14.00	☐ 1978S	17.50	12.50
☐ 1960 sm. date	36.00	26.00	☐ 1979S	21.25	15.25
☐ 1961	14.50	10.25	☐ 1979S Type II	72.00	52.00
☐ 1962	14.50	10.25	☐ 1980S	14.25	10.25
☐ 1963	14.50	10.25	☐ 1981S	16.00	11.50

MINT SETS

Mint sets consist of one coin of each denomination, from each mint, produced during a given year. These uncirculated quality coins may or may not have been assembled into a set by the Treasury's Bureau of the Mint. Treasury-assembled sets through 1958 were packaged in a die-cut cardboard holder with a high sulphur content, and as a result, the coins usually tarnished badly. These sets actually contained two examples of each coin of regular issue. Commencing in 1959 the Treasury's sets, offering only one specimen of each coin struck for the year, are sealed in pliable cellophane packets variously identified as to their origin. Nicely preserved "Treasury" sets of 1946 through 1964 generally command a 15 to 20 percent premium.

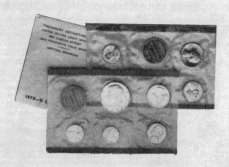

Date	Value	ABP	Date	Value	ABP
☐ 1940-P-D-S	—	—	☐ 1961-P-D	26.00	19.00
☐ 1941-P-D-S	—	—	☐ 1962-P-D	24.00	17.00
☐ 1942-P-D-S Both 5C	—	—	☐ 1963-P-D	24.00	17.00
☐ 1943-P-D-S	—	—	☐ 1964-P-D	19.00	13.50
☐ 1944-P-D-S	—	—	☐ 1965	5.70	4.05
☐ 1945-P-D-S	—	—	☐ 1966	6.75	4.50
☐ 1946-P-D-S	—	—	☐ 1967	14.00	9.50
☐ 1947-P-D-S (Est)	1000.	720.	☐ 1968-P-D-S	5.75	4.00
☐ 1948-P-D-S (Est.)	365.	260.	☐ 1969-P-D-S	5.75	4.00
☐ 1949-P-D-S (Est.)	2300.	1665.	☐ 1970-P-D-S Lg. Date	41.00	29.00
☐ 1950-P-D-S	—	—	☐ 1970-P-D-S Sm. Date	55.00	32.00
☐ 1951-P-D-S	750.	540.	☐ 1971-P-D-S	3.80	2.70
☐ 1952-P-D-S	390.	280.	☐ 1972-P-D-S	3.50	2.50
☐ 1953-P-D-S	315.	225.	☐ 1973-P-D-S	30.00	21.50
☐ 1954-P-D-S	170.	120.	☐ 1974-P-D-S	5.00	3.60
☐ 1955-P-D-S	82.00	58.00	☐ 1975-P-D-S	7.00	5.00
☐ 1956-P-D	63.00	45.00	☐ 1976 (3 pcs.)	14.75	10.50
☐ 1957-P-D	95.00	67.50	☐ 1976	5.35	3.80
☐ 1958-P-D	70.00	50.00	☐ 1977	7.30	5.20
☐ 1959-P-D	33.00	23.00	☐ 1978	7.75	5.50
☐ 1960-P-D Lg. Date	26.00	19.00	☐ 1979	7.75	5.50
☐ 1960-P-D Sm. Date	29.00	21.00	☐ 1980	8.75	6.30

MODERN SINGLES

Date	Cents Mintage	Unc.	Proof	Nickels Mintage	Unc.	Proof	Dimes Mintage	Unc.	Proof
1965	1,497,224,900	.15	NM	136,131,380	.15	NM	1,652,140,570	.20	NM
1966	2,188,147,783	.15	NM	156,208,283	.15	NM	1,382,734,540	.20	NM
1967	3,048,667,100	.15	NM	107,325,800	.15	NM	2,244,007,320	.20	NM
1968	1,707,880,970	.15	NM	----	NM	NM	424,470,000	.20	NM
1968D	2,886,269,600	.15	NM	91,227,880	.15	NM	480,748,280	.20	NM
1968S	261,311,510	.15	.25	103,437,510	.15	.40	Proof Only	NM	.75
1969	1,136,910,000	.25	NM	----	NM	NM	145,790,000	.20	NM
1969D	4,002,832,200	.15	NM	202,807,500	.15	NM	563,323,870	.20	NM
1969S	547,309,631	.15	.25	123,099,631	.15	.40	Proof Only	NM	.75
1970	1,898,315,000	.15	NM	----	NM	NM	345,570,000	.20	NM
1970D	2,891,438,900	.15	NM	515,485,380	.15	NM	754,942,100	.20	NM
1970S	693,192,814	.15	.65	241,464,814	.15	.65	Proof Only	NM	1.25
1971	1,919,490,000	.15	NM	106,884,000	.15	NM	162,690,000	.20	NM
1971D	2,911,045,600	.15	NM	316,144,800	.15	NM	377,914,240	.20	NM
1971S	528,354,192	.15	.25	Proof Only	NM	1.25	Proof Only	NM	.75
1972	2,933,255,000	.15	NM	202,036,000	.15	NM	431,540,000	.20	NM
1972D	2,665,071,400	.15	NM	351,694,600	.15	NM	330,290,000	.20	NM
1972S	380,200,104	.15	.25	Proof Only	NM	1.25	Proof Only	NM	.75
1973	3,728,245,000	.10	NM	384,396,000	.15	NM	315,670,000	.20	NM
1973D	3,549,576,588	.10	NM	261,405,400	.15	NM	455,032,426	.20	NM
1973S	319,937,634	.15	.75	Proof Only	NM	2.25	Proof Only	NM	1.75
1974	4,232,140,523	.10	NM	601,752,000	.15	NM	470,248,000	.20	NM
1974D	4,235,098,000	.10	NM	277,373,000	.15	NM	571,083,000	.20	NM
1974S	412,039,228	.15	.75	Proof Only	NM	3.75	Proof Only	NM	1.50
1975	5,451,476,142	.10	NM	181,772,000	.15	NM	585,673,900	.20	NM
1975D	4,505,245,300	.10	NM	401,875,300	.15	NM	313,705,300	.20	NM
1975S	Proof Only	NM	11.00	Proof Only	NM	2.50	Proof Only	NM	2.50
1976	4,674,292,426	.10	NM	367,124,000	.15	NM	568,760,000	.20	NM
1976D	4,221,592,455	.10	NM	563,964,147	.15	NM	695,222,774	.20	NM
1976S	Proof Only	NM	3.50	Proof Only	NM	1.50	Proof Only	NM	1.25
1977	4,469,930,000	.10	NM	585,376,000	.15	NM	796,930,000	.20	NM
1977D	4,149,062,300	.10	NM	297,313,460	.15	NM	376,607,228	.20	NM
1977S	Proof Only	NM	4.50	Proof Only	NM	1.50	Proof Only	NM	1.50
1978	5,558,605,000	.10	NM	391,308,000	.15	NM	663,980,000	.20	NM
1978D	4,280,233,400	.10	NM	313,092,780	.15	NM	282,847,540	.20	NM
1978S	Proof Only	NM	5.00	Proof Only	NM	1.35	Proof Only	NM	1.50

Quarters

Date	Mintage	Unc.	Proof	Date	Mintage	Unc.	Proof
1965	1,819,717,540	.80	NM	1974D	353,160,300	.40	NM
1966	821,101,500	.80	NM	1974S	Proof Only	NM	1.50
1967	1,524,031,848	.80	NM	1975	See Bicentennial	–	–
1968	220,731,500	.80	NM	1976	Issues	–	–
1968D	101,534,000	1.00	NM	1977	—	.50	–
1968S	Proof Only	NM	.75	1977D	—	.50	–
1969	176,212,000	.50	NM	1977S	Proof Only	–	1.00
1969D	114,372,000	1.25	NM	1978	—	.50	–
1969S	Proof Only	NM	.75	1978D	—	.50	–
1970	136,420,000	.50	NM	1978-S	Proof Only	–	1.00
1970D	417,341,364	.50	NM				
1970S	Proof Only	NM	1.00				
1971	109,284,000	.50	NM				
1971D	258,634,428	.50	NM				
1971S	Proof Only	NM	.75				
1972	215,048,000	.40	NM				
1972D	311,067,732	.40	NM				
1972S	Proof Only	NM	.75				
1973	346,924,000	.40	NM				
1973D	232,977,400	.40	NM				
1973S	Proof Only	NM	1.50				
1974	801,456,000	.40	NM				

Modern uncirculated single coins are generally in large supply in dealer's inventories and are not actively sought in the market place. Dealers normally obtain proof single coins for stock from complete sets purchased in open market transactions. (See page 115 for Proof Set prices.)

BICENTENNIAL COINAGE

The nation's quarter, half and dollar coinage was redesigned in 1975 to provide circulation issue commemoratives of the bicentennial of the American Revolution. While the obverses of these coins retained the familiar portraits of the Washington, Kennedy and Eisenhower, with the addition of commemorative - 1776/1976 - dual dating, the reverses were completely redesigned to feature themes reminiscent of the birth of the country.

To accomplish this change, assuring that sufficient quantities could be produced to attain active circulation and negate the possibility that a temporary shortage of any of the three denominations might develop, Congress authorized Mint officials to continue production of 1974 dated quarters, halves and dollars into mid-1975. The availability of this authority led to a decision not to produce 1975 dated counterparts of the regular issue designs.

All three coins were produced for circulation issue in the standard cupor-nickel clad copper composition, in which version they were also produced for inclusion in mint (uncirculated coin) and proof sets in combination with 1975 dated cents, nickels and dimes. Mint and proof sets will also be produced containing 1976 dated coins of the lower denominations. They were also made available in .400 fine silver versions, in sets only, each of which contained one specimen of each of the three coins in uncirculated or proof quality.

All versions of the dollar coin exist in two distinct varieties. Both the obverse and reverse dies were revised to facilitate production. The original design featured bold lettering on the reverse, on which the individual letters were squared off, excepting the letters A, M and N, which were pointed. The revised design features narrow lettering on the reverse, with light serifs on the individual letters, and blunted extremities on the letters A, M and N.

Coin	Philadelphia		Denver		San Francisco			
	Mintage	Unc.	Mintage	Unc.	Mintage	Unc.	Mintage	Proof
Clad Metal 25¢	—	.50	—	.50	—	—	—	1.25
.400 Silver 25¢	—	—	—	—	—	3.00	—	4.00
Clad Metal 50¢	—	1.00	—	1.00	—	—	—	2.00
.400 Silver 50¢ . . .	—	—	—	—	—	4.50	—	7.50

Variety 1

Variety 2

Clad Metal, Variety 1 $1								
	—	4.00	21,148,710	2.40	—	—	—	14.00
			(est.)					
Clad Metal, Variety 2 $1								
	—	2.00	—	1.75	—	—	—	5.00
.400 Silver, Variety 1 $1								
	—	—	—	—	—	14.00	—	14.50
Silver three coin uncirculated sets, variety dollar	—	—	—	—	—	15.75	—	—
Silver three coin proof sets, variety 1 dollar	—	—	—	—	—	—	—	16.00

COMMEMORATIVES

Date	Event	Mintage	XF/AU	MS-60	MS-65	ABP MS-60
☐ 1893	Isabella Quarter	24,214	185.	505.	2025.	405.
☐ 1900	Lafayette Dollar	36,026	360.	1460.	7000.	1170.

HALF DOLLARS

Date	Event	Mintage	XF/AU	MS-60	MS-65	ABP MS-60
☐ 1921	Alabama 2X2	6,006	125.	480.	1800.	380.
☐ 1921	Alabama	59,038	70.00	395.	1320.	315.
☐ 1936	Albany	17,671	150.	310.	545.	245.

Date	Event	Mintage	XF/AU	MS-60	MS-65	ABP MS-60
☐ 1937	Antietam	18,028	170.	420.	785.	335.
☐ 1935	Arkansas PDS Set	5,505	—	295.	630.	235.
☐ 1936	Arkansas PDS Set	9,660	—	295.	630.	235.
☐ 1937	Arkansas PDS Set	5,505	—	310.	665.	245.
☐ 1938	Arkansas PDS Set	3,155	—	535.	1575.	425.
☐ 1939	Arkansas PDS Set	2,104	—	1500.	3050.	1215.
	Arkansas - Type Coin	—	32.00	73.00	215.	58.00
☐	See Also Robinson-Arkansas					
☐ 1936	Bay Bridge	71,424	68.00	100.	335.	81.00
☐ 1934	Boone	10,007	50.00	118.	420.	95.00
☐ 1935	Boone - PDS Set w/1934	5,005	—	1575.	2900.	1250.
☐ 1935	Boone - PDS Set	2,003	—	340.	775.	270.
☐ 1936	Boone - PDS Set	5,005	—	340.	900.	270.
☐ 1937	Boone - PDS Set	2,506	—	700.	1575.	560.
☐ 1938	Boone - PDS Set	2,100	—	1400.	2800.	1125.
	Boone - Type Coin	—	50.00	135.	270.	108.

Date	Event	Mintage	XF/AU	MS-60	MS-65	ABP MS-60
☐ 1936	Bridgeport	25,015	58.00	160.	430.	125.
☐ 1925S	California Jubilee	86,594	55.00	170.	470.	135.

Date	Event	Mintage	XF/AU	MS-60	MS-65	ABP MS-60
☐ 1936	Cincinnati - PDS Set	5,005	—	1460.	2200.	1175.
☐ 1936	Cincinnati - Type Coin	—	190.	480.	720.	380.
☐ 1936	Cleveland - Great Lakes	50,030	27.00	85.00	220.	67.00
☐ 1936	Columbia PDS Set	9,007	—	1000.	2100.	810.
☐ 1936	Columbia - Type Coin	—	130.	310.	700.	250.
☐ 1892	Columbian Expo	950,000	7.25	26.00	225.	21.00
☐ 1893	Columbian Expo	1,550,405	7.25	23.00	225.	19.00
☐ 1935	Connecticut	25,018	112.	250.	675.	200.
☐ 1936	Delaware	20,993	112.	250.	500.	200.
☐ 1936	Elgin	20,015	84.00	230.	550.	185.
☐ 1936	Gettysburg	26,928	100.	330.	600.	265.
☐ 1922	Grant-With Star	4,256	365.	790.	6075.	630.
☐ 1922	Grant	67,405	36.00	105.	495.	85.00
☐ 1928	Hawaiian	10,008	760.	1545.	3650.	1240.
☐ 1935	Hudson	10,008	420.	790.	1490.	630.
☐ 1924	Huguenot-Walloon	142,080	47.00	105.	550.	85.00
☐ 1946	Iowa	100,057	40.00	90.00	260.	72.00
☐ 1925	Lexington-Concord	162,013	33.00	79.00	260.	63.00
☐ 1918	Lincoln-Illinois	100,058	37.00	95.00	450.	76.00
☐ 1936	Long Island	81,826	36.00	73.00	180.	58.00
☐ 1936	Lynchburg	20,013	84.00	210.	470.	165.
☐ 1920	Maine	50,028	46.00	112.	590.	90.00
☐ 1934	Maryland	25,015	75.00	180.	535.	145.
☐ 1921	Missouri - 2X4	5,000	250.	900.	2800.	720.
☐ 1921	Missouri	15,428	240.	870.	2600.	700.
☐ 1923S	Monroe	274,077	22.50	56.00	350.	45.00
☐ 1938	New Rochelle	15,266	225.	395.	700.	315.
☐ 1936	Norfolk	16,936	225.	395.	785.	315.

Date	Event	Mintage	XF/AU	MS-60	MS-65	ABP MS-60
☐ 1926	Oregon	47,955	52.00	125.	270.	100.
☐ 1926S	Oregon	83,055	52.00	125.	270.	100.
☐ 1928	Oregon	6,028	79.00	280.	700.	225.
☐ 1933D	Oregon	5,008	125.	350.	985.	280.
☐ 1934D	Oregon	7,006	62.00	235.	640.	190.
☐ 1936	Oregon	10,006	50.00	145.	490.	115.
☐ 1936S	Oregon	5,006	79.00	200.	845.	180.
☐ 1937D	Oregon	12,008	53.00	140.	485.	110.
☐ 1938	Oregon - PDS Set	6,005	—	560.	1690.	450.
☐ 1939	Oregon - PDS Set	3,004	—	930.	2360.	740.
	Oregon - Type Coin	—	52.00	125.	270.	100.
☐ 1915S	Panama - Pacific	27,134	195.	900.	4600.	720.
☐ 1920	Pilgrim	152,112	34.00	72.00	270.	57.00
☐ 1921	Pilgrim	20,053	58.00	195.	790.	155.
☐ 1936	Rhode Island - PDS Set	15,010	—	560.	790.	450.
☐ 1936	Rhode Island - Type Coin	—	39.00	170.	250.	135.
☐ 1937	Roanoke	29,030	62.00	170.	495.	135.

Date	Event	Mintage	XF/AU	MS-60	MS-65	ABP MS-60
☐ 1936	Robinson-Arkansas	25,265	62.00	140.	340.	110.
☐	(See Also Arkansas)					
☐ 1935S	San Diego	70,132	32.00	79.00	350.	63.00
☐ 1936D	San Diego	30,092	45.00	125.	550.	100.
☐ 1926	Sesquicentennial	141,120	25.00	56.00	300.	45.00

Date	Event	Mintage	XF/AU	MS-60	MS-65	ABP MS-60
☐ 1935	Spanish Trail	10,008	590.	950.	1850.	765.
☐ 1925	Stone Mountain	1,314,709	19.00	34.00	110.	27.00
☐ 1934	Texas	61,463	62.00	124.	250.	99.00
☐ 1935	Texas - PDS Set	9,994	—	270.	930.	215.
☐ 1936	Texas - PDS Set	8,911	—	270.	950.	215.
☐ 1937	Texas - PDS Set	6,571	—	335.	990.	270.
☐ 1938	Texas - PDS Set	3,775	—	645.	1660.	515.
	Texas - Type Coins	—	—	95.00	260.	76.00
☐ 1925	Ft. Vancouver	14,994	185.	590.	1700.	470.
☐ 1927	Vermont	28,142	79.00	280.	955.	225.
☐ 1946	B.T.W. - PDS Set	200,113	—	48.00	81.00	38.00
☐ 1947	B.T.W. - PDS Set	100,017	—	62.00	112.	49.00
☐ 1948	B.T.W. - PDS Set	8,005	—	112.	330.	90.00
☐ 1949	B.T.W. - PDS Set	6,004	—	215.	460.	170.
☐ 1950	B.T.W. - PDS Set	6,004	—	170.	340.	135.
☐ 1951	B.T.W. - PDS Set	7,004	—	135.	270.	110.
	B.T.W. - Type Coin	—	13.00	16.00	27.00	12.50
☐ 1951	Wash.-Carv. - PDS Set	10,004	—	100.	175.	81.00
☐ 1952	Wash.-Carv. - PDS Set	8,006	—	124.	225.	99.00
☐ 1953	Wash.-Carv. - PDS Set	8,003	—	170.	280.	135.
☐ 1954	Wash.-Carv. - PDS Set	12,006	—	100.	175.	81.00
	Wash.-Carver - Type Coin	—	12.50	15.00	27.00	12.00
☐ 1936	Wisconsin	25,015	84.00	195.	510.	155.
☐ 1936	York County	25,015	90.00	170.	460.	135.

GOLD DOLLARS

Date	Event	Mintage	XF/AU	MS-60	MS-65	ABP MS-60
☐ 1903	Louisiana, Jefferson	17,500	395.	900.	1400.	675.

Date	Event	Mintage	XF/AU	MS-60	MS-65	ABP MS-60
☐ 1903	Louisiana, Mckinley	17,500	395.	900.	1400.	675.
☐ 1904	Lewis and clark expo.	10,025	540.	2150.	3500.	1650.
☐ 1905	Lewis and clark expo.	10,041	540.	2150.	3500.	1650.
☐ 1915S	Pan-Pacific Expo.	15,000	350.	1150.	1875.	825.
☐ 1916	Mckinley Memorial	9,977	350.	950.	1525.	720.
☐ 1917	Mckinley Memorial	10,000	365.	1000.	1625.	765.
☐ 1922	Grant Mem. W/Star	5,016	625.	1500.	2600.	1175.
☐ 1922	Grant Mem. W/O Star	5,000	625.	1500.	2600.	1175.

GOLD TWO AND A HALF DOLLARS

Date	Event	Mintage	XF/AU	MS-60	MS-65	ABP MS-60
☐ 1915S	Pan-Pacific Expo.	6,749	825.	2350.	5850.	1800.
☐ 1926	Philadelphia Sesqui.	46,019	380.	760.	1050.	585.

GOLD FIFTY DOLLARS

Date	Event	Mintage	XF/AU	MS-60	MS-65	ABP MS-60
☐ 1915S	Pan-Pacific Expo., Round	483	22,500.	38,500.	50,000.	29,500.
☐ 1915S	Pan-Pacific Expo., Octagon	645	17,000.	28,000.	35,000.	21,500.

LARGE SIZE
PAPER MONEY
1861-1923

The collecting of U.S. paper money is divided into two distinct eras of interest; the old large size notes issued from 1861 to 1929, and the current small size note issue which was launched in mid-1929. The listings which follow are devoted exclusively to the former series, which displays a diversity in design which contrasts sharply with that projected on the small size issues of the past 50 years, but which has not been widely collected by series because of its general unavailability.

Although continental currency notes were issued under the authority of the Continental Congress to finance the Revolutionary War, the new nation forged out of that conflict did not immediately issue paper money, perhaps greatly due to the dishonor visited upon the concept by the vagaries of the wartime economy. When the first issue was authorized — Demand Notes on July 17, 1861 — it was created to meet the new fiscal demands brought on by the advent of the Civil War.

Americans of the mid-1800s accorded their new currency little more honor than did their counterparts three-quarters of a century earlier, instead placing their real trust in hard silver and gold coins. Ultimately, however, American paper money was to become the world's most honored and respected currency. The vehicle for this broadening spread were the attractive, varied and changing large size note issues of the late 1800s and early 1900s. At the time the standard note size was 7-3/8 by 3-1/8 inches, in contrast to our present currency size of 6-1/8 by 2-5/8 inches.

At various times over two-thirds of a century of issue — small size currency was first placed in circulation on July 10, 1929 — large size paper money was offered in twelve different basic obligations, not all of which were covered in the following listing. The first of these was the short lived Demand Notes series of 1861. Under two acts of that year the issue of $60 million in currency was authorized, with the resulting notes bearing vivid green reverse designs which gave to our nation's currency the lasting nickname "greenback."

This issue was followed by the Legal Tender or United States Note series which is now more than 110 years old and persists in the form of a single small size $100 note issue. The first Legal Tender note issue was authorized under a Congressional act of February 25, 1862, with the first issue carrying the date March 10, 1862. Interestingly the August 1 dated second series, the first to make provision for a government note issue in a unit of less than $5, was intended to include a $3 value.

The next two note issues authorized were designed to alleviate the deteriorated financial condition of the U.S. Treasury during the Civil War. The first of these was the Interest Bearing Note series, and the second the Compound Interest Treasury Note series. These $10 to $500 notes were released under various Congressional acts dating from July 17, 1861 to March 3, 1865. Following the war, on February 26, 1879, Congress enacted a law which authorized $10 unit Refunding Certificate notes as a means of placing government securities within the reach of the average citizen.

The nation's second longest lived paper money series, the Silver Certificate, was authorized on February 28, 1878, with the life of the series ending when its silver redemption provisions were drawn to a halt on June 24, 1968. This is a highly varied series, like that of the Legal Tender Note issues and was created to provide a circulating substitute for silver coins which the Treasury was required by law to produce. A Treasury or Coin Note series was created on July 14, 1890, which could be backed by either silver or gold coins, but it became obsolete in less than 15 years.

National Currency or National Bank Note issues, the nation's most extensive paper money series, came into being under a Congressional act of February 25, 1863, and their issue continued into the small currency series, being halted on May 20, 1935. The opportunity to issue these notes was individually extended to more than 14,000 banks chartered by Congress, several thousand of which exercised this option by depositing appropriate U.S. government securities with the Treasury. A closely allied and rare series is the National Gold Bank Note obligations circulated in 1870-84. The banks of issue were likewise required to deposit U.S. government obligations with the Treasury against note issues, with the obligations thereon specifying redemption in gold coin.

Although Federal Reserve Bank obligations today constitute all but an infinitesimal quantity of our circulating paper money the first notes were not issued until near the end of the large size currency era, as the Federal Reserve Act did not become law until December 23, 1913. A limited number of Federal Reserve Bank Notes were issued in 1915 and 1918 dated series on National Currency note blanks, while large distinctive Federal Reserve Note series were offered dated 1914 and 1918.

The twelfth large size currency obligation was the Gold Certificate series. Ten issues of Gold Certificates were offered from the first authorization on March 3, 1863, through the final series which bears the date 1922. The three issues of the 1865-75 period were primarily used by banks and clearing houses, with the fourth issue which is dated 1882 being the earliest released to general circulation. Most notes encountered today bear the series dates 1906, 1907, 1913 or 1922.

Series dates, signature combinations and identifications, along with other appropriate clarifications required for attribution are included in the listings which follow. Valuations are provided in the four most commonly collected paper money grades: Good — Specimens in badly deteriorated condition which may have edge tears, bad stains and missing corners (collectible only in the instance of rare or extremely scarce notes); Very Good — Considerable evidence of circulation, with heavy folds generally present sometimes along with fading, smears and smudges, but no tears or missing pieces; Fine — Noticeable evidence of circulation will be present, but the note will be intact and not otherwise badly abused, faded or stained; Very Fine — Only slight evidence of circulation or handling, with only faint folds or creases; Uncirculated — Never in circulation and generally crisp.

The following listings document the issue history and collector values of all obligation types issued during the large size currency eta. Detailed information is incorporated on all denominations of issue through $100; higher denomination notes are listed and priced by issue because they are extremely rare, and in some instances surviving examples are not known to exist.

Several detailed studies and listings of U.S. paper money are availabe to collectors desiring more comprehensive coverate than that provided here. These include the **Donlon Catalog, U.S. Large Size Paper Money, 1861 to 1923** by William P. Donlon and **Paper Money of the U.S.** by Robert Friedberg, which is heavily concentrated on the large size currency series. Recommended for the small size note series are the **Donlon Catalog of U.S. Small Size Paper Money,** along with **A Guide Book of Modern U.S. Currency** by Neil Shafer and **The Standard Handbook of Modern U.S. Paper Money** by Chuck O'Donnell.

DEMAND NOTES OF 1861

Five Dollars

Payable at:		Good	VG	ABP
☐ BOSTON	Type One	800.00	1500.00	400.00
☐ BOSTON	Type Two	600.00	900.00	325.00
☐ NEW YORK	Type One	800.00	1500.00	400.00
☐ NEW YORK	Type Two	550.00	800.00	300.00
☐ PHILADELPHIA	Type One	800.00	1500.00	400.00
☐ PHILADELPHIA	Type Two	550.00	800.00	300.00
☐ ST. LOUIS	Type One	1500.00	3000.00	750.00
☐ ST. LOUIS	Type Two	1250.00	2000.00	650.00
☐ CINCINNATI	Type One	2500.00	4000.00	1250.00
☐ CINCINNATI	Type Two	2000.00	3000.00	1100.00

Ten Dollars

Payable at:		Good	VG	ABP
☐ BOSTON	Type One	1000.00	2000.00	500.00
☐ BOSTON	Type Two	800.00	1400.00	450.00
☐ NEW YORK	Type One	900.00	1500.00	450.00
☐ NEW YORK	Type Two	750.00	1250.00	400.00
☐ PHILADELPHIA	Type One	900.00	1500.00	450.00
☐ PHILADELPHIA	Type Two	750.00	1250.00	400.00
☐ ST. LOUIS	Type One	2500.00	4500.00	1250.00
☐ ST. LOUIS	Type Two	2000.00	3000.00	1100.00
☐ CINCINNATI	Type One	2500.00	4500.00	1250.00
☐ CINCINNATI	Type Two	2000.00	3000.00	1100.00

Twenty Dollars

Payable at:		Good	VG	ABP
☐ BOSTON	Type One	VERY RARE	—	—
☐ BOSTON	Type Two	VERY RARE	—	—
☐ NEW YORK	Type One	5500.00	7500.00	3300.00
☐ NEW YORK	Type Two	5500.00	7000.00	3300.00
☐ PHILADELPHIA	Type One	5500.00	7500.00	3300.00
☐ PHILADELPHIA	Type Two	4000.00	7000.00	2400.00
☐ CINCINNATI	Type One	VERY RARE	—	—
☐ CINCINNATI	Type Two	VERY RARE	—	—

LEGAL TENDER NOTES

One Dollar

Series	Signatures	Seal	Fine	VF	ABP.
	Red. Numerals "1" "2" "3" vertically in center.				
☐ 1862	Chittenden-Spinner	Small red	85.00	125.00	50.00
	National Bank Note Co. American Bank Note Co., lower border. No Monogram.				
☐ 1862	Chittenden-Spinner	Small red	85.00	125.00	50.00
	As above with monogram ABN Co. upper right.				
☐ 1862	Chittenden-Spinner	Small red	80.00	120.00	45.00
	National Bank Note Co., twice in lower border. No Monogram.				
☐ 1862	Chittenden-Spinner	Small red	95.00	135.00	55.00
	As above, with monogram ABN Co. upper right.				
	Red serial numbers.				
☐ 1869	Allison-Spinner	Large red	75.00	155.00	40.00
	National Bank Note Co., lower portion back design.				

Series	Signatures	Seal	Fine	VF	ABP
Red Serial numbers. Red ornamentation at right, face design.					
☐ 1874	Allison-Spinner	Small red	35.00	85.00	20.00
Face, micro at right, "Engraved & Printed at the Bureau of Engraving & Printing."					
Back, Columbian Bank Note Co., twice in lower portion.					
☐ 1875	Allison-New	Small red	45.00	80.00	25.00
Above issued in five additional series, same design excepting Series letter.					
☐ 1875 Series "A"			90.00	170.00	50.00
☐ 1875 Series "B"			80.00	190.00	40.00
☐ 1875 Series "C"			80.00	190.00	40.00
☐ 1875 Series "D"			80.00	190.00	40.00
☐ 1875 Series "E"			100.00	225.00	50.00
☐ 1875	Allison-Wyman	Small red	35.00	65.00	20.00
☐ 1878	Allison-Gilfillan	Small red	40.00	65.00	22.00
"Series 1878" top margin, back design.					
"Printed by Bureau of Engraving & Printing" lower margin, back design.					

Series	Signatures	Seal	Fine	VF	ABP
Red Serial numbers. Ornamentation removed. Large Seal introduced.					
☐ 1880	Scofield-Gilfillan	Large brown	35.00	90.00	20.00
☐ 1880	Bruce-Gilfillan	Large brown	35.00	90.00	20.00
☐ 1880	Bruce-Wyman	Large brown	35.00	90.00	20.00
Blue Serial Numbers					
☐ 1880	Rosecrans-Huston	Large red	140.00	175.00	80.00
☐ 1880	Rosecrans-Huston	Large brown	150.00	200.00	85.00
☐ 1880	Rosecrans-Nebeker	Large brown	150.00	200.00	85.00
☐ 1880	Rosecrans-Nebeker	Small red	32.00	50.00	18.00
☐ 1880	Tillman-Morgan	Small red	32.00	50.00	18.00
Serial number panel dropped.					
☐ 1917	Teehee-Burke	Small red	18.00	26.00	10.00
☐ 1917	Elliott-Burke	Small red	18.00	26.00	10.00

Series	Signature	Seal	Fine	VF	ABP
☐ 1917	Burke-Elliott	Small red	40.00	70.00	20.00
☐ 1917	Elliott-White	Small red	18.00	26.00	10.00
☐ 1917	Speelman-White	Small red	18.00	26.00	10.00

Series	Signature	Seal	Fine	VF	ABP
☐ 1923	Speelman-White	Small red	28.00	50.00	14.00

Two Dollars

Series	Signatures	Seal	Fine	VF	ABP
	Red Numerals "1" "2" "3" vertically in center.				
☐ 1862	Chittenden-Spinner	Small red	150.00	225.00	80.00
	American Bank Note Co., vertically at left, face design.				
☐ 1862	Chittenden-Spinner	Small red	150.00	250.00	80.00
	National Bank Note Co., vertically at left, face design.				

Patented April 23, 1860, National Bank Note Co. in lower border, on both types.

Series	Signatures	Seal	Fine	VF	ABP
		Red Serial numbers			
☐ 1869	Allison-Spinner	Large red	135.00	450.00	85.00

"Engraved and printed at the Treasury Department," vertically at left, face design.
American Bank Note Co. bottom left, face design and twice below back design.

	Red Serial numbers. Red ornamentation at right.				
☐ 1874	Allison-Spinner	Small red	135.00	200.00	80.00
☐ 1875	Allison-New	Small red	65.00	100.00	35.00
	Issued in two additional series, same design:				
☐ 1875	Series A, lower right of face design.		135.00	265.00	80.00
☐ 1875	Series B		135.00	265.00	80.00
☐ 1875	Allison-Wyman	Small red	65.00	100.00	35.00
☐ 1878	Allison-Gilfillan	Small red	65.00	100.00	35.00
☐ 1878	Scofield-Gilfillan	Small red	1900.00	Rare	1000.00
	Red Serial numbers. Ornamentation removed.				
☐ 1880	Scofield-Gilfillan	Large brown	27.50	55.00	16.00
☐ 1880	Bruce-Gilfillan	Large brown	27.50	55.00	16.00
☐ 1880	Bruce-Wyman	Large brown	27.50	55.00	16.00
	Blue Serial numbers				
☐ 1880	Rosecrans-Huston	Large red	90.00	180.00	40.00
☐ 1880	Rosecrans-Huston	Large brown	80.00	160.00	40.00
☐ 1880	Rosecrans-Nebeker	Small red	35.00	60.00	15.00
☐ 1880	Tillman-Morgan	Small red	35.00	60.00	15.00
	Red Serial numbers.				
☐ 1917	Teehee-Burke	Small red	20.00	30.00	12.00
☐ 1917	Elliot-Burke	Small red	20.00	30.00	12.00
☐ 1917	Elliott-White	Small red	20.00	30.00	12.00
☐ 1917	Speelman-White	Small red	20.00	30.00	12.00

Five Dollars

Series	Signatures	Seal	Fine	VF	ABP
	First Obligation inscription on back. Red Serial numbers.				
☐ 1862	Chittenden-Spinner	Small red	110.00	175.00	60.00
	American Bank Note Co. in top border face design.				
	Second Obligation inscription. Red Serial numbers.				
☐ 1862	Chittenden-Spinner	Small red	100.00	175.00	55.00
	American Bank Note Co. National Bank Note Co. lower border face design.				
☐ 1863	Chittenden-Spinner	Small red	100.00	150.00	60.00
	American Bank Note Co., twice in lower border face design. One serial number.				
☐ 1863	Chittenden-Spinner	Small red	100.00	150.00	60.00
	American Bank Note Co. twice in lower border. Two serial numbers.				

Series	Signatures	Seal	Fine	VF	ABP
		Red Serial numbers.			
☐ 1869	Allison-Spinner	Large red	100.00	225.00	60.00

Face: Bureau, Engraving & Printing, upper left, face design.
Back: American Bank Note Co., upper and lower margin.

Red Serial numbers. Large "V" in red ornamentation at right.

☐ 1875	Allison-New	Small red	50.00	95.00	30.00
		Issued in two additional series, same design.			
☐ 1875	Series A in lower right of face design		80.00	110.00	17.50
☐ 1875	Series B		80.00	110.00	17.50
☐ 1875	Allison-Wyman	Small red	50.00	95.00	15.00
☐ 1878	Allison-Gilfillan	Small red	50.00	100.00	22.50
		Red Serial numbers.			
☐ 1880	Scofield-Gilfillan	Large brown	45.00	65.00	17.50
☐ 1880	Bruce-Gilfillan	Large brown	45.00	65.00	17.50
☐ 1880	Bruce-Wyman	Large brown	45.00	65.00	17.50
		Blue Serial numbers.			
☐ 1880	Bruce-Wyman	Large red	60.00	100.00	30.00
☐ 1880	Rosecrans-Jordan	Large red	60.00	100.00	30.00
☐ 1880	Rosecrans-Hyatt	Large red	65.00	100.00	30.00
☐ 1880	Rosecrans-Huston	Large red	85.00	135.00	40.00
☐ 1880	Rosecrans-Huston	Large brown	50.00	90.00	27.50
☐ 1880	Rosecrans-Nebeker	Large brown	70.00	135.00	35.00
☐ 1880	Rosecrans-Nebeker	Small red	35.00	60.00	20.00
☐ 1880	Tillman-Morgan	Small red	35.00	60.00	20.00
☐ 1880	Bruce-Roberts	Small red	35.00	60.00	20.00
☐ 1880	Lyons-Roberts	Small red	35.00	60.00	20.00

Series	Signatures	Seal	Fine	VF	ABP
		Red Serial numbers. Ornamental "V" at left.			
☐ 1907	Vernon-Treat	Small red	25.00	40.00	13.00
☐ 1907	Vernon-McClung	Small red	25.00	40.00	13.00
☐ 1907	Napier-McClung	Small red	25.00	40.00	13.00
☐ 1907	Napier-Thompson	Small red	100.00	200.00	55.00
☐ 1907	Parker-Burke	Small red	25.00	40.00	13.00
☐ 1907	Teehee-Burke	Small red	25.00	40.00	13.00
☐ 1907	Elliott-Burke	Small red	25.00	40.00	13.00
☐ 1907	Elliott-White	Small red	25.00	40.00	13.00
☐ 1907	Speelman-White	Small red	25.00	40.00	13.00
☐ 1907	Woods-White	Small red	30.00	40.00	15.00

Ten Dollars

Series	Signatures	Seal	Fine	VF	ABP
	First Obligation inscription on back. One red serial number.				
☐ 1862	Chittenden-Spinner	Small red	245.00	350.00	140.00
	American Bank Note Co. upper border.				

	Second Obligation inscription on back. One red serial number.				
☐ 1862	Chittenden-Spinner	Small red	245.00	365.00	140.00
	American Bank Note Co. upper border.				
	National Bank Note Co. lower border.				
	Second Obligation inscription on back. Two red serial numbers.				
☐ 1863	Chittenden-Spinner	Small red	265.00	400.00	155.00
	American Bank Note Co. upper and lower borders.				

Series	Signatures	Seal	Fine	VF	ABP
		Red Serial numbers.			
☐ 1869	Allison-Spinner	Large red	190.00	400.00	110.00

Face: Bureau of Engraving and Printing. Back National Bank Note Co.

☐ 1875	Allison-New	Small red	95.00	145.00	35.00
	Issued in one additional series, same design.				
☐ 1875	Series A in lower right of face design.		125.00	200.00	70.00
☐ 1878	Allison-Gilfillan	Small red	110.00	175.00	60.00
		Red Serial numbers			
☐ 1880	Scofield-Gilfillan	Large brown	65.00	100.00	35.00
☐ 1880	Bruce-Gilfillan	Large brown	65.00	100.00	35.00
☐ 1880	Bruce-Wyman	Large brown	65.00	100.00	35.00

Series	Signatures	Seal	Fine	VF	ABP
		Blue Serial numbers.			
☐ 1880	Bruce-Wyman	Large red	110.00	175.00	60.00
☐ 1880	Rosecrans-Jordan	Large red	110.00	175.00	60.00
☐ 1880	Rosecrans-Hyatt	Large red	110.00	175.00	60.00
☐ 1880	Rosecrans-Hyatt	Red spikes	110.00	200.00	60.00
☐ 1880	Rosecrans-Huston	Red spikes	110.00	200.00	60.00
☐ 1880	Rosecrans-Huston	Large brown	110.00	175.00	60.00
☐ 1880	Rosecrans-Nebeker	Large brown	110.00	175.00	60.00
☐ 1880	Rosecrans-Nebeker	Small red	100.00	120.00	55.00
☐ 1880	Tillman-Morgan	Small red	95.00	120.00	50.00
☐ 1880	Bruce-Roberts	Small red	95.00	120.00	50.00
☐ 1880	Lyons-Roberts	Small red	95.00	120.00	50.00

Red Serial numbers. Large "X" at left.

Series	Signatures	Seal	Fine	VF	ABP
☐ 1901	Lyons-Roberts	Small red	150.00	275.00	85.00
☐ 1901	Lyons-Treat	Small red	150.00	275.00	85.00
☐ 1901	Vernon-Treat	Small red	150.00	275.00	85.00
☐ 1901	Vernon-McClung	Small red	150.00	275.00	85.00
☐ 1901	Napier-McClung	Small red	150.00	275.00	85.00
☐ 1901	Parker-Burke	Small red	150.00	275.00	85.00
☐ 1901	Teehee-Burkee	Small red	150.00	275.00	85.00
☐ 1901	Elliott-White	Small red	150.00	275.00	85.00
☐ 1901	Speelman-White	Small red	150.00	275.00	85.00

Red Serial numbers. Large "X" at right.

Series	Signatures	Seal	Fine	VF	ABP
☐ 1923	Speelman-White	Small red	275.00	550.00	160.00

Twenty Dollars

Series	Signatures	Seal	Fine	VF	ABP
First Obligation inscription on back. One red serial number.					
☐ 1862	Chittenden-Spinner	Small red	350.00	525.00	200.00
	American Bank Note Co. lower border.				
Second Obligation inscription on back. One red serial number.					
☐ 1862	Chittenden-Spinner	Small red	400.00	550.00	225.00
	National Bank Note Co. American Bank Note Co.				
Second Obligation on back. Two red serial numbers.					
☐ 1863	Chittenden-Spinner	Small red	300.00	400.00	175.00
	American Bank Note Co. lower border.				

Series	Signatures	Seal	Fine	VF	ABP
	Blue Serial numbers.				
☐ 1869	Allison-Spinner	Large red	550.00	950.00	300.00
Blue serial numbers. "XX" twice on face of note.					
☐ 1875	Allison-New	Small red	195.00	385.00	110.00
☐ 1878	Allison-Gilfillan	Small red	225.00	350.00	130.00

Series		Signatures	Seal	Fine	VF	ABP
		Blue Serial numbers. "XX" removed.				
☐	1880	Scofield-Gilfillan	Large brown	125.00	200.00	70.00
☐	1880	Bruce-Gilfillan	Large brown	125.00	200.00	70.00
☐	1880	Bruce-Wyman	Large brown	125.00	200.00	70.00
☐	1880	Bruce-Wyman	Large red	135.00	200.00	75.00
☐	1880	Rosecrans-Jordan	Large red	120.00	150.00	65.00
☐	1880	Rosecrans-Hyatt	Large red	120.00	150.00	65.00
☐	1880	Rosecrans-Hyatt	Red spikes	120.00	200.00	65.00
☐	1880	Rosecrans-Huston	Red spikes	120.00	200.00	65.00
☐	1880	Rosecrans-Huston	Large brown	165.00	250.00	95.00
☐	1880	Rosecrans-Nebeker	Large brown	165.00	250.00	95.00
☐	1880	Rosecrans-Nebeker	Small red	100.00	120.00	55.00
☐	1880	Tillman-Morgan	Small red	100.00	120.00	55.00
☐	1880	Bruce-Roberts	Small red	100.00	120.00	55.00
☐	1880	Lyons-Roberts	Small red	100.00	120.00	55.00
☐	1880	Vernon-Treat	Small red	100.00	120.00	55.00
☐	1880	Vernon-McClung	Small red	100.00	120.00	55.00
		Red Serial numbers.				
☐	1880	Teehee-Burke	Small red	100.00	120.00	55.00
☐	1880	Elliott-Burke	Small red	100.00	120.00	55.00

$50 denominations also were produced in Series of 1862, 1863, 1869, 1874, 1875, 1878 and 1880 and all but 1874 were produced in $100 denominations.

SILVER CERTIFICATES

Silver Certificate notes are easily identified, as all carry the words Silver Certificate prominently displayed on the face and/or back side, and additionally proclaim their value in "silver dollars." Serial numbers always appear in blue, while the Treasury seals appear in red or brown, with a switch to blue coming in the 1891 and 1899 series, in varying positions and sizes. In addition to the denominations incorporated in the following listing, $500 and $1,000 notes are known in the 1878 and 1880 series, and the $1,000 unit along in the 1891 series, and all are very rare. Some of the finest engraving work and most attractive designs were incorporated in the Silver Certificate series which features the series 1886 "five silver dollars" back, the series 1896 "educational" notes and the series 1899 "Onepapa" Indian design.

One Dollar

Series		Signatures	Seal	Fine	VF	ABP
		Blue Serial numbers on all Silver Certificates, all denominations.				
☐	1886	Rosecrans-Jordan	Small red	75.00	200.00	45.00

Series	Signatures	Seal	Fine	VF	ABP
☐ 1886	Rosecrans-Hyatt	Small red	75.00	200.00	50.00
☐ 1886	Rosecrans-Hyatt	Large red	77.00	200.00	50.00
☐ 1886	Rosecrans-Huston	Large red	77.00	200.00	50.00
☐ 1886	Rosecrans-Huston	Large brown	85.00	200.00	50.00
☐ 1886	Rosecrans-Nebeker	Large brown	75.00	200.00	50.00
☐ 1886	Rosecrans-Nebeker	Small red	100.00	200.00	60.00
☐ 1891	Rosecrans-Nebeker	Small red	80.00	135.00	55.00
☐ 1891	Tillman-Morgan	Small red	87.50	135.00	55.00

☐ 1896	Tillman-Morgan	Small red	85.00	120.00	50.00
☐ 1896	Bruce-Roberts	Small red	85.00	120.00	50.00

Series	Signatures	Seal	Fine	VF	ADP
	Series eate above serial number, upper right.				
☐ 1899	Lyons-Roberts	Small blue	25.00	35.00	13.00
	Series date below serial number.				
☐ 1899	Lyons-Roberts	Small blue	25.00	35.00	12.00
☐ 1899	Lyons-Treat	Small blue	25.00	35.00	12.00
☐ 1899	Vernon-Treat	Small blue	20.00	35.00	11.00
☐ 1899	Vernon-McClung	Small blue	20.00	35.00	11.00
	Series date vertically at right, on the following:				
☐ 1899	Napier-McClung	Small blue	20.00	30.00	11.00
☐ 1899	Napier-Thompson	Small blue	75.00	175.00	30.00
☐ 1899	Parker-Burke	Small blue	20.00	30.00	11.00
☐ 1899	Teehee-jburke	Small blue	20.00	30.00	11.00
☐ 1899	Elliott-Burke	Small blue	20.00	30.00	11.00
☐ 1899	Elliott-White	Small blue	20.00	30.00	11.00
☐ 1899	Speelman-White	Small blue	20.00	30.00	11.00

Series	Signatures	Seal	Fine	VF	ADP
☐ 1923	Speelman-White	Small blue	14.00	17.50	8.00
☐ 1923	Woods-White	Small blue	16.00	20.00	9.00
☐ 1923	Woods-Tate	Small blue	35.00	65.00	20.00

Two Dollars

Series	Signatures	Seal	Fine	VF	ABP
☐ 1886	Rosecrans-Jordan	Small red	115.00	210.00	75.00
☐ 1886	Rosecrans-Hyatt	Small red	115.00	210.00	77.50
☐ 1886	Rosecrans-Hyatt	Large red	125.00	230.00	80.00
☐ 1886	Rosecrans-Huston	Large red	145.00	240.00	80.00
☐ 1886	Rosecrans-Huston	Large brown	155.00	240.00	85.00

Series	Signatures	Seal	Fine	VF	ABP
☐ 1891	Rosecrans-Nebeker	Small red	140.00	335.00	80.00
☐ 1891	Tillman-Morgan	Small red	140.00	300.00	80.00

| ☐ 1896 | Tillman-Morgan | Small red | 135.00 | 350.00 | 85.00 |
| ☐ 1896 | Bruce-Roberts | Small red | 135.00 | 350.00 | 85.00 |

☐ 1899	Lyons-Roberts	Small blue	75.00	125.00	45.00
☐ 1899	Lyons-Treat	Small blue	75.00	125.00	45.00
☐ 1899	Vernon-Treat	Small blue	75.00	125.00	45.00
☐ 1899	Vernon-McClung	Small blue	75.00	125.00	4 .00
☐ 1899	Napier-McClung	Small blue	75.00	125.00	45.00
☐ 1899	Napier-Thompson	Small blue	100.00	200.00	60.00
☐ 1899	Parker-Burke	Small blue	75.00	125.00	45.00
☐ 1899	Teehee-Burke	Small blue	75.00	125.00	45.00
☐ 1899	Elliott-Burke	Small blue	75.00	125.00	45.00
☐ 1899	Speelman-White	Small blue	75.00	125.00	45.00

Five Dollars

Series	Signatures	Seal	Fine	VF	ABP
		Blue Serial numbers.			
☐ 1886	Rosecrans-Jordan	Small red	250.00	450.00	150.00
☐ 1886	Rosecrans-Hyatt	Small red	250.00	450.00	150.00
☐ 1886	Rosecrans-Hyatt	Large red	250.00	450.00	150.00
☐ 1886	Rosecrans-Huston	Large red	250.00	450.00	150.00
☐ 1886	Rosecrans-Huston	Large brown	275.00	475.00	160.00
☐ 1886	Rosecrans-Nebeker	Large brown	275.00	475.00	160.00
☐ 1886	Rosecrans-Nebeker	Small red	400.00	700.00	225.00

| ☐ 1891 | Rosecrans-Nebeker | Small red | 150.00 | 350.00 | 85.00 |
| ☐ 1891 | Tillman-Morgan | Small red | 150.00 | 300.00 | 85.00 |

☐ 1896	Tillman-Morgan	Small red	300.00	750.00	170.00
☐ 1896	Bruce-Roberts	Small red	300.00	750.00	170.00
☐ 1896	Lyons-Roberts	Small red	400.00	1000.00	225.00

Series	Signatures	Seal	Fine	VF	ABP
☐ 1899	Lyons-Roberts	Small blue	75.00	145.00	45.00
☐ 1899	Lyons-Treat	Small blue	75.00	145.00	45.00
☐ 1899	Vernon-Treat	Small blue	75.00	135.00	45.00
☐ 1899	Vernon-McClung	Small blue	75.00	135.00	45.00
☐ 1899	Napier-McClung	Small blue	75.00	135.00	45.00
☐ 1899	Napier-Thompson	Small blue	125.00	225.00	70.00
☐ 1899	Parker-Burke	Small blue	75.00	135.00	45.00
☐ 1899	Teehee-Burke	Small blue	75.00	135.00	45.00
☐ 1899	Elliott-Burke	Small blue	75.00	135.00	45.00
☐ 1899	Elliott-White	Small blue	75.00	135.00	45.00
☐ 1899	Speelman-White	Small blue	75.00	135.00	45.00

☐ 1923	Speelman-White	Small blue	185.00	450.00	110.00

Ten Dollars
The Countersigned Series
Scofield-Gilfillan signatures. Blue serial numbers.
Types 1, 2, 4 and 5, place of deposit: New York.
Type 3 place of deposit: Washington, D.C.
Series 1878 Large red seal and large red "TEN" below seal.
Series 1880 Large brown seal and large "X" below seal.

Type III Note Illustrated

Series	Countersigned by:	Type	VG	ABP
☐ 1878	J.C. Hopper, Asst. U.S. Treas.	I	3750.00	2000.00
☐ 1878	W.G. White, Asst. U.S. Treas.	II	3750.00	2000.00
☐ 1878	A.V. Wyman, Asst. U.S. Treas.	III	3750.00	2000.00
☐ 1878	T. Hillhouse, Asst. U.S. Treas.	IV	V. RARE	—
☐ 1880	T. Hillhouse, Asst. U.S. Treas.	V	3500.00	1800.00

Series	Signatures	Seal	Fine	VF	ABP
	Blue Serial numbers. Large "X" below center seal.				
☐ 1880	Scofield-Gilfillan	Large brown	325.00	975.00	185.00
☐ 1880	Bruce-Gilfillan	Large brown	325.00	975.00	185.00
☐ 1880	Bruce-Wyman	Large brown	325.00	975.00	185.00

	Blue Serial numbers, without large "X" below center seal.				
☐ 1880	Bruce-Wyman	Large red	500.00	1100.00	275.00

Series	Signatures	Seal	Fine	VF	ABP
☐ 1886	Rosecrans-Jordan	Small red	195.00	325.00	110.00
☐ 1886	Rosecrans-Hyatt	Small red	195.00	325.00	110.00
☐ 1886	Rosecrans-Hyatt	Large red	195.00	350.00	110.00
☐ 1886	Rosecrans-Huston	Large red	195.00	350.00	110.00
☐ 1886	Rosecrans-Huston	Large brown	210.00	375.00	115.00
☐ 1886	Rosecrans-Nebeker	Large brown	225.00	375.00	120.00
☐ 1886	Rosecrans-Nebeker	Small red	300.00	450.00	175.00
☐ 1891	Rosecrans-Nebeker	Small red	110.00	160.00	65.00
☐ 1891	Tillman-Morgan	Small red	110.00	160.00	65.00
☐ 1891	Bruce-Roberts	Small red	120.00	175.00	70.00
☐ 1891	Lyons-Roberts	Small red	110.00	160.00	65.00
☐ 1908	Vernon-Treat	Small blue	100.00	150.00	60.00
☐ 1908	Vernon-McClung	Small blue	100.00	150.00	60.00
☐ 1908	Parker-Burke	Small blue	100.00	150.00	60.00

Twenty Dollars

The Countersigned Series

Scofield-Gilfillan signatures. Blue serial numbers.
Types 1, 4 and 5: Place of deposit, New York.
Type 3: Place of deposit, Washington, D.C.
Series 1878 Large red "TWENTY" below red seal.
Series 1880 Large "XX" below brown seal.

Type III Note Illustrated

Series	Countersigned by:	Type	VG	ABP
☐ 1878	J.C. Hopper, Asst. U.S. Treas.	I	2200.00	1300.00
☐ 1878	A.V. Wyman, Asst. Treas.	III	2500.00	1500.00
☐ 1878	T. Hillhouse, Asst. U.S. Treas.	IV	2200.00	1300.00
☐ 1880	T. Hillhouse, Asst. U.S. Treas.	V	2000.00	1200.00

Series	Signatures	Seal	Fine	VF	ABP
☐ 1880	Scofield-Gilfillan	Large brown	675.00	1750.00	375.00
☐ 1880	Bruce-Gilfillan	Large brown	650.00	1150.00	360.00
☐ 1880	Bruce-Wyman	Large brown	650.00	1150.00	360.00

		Large "XX" removed.			
☐ 1880	Bruce-Wyman	Small red	1850.00	3000.00	1000.00

Series	Signatures	Seal	Fine	VF	ABP
☐ 1886	Rosecrans-Hyatt	Large red	1200.00	2000.00	700.00
☐ 1886	Rosecrans-Huston	Large brown	1200.00	2000.00	700.00
☐ 1886	Rosecrans-Nebeker	Large brown	1200.00	2000.00	700.00
☐ 1886	Rosecans-Nebeker	Small red	1500.00	2500.00	800.00

"Series 1891" upper right, and lower left.

Series	Signatures	Seal	Fine	VF	ABP
☐ 1891	Rosecrans-Nebeker	Small red	175.00	300.00	100.00
☐ 1891	Tillman-Morgan	Small red	175.00	300.00	100.00
☐ 1891	Bruce-Roberts	Small red	175.00	300.00	100.00
☐ 1891	Lyons-Roberts	Small red	175.00	300.00	100.00

Large blue "XX" at left.

Series	Signatures	Seal	Fine	VF	ABP
☐ 1891	Parker-Burke	Small blue	145.00	250.00	85.00
☐ 1891	Teehee-Burke	Small blue	145.00	250.00	85.00

$50 and $100 Silver Certificates of similar design and type were also produced.

TREASURY NOTES

Treasury or coin notes resulted from the Legal Tender Act of July 14, 1890, which provided for their backing by gold or silver coin. The words Treasury Note are worked into the borders on the face side. They bear both brown and red seals, in both large and small sizes. In addition to the denominations incorporated in the following listing, $1,000 notes were issued in both series, but they are practically non-collectible, as less than 25 were not redeemed.

One Dollar

Series	Signatures	Seal	VG	VF	ABP
☐ 1890	Rosecrans-Huston	Large brown	100.00	375.00	60.00
☐ 1890	Rosecrans-Nebeker	Large brown	175.00	600.00	100.00
☐ 1890	Rosecrans-Nebeker	Small red	150.00	525.00	90.00

Series	Signatures	Seal	VG	VF	ABP
☐ 1891	Rosecrans-Nebeker	Small red	65.00	135.00	35.00
☐ 1891	Tillman-Morgan	Small red	65.00	135.00	35.00
☐ 1891	Bruce-Roberts	Small red	65.00	135.00	35.00

Two Dollars

Series	Signatures	Seal	VG	VF	ABP
☐ 1890	Rosecrans-Huston	Large brown	165.00	450.00	95.00
☐ 1890	Rosecrans-Nebeker	Large brown	175.00	500.00	100.00
☐ 1890	Rosecrans-Nebeker	Small red	140.00	450.00	80.00
☐ 1891	Rosecrans-Nebeker	Small red	100.00	225.00	60.00
☐ 1891	Tillman-Morgan	Small red	100.00	225.00	60.00
☐ 1891	Bruce-Roberts	Small red	100.00	260.00	60.00

Five Dollars

Series	Signatures	Seal	VG	VF	ABP
☐ 1890	Rosecrans-Huston	Large brown	150.00	525.00	85.00

Series	Signatures	Seal	VG	VF	ABP
☐ 1890	Rosecrans-Nebeker	Large brown	150.00	525.00	85.00
☐ 1890	Rosecrans-Nebeker	Small red	150.00	525.00	85.00
☐ 1891	Rosecrans-Nebeker	Small red	115.00	225.00	65.00
☐ 1891	Tillman-Morgan	Small red	115.00	225.00	65.00
☐ 1891	Bruce-Roberts	Small red	115.00	225.00	65.00
☐ 1891	Lyons-Roberts	Small red	200.00	650.00	120.00

Ten Dollars

Series	Signatures	Seal	VG	VF	ABP
☐ 1890	Rosecrans-Huston	Large brown	185.00	525.00	110.00
☐ 1890	Rosecrans-Nebeker	Large brown	185.00	525.00	110.00
☐ 1890	Rosecrans-Nebeker	Small red	185.00	525.00	110.00
☐ 1891	Rosecrans-Nebeker	Small red	135.00	225.00	80.00
☐ 1891	Tillman-Morgan	Small red	135.00	225.00	80.00
☐ 1891	Bruce-Roberts	Small red	135.00	225.00	80.00

Twenty Dollars

Series	Signatures	Seal	VG	VF	ABP
☐ 1890	Rosecrans-Huston	Large brown	550.00	2700.00	300.00
☐ 1890	Rosecrans-Nebeker	Large brown	575.00	2700.00	300.00
☐ 1890	Rosecrans-Nebeker	Small red	550.00	2700.00	300.00

Series 1891 — Back Similar To Other 1891 Issues

☐ 1891	Tillman-Morgan	Small red	1000.00	4000.00	550.00
☐ 1891	Bruce-Roberts	Small red	1000.00	4000.00	550.00

$50, $100 and $1000 were also produced and are considered quite rare.

NATIONAL BANK NOTES

National bank notes can always be identified by the presence of the words National Currency within the border on the face side, and additionally by the presence of an imprint of the specific bank of issue, along with its city and state of business. They also generally carry an overprint of the bank's charter number, in addition to the serial number. There are seven distinctive issue periods. First charter notes are overprinted with red seals and serial numbers, and the backs bear black vignettes of famous paintings, with green borders, which hang in the nation's Capitol.

Second charter, first issue notes are overprinted with brown seals and charter numbers, and blue or red serial numbers, while the brown backs bear bold engravings of the bank charter numbers. Second charter, second issue notes are overprinted with blue seal, charter and serial numbers, and the green backs display the dates 1882-1908 in plain field. Second charter, third issue notes are similar, except the denomination is displayed in the back field. Third charter, first issue notes have red seal and charter numbers, along with blue serial numbers, and the backs again offer vignettes. Third charter, second issue notes are the same, except the seals are overprinted in blue and the dates 1902 and 1908 flank the vignettes on the back. Third charter, third issue notes also have blue seals, but the backs are without the dates as was the case with the third charter, first issue notes. First charter notes were issued in denominations from $1 to $1,000 and the other issues only in $5 to $100 denominations. Although over 150 $500 notes are unredeemed, only one is known, while none of about 20 unredeemed $1000 notes are known.

The rarity, and accordingly value, of National Bank Note issues vary widely from state to state. The values stated in the following listings are for the most common specimens of each type. These would generally be the notes from banks in those states tabulated under rarity one in the table which follows, although it must be remembered that rarity also varies from bank to bank within a given state. In the other rarity categories values should generally be increased on the following scale:

Rarity 2: 20% Rarity 3: 30% Rarity 4: 40% Rarity 5: 50% Rarity 6: 60% Rarity 7: 2-4 times Rarity 8: 3-5 times Rarity 9: 5-10 times.

Rarity 1	Rarity 2	Rarity 3	Rarity 4
California	Indiana	Kansas	Alabama
Illinois	Iowa	Kentucky	Connecticut
New York	Massachusetts	Michigan	Maryland
Ohio	New Jersey	Minnesota	Nebraska
Pennsylvania	Texas	Missouri	Tennessee
	Wisconsin		Virginia

Rarity 5	Rarity 6	Rarity 7	Rarity 8
Colorado	Florida	Arkansas	Arizona
Dist. of Columbia	Georgia	Delaware	Colorado Terr.
New Hampshire	Louisiana	Hawaii	Mississippi
North Carolina	Maine	Montana	Nevada
Oklahoma	North Dakota	Rhode Island	New Mexico
Washington	Oregon	South Dakota	
West Virginia	South Carolina	Utah	
	Vermont	Wyoming	

Rarity 9	Rarity 10
District of Alaska	Nebraska Terr.
Territorial Notes	Porto Rico
(except Colorado, Nebraska and Washington)	Washington Terr.

One Dollar
First Charter Period

Series	Signatures	Seal	VG	VF	ABP
☐ Original	Colby-Spinner	Small red	95.00	150.00	55.00
☐ Original	Jeffries-Spinner	Small red	600.00	1100.00	250.00
☐ Original	Allison-Spinner	Small red	85.00	150.00	50.00

Charter number and "Series 1875" added.

Series	Signatures	Seal	VG	VF	ABP
☐ 1875	Allison-New	Red	85.00	150.00	50.00
☐ 1875	Allison-Wyman	Red	85.00	150.00	50.00
☐ 1875	Allison-Gilfillan	Red	85.00	150.00	50.00
☐ 1875	Scofield-Gilfillan	Red	90.00	175.00	55.00

Two Dollars
First Charter Period

Series	Signatures	Seal	VG	VF	ABP
☐ Original	Colby-Spinner	Small red	235.00	425.00	140.00
☐ Original	Jeffries-Spinner	Small red	1250.00	1850.00	550.00
☐ Original	Allison-Spinner	Small red	235.00	425.00	140.00
☐ 1875	Allison-New	Red	235.00	425.00	140.00
☐ 1875	Allison-Wyman	Red	235.00	425.00	140.00
☐ 1875	Allison-Gilfillan	Red	250.00	450.00	145.00
☐ 1875	Scofield-Gilfillan	Red	250.00	450.00	145.00

Five Dollars
First Charter Period

Series	Signatures	Seal	VG	VF	ABP
☐ Original	Chittenden-Spinner	Small red	100.00	300.00	60.00
☐ Original	Colby-Spinner	Small red	100.00	300.00	60.00
☐ Original	Jeffries-Spinner	Small red	600.00	1500.00	300.00
☐ Original	Allison-Spinner	Small red	100.00	290.00	60.00

Series	Signatures	Seal	VG	VF	ABP
		Charter number and "Series 1875" added.			
☐ 1875	Allison-New	Red	100.00	290.00	55.00
☐ 1875	Allison-Wyman	Red	100.00	290.00	55.00
☐ 1875	Allison-Gilfillan	Red	100.00	290.00	55.00
☐ 1875	Scofield-Gilfillan	Red	100.00	290.00	55.00
☐ 1875	Bruce-Gilfillan	Red	100.00	290.00	55.00
☐ 1875	Bruce-Wyman	Red	110.00	300.00	60.00
☐ 1875	Bruce-Jordan	Red	600.00	1500.00	300.00
☐ 1875	Rosecrans-Jordan	Red	125.00	300.00	75.00
☐ 1875	Rosecrans-Huston	Red	100.00	290.00	55.00

Series 1882, Second Charter, First Issue

Signatures	VG	VF	ABP
☐ Bruce-Gilfillan	40.00	70.00	24.00
☐ Bruce-Wyman	40.00	70.00	24.00
☐ Bruce-Jordan	40.00	90.00	24.00
☐ Rosecrans-Jordan	40.00	70.00	24.00
☐ Rosecrans-Hyatt	40.00	70.00	24.00
☐ Rosecrans-Huston	40.00	70.00	24.00
☐ Rosecrans-Nebeker	40.00	70.00	24.00
☐ Rosecrans-Morgan	250.00	475.00	125.00
☐ Tillman-Morgan	40.00	75.00	24.00
☐ Tillman-Roberts	40.00	90.00	24.00
☐ Bruce-Roberts	40.00	70.00	24.00
☐ Lyons-Robert	40.00	70.00	24.00
☐ Vernon-Treat	50.00	90.00	30.00

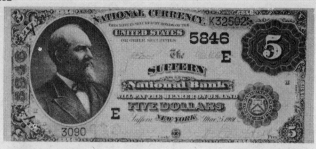

Series 1882, Second Charter, Second Issue

Signatures	VG	VF	ABP
☐ Rosecrans-Huston	45.00	90.00	26.00
☐ Rosecrans-Nebeker	50.00	90.00	30.00
☐ Tillman-Morgan	45.00	90.00	26.00
☐ Tillman-Roberts	45.00	90.00	26.00
☐ Bruce-Roberts	50.00	100.00	30.00
☐ Lyons-Roberts	45.00	90.00	26.00
☐ Vernon-Treat	60.00	125.00	35.00
☐ Napier-McClung	250.00	500.00	115.00

Series 1882, Second Charter, Third Issue

Signatures	VG	VF	ABP
☐ Tillman-Morgan	85.00	200.00	47.50
☐ Tillman-Roberts	125.00	300.00	70.00
☐ Bruce-Roberts	125.00	300.00	70.00

Signatures	VG	VF	ABP
☐ Lyons-Roberts	85.00	175.00	47.50
☐ Vernon-Treat	100.00	200.00	55.00
☐ Napier-McClung	90.00	225.00	50.00
☐ Teehee-Burke	125.00	300.00	70.00

Series 1902, Third Charter, First Issue (Red Seal)

Signatures	VG	VF	ABP
☐ Lyons-Roberts	65.00	125.00	35.00
☐ Lyons-Treat	70.00	135.00	40.00
☐ Vernon-Treat	75.00	175.00	45.00

Series 1902, Third Charter, Second Issue (Blue Seal)

Signatures	VG	VF	ABP
☐ Lyons-Roberts	17.50	25.00	11.00
☐ Lyons-Treat	20.00	27.50	11.00
☐ Vernon-Treat	17.50	25.00	11.00
☐ Vernon-McClung	17.50	25.00	11.00
☐ Napier-McClung	20.00	27.50	11.00
☐ Napier-Thompson	27.50	60.00	13.50
☐ Napier-Burke	20.00	27.50	11.00
☐ Parker-Burke	20.00	27.50	11.00
☐ Teehee-Burke	40.00	100.00	18.50

Series 1902, Third Charter, Third Issue (Blue Seal)
Without "1902-1908" on back

Signatures	VG	VF	ABP
☐ Lyons-Roberts	17.50	25.00	10.00
☐ Lyons-Treat	17.50	27.50	10.00
☐ Vernon-Treat	17.50	25.00	10.00

Signatures	VG	VF	ABP
☐ Vernon-McClung	17.50	25.00	10.00
☐ Napier-McClung	17.50	25.00	10.00
☐ Napier-Thompson	25.00	60.00	12.50
☐ Napier-Burke	17.50	25.00	10.00
☐ Parker-Burke	17.50	25.00	10.00
☐ Teehee-Burke	17.50	25.00	10.00
☐ Elliott-Burke	17.50	25.00	10.00
☐ Elliott-White	17.50	25.00	10.00
☐ Speelman-White	17.50	25.00	10.00
☐ Woods-White	20.00	30.00	12.00
☐ Woods-Tate	20.00	40.00	12.00
☐ Jones-Woods	100.00	175.00	45.00

Ten Dollars
First Charter Period

Series	Signatures	Seal	Fine	VF	ABP
☐ Original	Chittenden-Spinner	Small red	100.00	225.00	55.00
☐ Original	Colby-Spinner	Small red	95.00	200.00	50.00
☐ Original	Jeffries-Spinner	Small red	400.00	1000.00	225.00
☐ Original	Allison-Spinner	Small red	95.00	200.00	50.00
☐ 1875	Allison-New	Red	90.00	200.00	50.00
☐ 1875	Allison-Wyman	Red	90.00	200.00	50.00
☐ 1875	Allison-Gilfillan	Red	90.00	200.00	50.00
☐ 1875	Scofield-Gilfillan	Red	90.00	200.00	50.00
☐ 1875	Bruce-Gilfillan	Red	90.00	200.00	50.00
☐ 1875	Bruce-Wyman	Red	100.00	225.00	55.00
☐ 1875	Rosecrans-Huston	Red	100.00	225.00	55.00
☐ 1875	Rosecrans-Nebeker	Red	100.00	225.00	55.00

Series 1882, Second Charter, First Issue

Signatures	VG	VF	ABP.
☐ Bruce-Gilfillan	45.00	75.00	25.00
☐ Bruce-Wyman	45.00	75.00	25.00
☐ Bruce-Jordan	55.00	100.00	30.00
☐ Rosecrans-Jordan	45.00	80.00	25.00
☐ Rosecrans-Hyatt	45.00	90.00	25.00
☐ Rosecrans-Huston	45.00	80.00	25.00
☐ Rosecrans-Nebeker	45.00	80.00	25.00
☐ Rosecrans-Morgan	300.00	700.00	175.00
☐ Tillman-Morgan	45.00	80.00	25.00
☐ Tillman-Roberts	45.00	90.00	25.00
☐ Bruce-Roberts	45.00	80.00	25.00

Signatures	VG	VF	ABP
☐ Lyons-Roberts	45.00	75.00	25.00
☐ Lyons-Treat	70.00	120.00	35.00
☐ Vernon-Treat	55.00	100.00	30.00

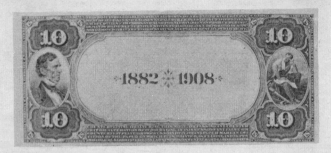

Series 1882, Second Charter, Second Issue

Signatures	VG	VF	ABP
☐ Rosecrans-Huston	50.00	95.00	27.50
☐ Rosecrans-Nebeker	50.00	95.00	27.50
☐ Rosecrans-Morgan	225.00	600.00	125.00
☐ Tillman-Morgan	50.00	95.00	27.50
☐ Tillman-Roberts	55.00	100.00	30.00
☐ Bruce-Roberts	55.00	110.00	30.00
☐ Lyons-Roberts	50.00	95.00	27.50
☐ Vernon-Treat	70.00	125.00	35.00
☐ Vernon-McClung	85.00	175.00	45.00
☐ Napier-McClung	85.00	175.00	45.00

Series 1882, Second Charter, Third Issue

Signatures	VG	VF	ABP
☐ Tillman-Morgan	200.00	350.00	100.00
☐ Tillman-Roberts	150.00	350.00	80.00
☐ Bruce-Roberts	200.00	350.00	100.00
☐ Lyons-Roberts	150.00	300.00	67.50
☐ Vernon-Treat	175.00	325.00	90.00
☐ Napier-McClung	150.00	350.00	80.00
☐ Teehee-Burke	200.00	350.00	100.00

Series 1902, Third Charter, First Issue (Red Seal)

Signatures	VG	VF	ABP
☐ Lyons-Roberts	40.00	100.00	22.00
☐ Lyons-Treat	65.00	135.00	35.00
☐ Vernon-Treat	75.00	175.00	35.00

Series 1902, Third Charter, Second Issue (Blue Seal)

Signatures	VG	VF	ABP
☐ Lyons-Roberts	25.00	35.00	14.00
☐ Lyons-Treat	25.00	40.00	14.00
☐ Vernon-Treat	25.00	35.00	14.00
☐ Vernon-McClung	25.00	35.00	14.00
☐ Napier-McClung	25.00	40.00	14.00
☐ Napier-Thompson	35.00	75.00	16.00
☐ Napier-Burke	30.00	45.00	15.00
☐ Parker-Burke	30.00	45.00	15.00
☐ Teehee-Burke	40.00	80.00	18.50

Series 1902, Third Charter, Third Issue (Blue Seal)
Without "1902-1908" on back

Signatures	VG	VF	ABP
☐ Lyons-Roberts	22.50	32.50	13.00
☐ Lyons-Treat	22.50	35.00	13.00
☐ Vernon-Treat	22.50	32.50	13.00
☐ Vernon-McClung	22.50	32.50	13.00
☐ Napier-McClung	22.50	35.00	13.00
☐ Napier-Thompson	30.00	60.00	15.00
☐ Napier-Burke	22.50	40.00	13.00
☐ Parker-Burke	22.50	40.00	13.00
☐ Teehee-Burke	22.50	35.00	13.00
☐ Elliott-Burke	22.50	32.50	13.00
☐ Elliott-White	22.50	32.50	13.00
☐ Speelman-White	22.50	32.50	13.00
☐ Woods-White	27.50	45.00	14.00
☐ Woods-Tate	30.00	60.00	15.00
☐ Jones-Woods	100.00	250.00	55.00

Twenty Dollars
First Charter Period

Series	Signatures	Seal	VG	VF	ABP
☐ Original	Chittenden-Spinner	Small red	275.00	600.00	160.00
☐ Original	Colby-Spinner	Small red	275.00	600.00	160.00
☐ Original	Jeffries-Spinner	Small red	1500.00	2250.00	700.00
☐ Original	Allison-Spinner	Small red	275.00	600.00	160.00

Series	Signatures	Seal	VG	VF	ABP
☐ 1875	Allison-New	Red	275.00	600.00	160.00
☐ 1875	Allison-Wyman	Red	275.00	600.00	160.00
☐ 1875	Allison-Gilfillan	Red	275.00	600.00	160.00
☐ 1875	Scofield-Gilfillan	Red	275.00	600.00	160.00
☐ 1875	Bruce-Gilfillan	Red	275.00	600.00	160.00
☐ 1875	Bruce-Wyman	Red	275.00	600.00	160.00
☐ 1875	Rosecrans-Huston	Red	275.00	600.00	160.00
☐ 1875	Rosecrans-Nebeker	Red	275.00	600.00	160.00
☐ 1875	Tillman-Morgan	Red	275.00	600.00	160.00

Series 1882, Second Charter, First Issue

Signatures	VG	VF	ABP
☐ Bruce-Gilfillan	75.00	125.00	40.00
☐ Bruce-Wyman	75.00	125.00	40.00
☐ Bruce-Jordan	90.00	150.00	50.00
☐ Rosecrans-Jordan	75.00	125.00	40.00
☐ Rosecrans-Hyatt	75.00	125.00	40.00
☐ Rosecrans-Huston	75.00	125.00	40.00
☐ Rosecrans-Nebeker	75.00	125.00	40.00
☐ Rosecrans-Morgan	350.00	850.00	200.00
☐ Tillman-Morgan	75.00	125.00	40.00
☐ Tillman-Roberts	75.00	125.00	40.00
☐ Bruce-Roberts	75.00	125.00	40.00
☐ Lyons-Roberts	75.00	125.00	40.00
☐ Lyons-Treat	100.00	225.00	60.00
☐ Vernon-Treat	100.00	150.00	60.00

Series 1882, Second Charter, Second Issue

Signatures	VG	VF	ABP
☐ Rosecrans-Huston	95.00	175.00	50.00
☐ Rosecrans-Nebeker	85.00	135.00	45.00
☐ Rosecrans-Morgan	400.00	850.00	225.00
☐ Tillman-Morgan	85.00	135.00	45.00
☐ Tillman-Roberts	85.00	150.00	45.00
☐ Bruce-Roberts	95.00	150.00	50.00
☐ Lyons-Roberts	85.00	135.00	45.00
☐ Vernon-Treat	95.00	175.00	45.00
☐ Napier-McClung	100.00	200.00	60.00

Series 1882, Second Charter, Third Issue

Signatures	VG	VF	ABP
☐ Tillman-Morgan	150.00	350.00	85.00
☐ Tillman-Roberts	250.00	600.00	140.00
☐ Bruce-Roberts	250.00	600.00	140.00
☐ Lyons-Roberts	125.00	300.00	70.00
☐ Lyons-Treat	175.00	450.00	100.00
☐ Vernon-Treat	175.00	450.00	100.00
☐ Napier-McClung	150.00	350.00	85.00
☐ Teehee-Burke	175.00	450.00	100.00

Series 1902, Third Charter, First Issue (Red Seal)

Signatures	VG	VF	ABP
☐ Lyons-Roberts	75.00	150.00	42.50
☐ Lyons-Treat	80.00	150.00	45.00
☐ Vernon-Treat	100.00	200.00	60.00

Series 1902, Third Charter, Second Issue (Blue Seal)

Signatures	VG	VF	ABP
☐ Lyons-Roberts	30.00	45.00	22.00
☐ Lyons-Treat	30.00	50.00	22.00
☐ Vernon-Treat	30.00	45.00	22.00
☐ Vernon-McClung	30.00	45.00	22.00
☐ Napier-McClung	30.00	50.00	22.00
☐ Napier-Thompson	40.00	85.00	25.00
☐ Napier-Burke	35.00	60.00	22.50
☐ Parker-Burke	35.00	60.00	22.50
☐ Teehee-Burke	50.00	100.00	27.00

Series 1902, Third Charter, Third Issue (Blue Seal)
Without "1902-1908" on back

Signatures	VG	VF	ABP
☐ Lyons-Roberts	27.50	45.00	21.50
☐ Lyons-Treat	27.50	50.00	21.50
☐ Vernon-Treat	27.50	45.00	21.50
☐ Vernon-McClung	27.50	45.00	21.50
☐ Napier-McClung	27.50	50.00	21.50
☐ Napier-Thompson	40.00	80.00	25.00
☐ Napier-Burke	27.50	50.00	21.50
☐ Parker-Burke	27.50	55.00	21.50
☐ Teehee-Burke	27.50	55.00	22.50
☐ Elliott-Burke	27.50	55.00	21.50
☐ Elliott-White	27.50	55.00	21.50
☐ Speelman-White	27.50	55.00	21.50
☐ Woods-White	35.00	100.00	22.50
☐ Woods-Tate	50.00	175.00	25.00
☐ Jones-Woods	500.00	1000.00	300.00

Fifty Dollars
First Charter Period

Series	Signatures	Seal	VG	VF	ABP
☐ Original	Chittenden-Spinner	Small red	350.00	1000.00	200.00
☐ Original	Colby-Spinner	Small red	350.00	1000.00	200.00
☐ Original	Allison-Spinner	Small red	350.00	1000.00	200.00
☐ 1875	Allison-New	Scalloped red	350.00	1000.00	200.00
☐ 1875	Allison-Wyman	Scalloped red	450.00	1250.00	250.00
☐ 1875	Allison-Gilfillan	Scalloped red	350.00	1000.00	200.00
☐ 1875	Scofield-Gilfillan	Scalloped red	350.00	1000.00	200.00
☐ 1875	Bruce-Gilfillan	Scalloped red	350.00	1000.00	200.00
☐ 1875	Bruce-Wyman	Scalloped red	350.00	1000.00	200.00
☐ 1875	Rosecrans-Huston	Scalloped red	350.00	1000.00	200.00
☐ 1875	Rosecrans-Nebeker	Scalloped red	400.00	1100.00	225.00
☐ 1875	Tillman-Morgan	Scalloped red	350.00	1000.00	200.00

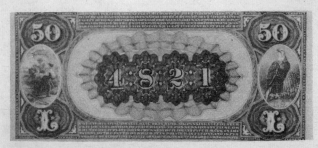

Series 1882, Second Charter, First Issue

Signatures	VG	VF	ABP
☐ Bruce-Gilfillan	175.00	300.00	100.00
☐ Bruce-Wyman	175.00	300.00	100.00
☐ Bruce-Jordan	175.00	300.00	100.00
☐ Rosecrans-Jordan	175.00	300.00	100.00
☐ Rosecrans-Hyatt	175.00	300.00	100.00
☐ Rosecrans-Huston	175.00	300.00	100.00
☐ Rosecrans-Nebeker	175.00	300.00	100.00
☐ Rosecrans-Morgan	600.00	1100.00	325.00
☐ Tillman-Morgan	175.00	300.00	100.00
☐ Tillman-Roberts	175.00	300.00	100.00
☐ Bruce-Roberts	175.00	300.00	100.00
☐ Lyons-Roberts	175.00	300.00	100.00
☐ Vernon-Treat	650.00	1200.00	375.00

Series 1882, Second Charter, Second Issue

Signatures	VG	VF	ABP
☐ Rosecrans-Huston	150.00	275.00	90.00
☐ Rosecrans-Nebeker	150.00	275.00	90.00
☐ Tillman-Morgan	150.00	275.00	90.00
☐ Tillman-Roberts	165.00	300.00	95.00
☐ Bruce-Roberts	165.00	300.00	95.00
☐ Lyons-Roberts	150.00	275.00	90.00
☐ Vernon-Treat	165.00	300.00	95.00
☐ Napier-McClung	185.00	400.00	100.00

Series 1882, Second Charter, Third Issue

Only one signature combination (Lyons-Roberts) was issued in the $50 and $100 denomination of the Second Charter, Third Issue (Denomination Back) notes, and only two banks issued the type in those denominations. Currently only four $50 and one $100 notes of this type are known and all reside in one collection.

Series 1902, Third Charter, First Issue (Red Seal)

Signatures	VG	VF	ABP
☐ Lyons-Roberts	175.00	450.00	100.00
☐ Lyons-Treat	185.00	500.00	110.00
☐ Vernon-Treat	200.00	600.00	120.00

Series 1902, Third Charter, Second Issue (Blue Seal)

Signatures	VG	VF	ABP
☐ Lyons-Roberts	75.00	125.00	55.00
☐ Lyons-Treat	75.00	130.00	55.00
☐ Vernon-Treat	75.00	125.00	55.00
☐ Vernon-McClung	75.00	125.00	55.00
☐ Napier-McClung	75.00	130.00	55.00
☐ Napier-Thompson	85.00	185.00	57.50
☐ Napier-Burke	75.00	130.00	55.00
☐ Parker-Burke	75.00	130.00	55.00
☐ Teehee-Burke	125.00	275.00	65.00

Series 1902, Third Charter, Third Issue (Blue Seal)
Without "1902-1908" on back

Signatures	VG	VF	ABP
☐ Lyons-Roberts	75.00	110.00	55.00
☐ Lyons-Treat	80.00	115.00	55.00
☐ Vernon-Treat	75.00	110.00	55.00
☐ Vernon-McClung	75.00	110.00	55.00
☐ Napier-McClung	75.00	110.00	55.00
☐ Napier-Thompson	85.00	160.00	57.50
☐ Napier-Burke	80.00	115.00	55.00
☐ Parker-Burke	80.00	115.00	55.00
☐ Teehee-Burke	75.00	110.00	55.00
☐ Elliott-Burke	75.00	110.00	55.00
☐ Elliott-White	75.00	110.00	55.00
☐ Speelman-White	75.00	110.00	55.00
☐ Woods-White	100.00	250.00	60.00

One Hundred Dollars
First Charter Period

Series	Signatures	Seal	VG	VF	ABP
☐ Original	Chittenden-Spinner	Sm. red	1000.00	4500.00	550.00
☐ Original	Colby-Spinner	Sm. red	1000.00	4500.00	550.00
☐ Original	Allison-Spinner	Sm. red	1000.00	4500.00	550.00
☐ 1875	Allison-New	Red	1000.00	4500.00	550.00
☐ 1875	Allison-Wyman	Red	1000.00	4500.00	550.00
☐ 1875	Allison-Gilfillan	Red	1000.00	4500.00	550.00
☐ 1875	Scofield-Gilfillan	Red	1000.00	4500.00	550.00
☐ 1875	Bruce-Gilfillan	Red	1000.00	4500.00	500.00
☐ 1875	Bruce-Wyman	Red	1000.00	4500.00	500.00
☐ 1875	Rosecrans-Huston	Red	1000.00	4500.00	500.00
☐ 1875	Rosecrans-Nebeker	Red	1000.00	4500.00	500.00
☐ 1875	Tillman-Morgan	Red	1000.00	4500.00	500.00

Series 1882, Second Charter, First Issue

Signature	VG	VF	ABP
☐ Bruce-Gilfillan	325.00	600.00	190.00
☐ Bruce-Wyman	325.00	600.00	190.00
☐ Bruce-Jordan	325.00	600.00	190.00
☐ Rosecrans-Jordan	325.00	600.00	190.00
☐ Rosecrans-Hyatt	325.00	600.00	190.00
☐ Rosecrans-Huston	325.00	600.00	190.00
☐ Rosecrans-Nebeker	325.00	600.00	190.00
☐ Rosecrans-Morgan	500.00	1200.00	250.00
☐ Tillman-Morgan	325.00	600.00	190.00
☐ Tillman-Roberts	325.00	600.00	190.00
☐ Bruce-Roberts	325.00	600.00	190.00
☐ Lyons-Roberts	325.00	600.00	190.00
☐ Vernon-Treat	500.00	1200.00	250.00

Series 1882, Second Charter, Second Issue
Similar to $50 note illustrated page 163

Signatures	VG	VF	ABP
☐ Rosecrans-Huston	350.00	675.00	200.00
☐ Rosecrans-Nebeker	350.00	675.00	200.00
☐ Tillman-Morgan	350.00	675.00	200.00
☐ Tillman-Roberts	350.00	675.00	200.00
☐ Bruce-Roberts	350.00	675.00	200.00
☐ Lyons-Roberts	350.00	675.00	200.00
☐ Vernon-Treat	350.00	675.00	200.00
☐ Napier-McClung	350.00	675.00	200.00

Series 1882, Second Charter, Third Issue

Only one signature combination (Lyons-Roberts) was issued in the $50 and $100 denomination of the Second Charter, Third Issue (Denomination Back) notes, and only two banks issued the type in those denominations. Currently only four $50 and one $100 notes of this type are known and all reside in one collection.

Series 1902, Third Charter, First Issue (Red Seal)

Signatures	VG	VF	ABP
☐ Lyons-Roberts	500.00	1000.00	300.00
☐ Lyons-Treat	500.00	1000.00	300.00
☐ Vernon-Treat	500.00	1000.00	300.00

Series 1902, Third Charter, Second Issue (Blue Seal)

Signatures	VG	VF	ABP
☐ Lyons-Roberts	160.00	300.00	120.00
☐ Lyons-Treat	160.00	300.00	120.00
☐ Vernon-Treat	160.00	300.00	120.00
☐ Vernon-McClung	160.00	300.00	120.00
☐ Napier-McClung	160.00	300.00	120.00
☐ Napier-Thompson	200.00	300.00	125.00
☐ Napier-Burke	175.00	300.00	122.50
☐ Parker-Burke	175.00	300.00	122.50
☐ Teehee-Burke	200.00	300.00	125.00

Series 1902, Third Charter, Third Issue (Blue Seal)
Without "1902-1908" on back

Signatures	VG	VF	ABP
☐ Lyons-Roberts	150.00	275.00	115.00
☐ Lyons-Treat	150.00	275.00	115.00
☐ Vernon-Treat	150.00	275.00	115.00
☐ Vernon-McClung	150.00	275.00	115.00
☐ Napier-McClung	150.00	275.00	115.00
☐ Napier-Thompson	200.00	325.00	125.00
☐ Parker-Burke	160.00	275.00	117.50
☐ Teehee-Burke	150.00	275.00	115.00
☐ Elliott-Burke	150.00	275.00	115.00
☐ Elliott-White	150.00	275.00	115.00
☐ Speelman-White	150.00	275.00	115.00

GOLD BANK NOTES

Five Dollars

Series	Issuing Bank	Location	Good	ABP
☐ 1870	First Nat'l Gold Bank	San Francisco	550.00	325.00
☐ 1872	Nat'l Gold Bank & Trust Co.	San Francisco	550.00	325.00
☐ 1872	Nat'l Gold Bank of D.O. Mills	Sacramento	550.00	325.00
☐ 1873	First Nat'l Gold Bank	Stockton	550.00	325.00
☐ 1873	First Nat'l Gold Bank	Santa Barbara	550.00	325.00
☐ 1874	Farmers' Nat'l Gold Bank	San Jose	550.00	325.00

Ten Dollars

Series	Issuing Bank	Location	Good	ABP
☐ 1870	First Nat'l Gold Bank	San Francisco	600.00	350.00
☐ 1872	Nat'l Gold Bank & Trust Co.	San Francisco	600.00	350.00
☐ 1872	Nat'l Gold Bank of D.O. Mills	Sacramento	600.00	350.00
☐ 1873	First Nat'l Gold Bank	Stockton	600.00	350.00
☐ 1875	First Nat'l Gold Bank	Stockton	600.00	350.00
☐ 1873	First Nat'l Gold Bank	Santa Barbara	750.00	450.00
☐ 1874	Farmers' Nat'l Gold Bank	San Jose	600.00	350.00
☐ 1874	First Nat'l Gold Bank	Petaluma	600.00	350.00
☐ 1875	First Nat'l Gold Bank	Petaluma	600.00	350.00
☐ 1875	First Nat'l Gold Bank	Oakland	600.00	350.00
☐ 1875	Union Nat'l Gold Bank	Oakland	700.00	400.00

Twenty Dollars

Series	Issuing Bank	Location	Good	ABP
☐ 1870	First Nat'l Gold Bank	San Francisco	1250.00	700.00
☐ 1875	First Nat'l Gold Bank	San Francisco	1250.00	700.00
☐ 1872	Nat'l Gold Bank of D.O. Mills	Sacramento	1250.00	700.00
☐ 1873	First Nat'l Gold Bank	Stockton	1250.00	700.00
☐ 1873	First Nat'l Gold Bank	Santa Barbara	1400.00	825.00
☐ 1874	Farmers' Nat'l Gold Bank	San Jose	1250.00	700.00
☐ 1875	First Nat'l Gold Bank	San Francisco	1250.00	700.00
☐ 1875	First Nat'l Gold Bank	Petaluma	1250.00	700.00
☐ 1875	First Nat'l Gold Bank	Oakland	1350.00	800.00
☐ 1875	Union Nat'l Gold Bank	Oakland	1350.00	800.00

Fifty Dollars

Series	Issuing Bank	Location	Good	ABP
☐ 1870	First Nat'l Gold Bank	San Francisco	3000.00	1800.00
☐ 1874	Nat'l Gold Bank	San Jose	3000.00	1800.00

One Hundred Dollars

Series	Issuing Bank	Location	Good	ABP
☐ 1870	First Nat'l Gold Bank	San Francisco	4000.00	2200.00
☐ 1875	First Nat'l Gold Bank	San Francisco	4000.00	2200.00
☐ 1873	First Nat'l Gold Bank	Santa Barbara	4000.00	2200.00
☐ 1874	First Nat'l Gold Bank	Petaluma	4000.00	2200.00
☐ 1875	Union Nat'l Gold Bank	Oakland	4000.00	2200.00

FEDERAL RESERVE NOTES

Typical Obverse, all Denominations

Five Dollars, Series 1914, Red Seals

Bank	Signatures	VG	VF	Unc.	ABP
☐ BOSTON	Burke-McAdoo	25.00	60.00	600.00	14.00
☐ NEW YORK	Burke-McAdoo	30.00	50.00	600.00	16.00
☐ PHILADELPHIA	Burke-McAdoo	20.00	50.00	600.00	12.00
☐ CLEVELAND	Burke-McAdoo	20.00	50.00	600.00	12.00
☐ RICHMOND	Burke-McAdoo	20.00	50.00	600.00	12.00
☐ ATLANTA	Burke-McAdoo	20.00	50.00	600.00	12.00
☐ CHICAGO	Burke-McAdoo	20.00	50.00	600.00	12.00
☐ ST. LOUIS	Burke-McAdoo	20.00	50.00	600.00	12.00
☐ MINNEAPOLIS	Burke-McAdoo	20.00	50.00	600.00	12.00
☐ KANSAS CITY	Burke-McAdoo	20.00	50.00	600.00	12.00
☐ DALLAS	Burke-McAdoo	20.00	50.00	600.00	12.00
☐ SAN FRANCISCO	Burke-McAdoo	25.00	60.00	600.00	14.00

Blue Seals

Bank	Signatures	VG	VF	Unc.	ABP
☐ BOSTON	Burke-McAdoo	14.50	30.00	150.00	8.00
☐ BOSTON	Burke-Glass	14.50	30.00	150.00	8.00
☐ BOSTON	Burke-Houston	14.50	30.00	150.00	8.00
☐ BOSTON	White-Mellon	14.50	30.00	150.00	8.00
☐ NEW YORK	Burke-McAdoo	14.50	30.00	150.00	8.00
☐ NEW YORK	Burke-Glass	14.50	30.00	150.00	8.00
☐ NEW YORK	Burke-Houston	14.50	30.00	150.00	8.00
☐ NEW YORK	White-Mellon	14.50	30.00	150.00	8.00
☐ PHILADELPHIA	Burke-McAdoo	14.50	30.00	150.00	8.00
☐ PHILADELPHIA	Burke-Glass	14.50	30.00	150.00	8.00
☐ PHILADELPHIA	Burke-Houston	14.50	30.00	150.00	8.00
☐ PHILADELPHIA	White-Mellon	14.50	30.00	150.00	8.00
☐ CLEVELAND	Burke-McAdoo	14.50	30.00	150.00	8.00
☐ CLEVELAND	Burke-Glass	14.50	30.00	150.00	8.00
☐ CLEVELAND	Burke-Houston	14.50	30.00	150.00	8.00
☐ CLEVELAND	White-Mellon	14.50	30.00	150.00	8.00
☐ RICHMOND	Burke-McAdoo	15.00	30.00	150.00	8.50
☐ RICHMOND	Burke-Glass	15.00	30.00	150.00	8.50
☐ RICHMOND	Burke-Houston	14.50	30.00	150.00	8.00
☐ RICHMOND	White-Mellon	14.50	30.00	150.00	8.00
☐ ATLANTA	Burke-McAdoo	14.50	30.00	150.00	8.00
☐ ATLANTA	Burke-Glass	17.00	30.00	150.00	9.00
☐ ATLANTA	Burke-Houston	14.50	30.00	150.00	8.00
☐ ATLANTA	White-Mellon	14.50	30.00	150.00	8.00
☐ CHICAGO	Burke-McAdoo	14.50	30.00	150.00	8.00
☐ CHICAGO	Burke-Glass	14.50	30.00	150.00	8.00
☐ CHICAGO	Burke-Houston	14.50	30.00	150.00	8.00
☐ CHICAGO	White-Mellon	14.50	30.00	150.00	8.00
☐ ST. LOUIS	Burke-McAdoo	14.50	30.00	150.00	8.00
☐ ST. LOUIS	Burke-Glass	15.00	30.00	150.00	8.50
☐ ST. LOUIS	Burke-Houston	14.50	30.00	150.00	8.00
☐ ST. LOUIS	White-Mellon	14.50	30.00	150.00	8.00
☐ MINNEAPOLIS	Burke-McAdoo	14.50	30.00	150.00	8.00
☐ MINNEAPOLIS	Burke-Glass	14.50	30.00	150.00	8.00
☐ MINNEAPOLIS	Burke-Houston	14.50	30.00	150.00	8.00
☐ MINNEAPOLIS	White-Mellon	14.50	30.00	150.00	8.00
☐ KANSAS CITY	Burke-McAdoo	14.50	30.00	150.00	8.00
☐ KANSAS CITY	Burke-Glass	14.50	30.00	150.00	8.00
☐ KANSAS CITY	Burke-Houston	14.50	30.00	150.00	8.00
☐ KANSAS CITY	White-Mellon	14.50	30.00	150.00	8.00

Bank	Signatures	VG	VF	Unc	ABP
☐ DALLAS	Burke-McAdoo	18.00	30.00	150.00	10.00
☐ DALLAS	Burke-Glass	17.00	30.00	150.00	9.00
☐ DALLAS	Burke-Houston	14.50	30.00	150.00	8.00
☐ DALLAS	White-Mellon	14.50	30.00	150.00	8.00
☐ SAN FRANCISCO	Burke-McAdoo	14.50	30.00	150.00	8.00
☐ SAN FRANCISCO	Burke-Glass	18.00	30.00	150.00	9.00
☐ SAN FRANCISCO	Burke-Houston	14.50	30.00	150.00	8.00
☐ SAN FRANCISCO	White-Mellon	14.50	30.00	150.00	8.00
☐ SAN FRANCISCO	White-Mellon	14.50	30.00	150.00	8.00

Ten Dollars

Typical Reverse, All Denominations
1914, Red Seals

Bank	Signatures	VG	VF	Unc.	ABP
☐ BOSTON	Burke-McAdoo	35.00	125.00	875.00	17.00
☐ NEW YORK	Burke-McAdoo	30.00	125.00	875.00	16.00
☐ PHILADELPHIA	Burke-McAdoo	30.00	125.00	875.00	16.00
☐ CLEVELAND	Burke-McAdoo	30.00	125.00	875.00	16.00
☐ RICHMOND	Burke-McAdoo	30.00	125.00	875.00	16.00
☐ ATLANTA	Burke-McAdoo	30.00	125.00	875.00	16.00
☐ CHICAGO	Burke-McAdoo	30.00	125.00	875.00	16.00
☐ ST. LOUIS	Burke-McAdoo	30.00	125.00	875.00	16.00
☐ MINNEAPOLIS	Burke-McAdoo	30.00	125.00	875.00	16.00
☐ KANSAS CITY	Burke-McAdoo	30.00	125.00	875.00	16.00
☐ DALLAS	Burke-McAdoo	35.00	125.00	875.00	17.00
☐ SAN FRANCISCO	Burke-McAdoo	35.00	125.00	875.00	17.00

Blue Seals

Bank	Signatures	VG	VF	Unc.	ABP
☐ BOSTON	Burke-McAdoo	19.00	32.00	150.00	12.00
☐ BOSTON	Burke-Glass	19.00	32.00	150.00	12.00
☐ BOSTON	Burke-Houston	19.00	32.00	150.00	12.00
☐ BOSTON	White-Mellon	19.00	32.00	150.00	12.00
☐ NEW YORK	Burke-McAdoo	19.00	32.00	150.00	12.00
☐ NEW YORK	Burke-Glass	19.00	32.00	150.00	12.00
☐ NEW YORK	Burke-Houston	19.00	32.00	150.00	12.00
☐ NEW YORK	White-Mellon	19.00	32.00	150.00	12.00
☐ PHILADELPHIA	Burke-McAdoo	19.00	32.00	150.00	12.00
☐ PHILADELPHIA	Burke-Glass	19.00	32.00	150.00	12.00
☐ PHILADELPHIA	Burke-Houston	19.00	32.00	150.00	12.00
☐ PHILADELPHIA	White-Mellon	19.00	32.00	150.00	12.00
☐ CLEVELAND	Burke-McAdoo	19.00	32.00	150.00	12.00
☐ CLEVELAND	Burke-Glass	19.00	32.00	150.00	12.00
☐ CLEVELAND	Burke-Houston	19.00	32.00	150.00	12.00
☐ CLEVELAND	White-Mellon	19.00	32.00	150.00	12.00

Bank	Signatures	VG	VF	Unc	ABP
☐ RICHMOND	Burke-McAdoo	19.00	32.00	150.00	12.00
☐ RICHMOND	Burke-Glass	19.00	32.00	150.00	12.00
☐ RICHMOND	Burke-Houston	19.00	32.00	150.00	12.00
☐ RICHMOND	White-Mellon	19.00	32.00	150.00	12.00
☐ ATLANTA	Burke-McAdoo	19.00	32.00	150.00	12.00
☐ ATLANTA	Burke-Glass	19.00	32.00	150.00	12.00
☐ ATLANTA	Burke-Houston	19.00	30.00	150.00	12.00
☐ ATLANTA	White-Mellon	19.00	30.00	150.00	12.00
☐ CHICAGO	Burke-McAdoo	19.00	30.00	150.00	12.00
☐ CHICAGO	Burke-Glass	19.00	30.00	150.00	12.00
☐ CHICAGO	Burke-Houston	19.00	30.00	150.00	12.00
☐ CHICAGO	White-Mellon	19.00	30.00	150.00	12.00
☐ ST. LOUIS	Burke-McAdoo	19.00	30.00	150.00	12.00
☐ ST. LOUIS	Burke-Glass	19.00	30.00	150.00	12.00
☐ ST. LOUIS	Burke-Houston	19.00	30.00	150.00	12.00
☐ ST. LOUIS	White-Mellon	19.00	30.00	150.00	12.00
☐ MINNEAPOLIS	Burke-McAdoo	19.00	30.00	150.00	12.00
☐ MINNEAPOLIS	Burke-Glass	19.00	30.00	150.00	12.00
☐ MINNEAPOLIS	Burke-Houston	19.00	30.00	150.00	12.00
☐ MINNEAPOLIS	White-Mellon	19.00	30.00	150.00	12.00
☐ KANSAS CITY	Burke-McAdoo	19.00	30.00	150.00	12.00
☐ KANSAS CITY	Burke-Glass	19.00	30.00	150.00	12.00
☐ KANSAS CITY	Burke-Houston	19.00	30.00	150.00	12.00
☐ KANSAS CITY	White- Mellon	19.00	30.00	150.00	12.00
☐ DALLAS	Burke-McAdoo	19.00	30.00	150.00	12.00
☐ DALLAS	Burke-Glass	19.00	30.00	150.00	12.00
☐ DALLAS	Burke-Houston	19.00	30.00	150.00	12.00
☐ DALLAS	White-Mellon	19.00	30.00	150.00	12.00
☐ SAN FRANCISCO	Burke-McAdoo	19.00	30.00	150.00	12.00
☐ SAN FRANCISCO	Burke-Glass	19.00	30.00	150.00	12.00
☐ SAN FRANCISCO	Burke-Houston	19.00	30.00	150.00	12.00
☐ SAN FRANCISCO	White-Mellon	19.00	30.00	150.00	12.00

Twenty Dollars, Series 1914, Red Seals

Bank	Signatures	VG	VF	Unc.	ABP
☐ BOSTON	Burke-McAdoo	40.00	100.00	950.00	27.50
☐ NEW YORK	Burke-McAdoo	35.00	75.00	950.00	25.00
☐ PHILADELPHIA	Burke-McAdoo	35.00	75.00	950.00	25.00
☐ CLEVELAND	Burke-McAdoo	35.00	75.00	950.00	25.00
☐ RICHMOND	Burke-McAdoo	35.00	85.00	950.00	25.00
☐ ATLANTA	Burke-McAdoo	35.00	85.00	950.00	25.00
☐ CHICAGO	Burke-McAdoo	35.00	75.00	950.00	25.00
☐ ST. LOUIS	Burke-McAdoo	35.00	85.00	950.00	25.00
☐ MINNEAPOLIS	Burke-McAdoo	35.00	85.00	950.00	25.00
☐ KANSAS CITY	Burke-McAdoo	35.00	90.00	950.00	25.00
☐ DALLAS	Burke-McAdoo	35.00	85.00	950.00	25.00
☐ SAN FRANCISCO	Burke-McAdoo	35.00	90.00	950.00	25.00

Blue Seals

☐ BOSTON	Burke-McAdoo	30.00	40.00	200.00	23.00
☐ BOSTON	Burke-Glass	30.00	40.00	200.00	23.00
☐ BOSTON	Burke-Houston	30.00	40.00	200.00	23.00

Bank	Signatures	VG	VF	Unc	ABP
☐ BOSTON	White-Mellon	30.00	40.00	125.00	23.00
☐ NEW YORK	Burke-McAdoo	30.00	40.00	125.00	23.00
☐ NEW YORK	Burke-Glass	30.00	40.00	125.00	23.00
☐ NEW YORK	Burke-Houston	30.00	40.00	125.00	23.00
☐ NEW YORK	White-Mellon	30.00	40.00	125.00	23.00
☐ PHILADELPHIA	Burke-McAdoo	30.00	40.00	125.00	23.00
☐ PHILADELPHIA	Burke-Glass	30.00	40.00	125.00	23.00
☐ PHILADELPHIA	Burke-Houston	30.00	40.00	125.00	23.00
☐ PHILADELPHIA	White-Mellon	30.00	40.00	125.00	23.00
☐ CLEVELAND	Burke-McAdoo	30.00	40.00	125.00	23.00
☐ CLEVELAND	Burke-Glass	30.00	40.00	125.00	23.00
☐ CLEVELAND	Burke-Houston	30.00	40.00	125.00	23.00
☐ CLEVELAND	White-Mellon	30.00	40.00	125.00	23.00
☐ RICHMOND	Burke-McAdoo	31.00	40.00	125.00	24.00
☐ RICHMOND	Burke-Glass	31.00	40.00	125.00	24.00
☐ RICHMOND	Burke-Houston	30.00	40.00	125.00	23.00
☐ RICHMOND	White-Mellon	30.00	40.00	125.00	23.00
☐ ATLANTA	Burke-McAdoo	30.00	40.00	125.00	23.00
☐ ATLANTA	Burke-Glass	31.00	40.00	125.00	24.00
☐ ATLANTA	Burke-Houston	30.00	40.00	125.00	23.00
☐ ATLANTA	White-Mellon	30.00	40.00	125.00	23.00
☐ CHICAGO	Burke-McAdoo	30.00	40.00	125.00	23.00
☐ CHICAGO	Burke-Glass	30.00	40.00	125.00	23.00
☐ CHICAGO	Burke-Houston	30.00	40.00	125.00	23.00
☐ CHICAGO	White-Mellon	30.00	40.00	125.00	23.00
☐ ST. LOUIS	Burke-McAdoo	30.00	40.00	125.00	23.00
☐ ST. LOUIS	Burke-Glass	30.00	40.00	125.00	23.00
☐ ST. LOUIS	Burke-Houston	30.00	40.00	125.00	23.00
☐ ST. LOUIS	White-Mellon	30.00	40.00	125.00	23.00
☐ MINNEAPOLIS	Burke-McAdoo	30.00	40.00	125.00	23.00
☐ MINNEAPOLIS	Burke-Glass	31.00	40.00	125.00	24.00
☐ MINNEAPOLIS	Burke-Houston	30.00	40.00	125.00	23.00
☐ MINNEAPOLIS	White-Mellon	30.00	40.00	125.00	23.00
☐ KANSAS CITY	Burke-McAdoo	30.00	40.00	125.00	23.00
☐ KANSAS CITY	Burke-Glass	31.00	40.00	125.00	24.00
☐ KANSAS CITY	Burke-Houston	30.00	40.00	125.00	23.00
☐ KANSAS CITY	White-Mellon	30.00	40.00	125.00	23.00
☐ DALLAS	Burke-McAdoo	30.00	40.00	125.00	23.00
☐ DALLAS	Burke-Glass	32.00	40.00	125.00	25.00
☐ DALLAS	Burke-Houston	30.00	40.00	125.00	23.00
☐ DALLAS	White-Mellon	30.00	40.00	125.00	23.00
☐ SAN FRANCISCO	Burke-McAdoo	32.00	40.00	125.00	25.00
☐ SAN FRANCISCO	Burke-Glass	32.00	40.00	125.00	25.00
☐ SAN FRANCISCO	Burke-Houston	30.00	40.00	125.00	23.00
☐ SAN FRANCISCO	White-Mellon	30.00	40.00	125.00	33.00

$50 and $100 denomination also received wide circulations. $500, $1000, $5000 and $10,000 denominations were also produced.

FEDERAL RESERVE BANK NOTES

One Dollar, Series 1918

Bank	Federal Sigs.	Bank Sigs.	VF	ABP
☐ BOSTON	Teehee-Burke	Bullen-Morss	35.00	19.00
☐ BOSTON	Teehee-Burke	Willett-Morss	75.00	35.00
☐ BOSTON	Elliot-Burke	Willett-Morss	35.00	19.00
☐ NEW YORK	Teehee-Burke	Sailer-Strong	35.00	19.00
☐ NEW YORK	Teehee-Burke	Hendricks-Strong	35.00	19.00
☐ NEW YORK	Teehee-Burke	Hendricks-Strong	35.00	19.00
☐ PHILADELPHIA	Teehee-Burke	Hardt-Passmore	35.00	19.00
☐ PHILADELPHIA	Teehee-Burke	Dyer-Passmore	37.50	20.00
☐ PHILADELPHIA	Elliott-Burke	Dyer-Passmore	35.00	19.00
☐ PHILADELPHIA	Elliott-Burke	Dyer-Norris	35.00	19.00
☐ CLEVELAND	Teehee-Burke	Baxter-Fancher	35.00	19.00
☐ CLEVELAND	Teehee-Burke	Davis-Fancher	35.00	19.00
☐ CLEVELAND	Elliot-Burke	Davis-Fancher	35.00	19.00
☐ RICHMOND	Teehee-Burke	Keesee-Seay	35.00	19.00
☐ RICHMOND	Elliot-Burke	Keesee-Seay	35.00	19.00
☐ ATLANTA	Teehee-Burke	Pike-McCord	35.00	19.00
☐ ATLANTA	Teehee-Burke	Bell-McCord	37.50	20.00
☐ ATLANTA	Teehee-Burke	Bell-Wellborn	35.00	19.00
☐ ATLANTA	Elliott-Burke	Bell-Wellborn	35.00	19.00
☐ CHICAGO	Teehee-Burke	McCloud-McDougall	35.00	19.00
☐ CHICAGO	Teehee-Burke	Cramer-McDougall	35.00	19.00
☐ CHICAGO	Elliott-Burke	Cramer-McDougall	35.00	19.00
☐ ST. LOUIS	Teehee-Burke	Attebery-Wells	37.50	20.00
☐ ST. LOUIS	Teehee-Burke	Attebery-Biggs	35.00	19.00
☐ ST. LOUIS	Elliott-Burke	Attebery-Biggs	35.00	19.00
☐ ST. LOUIS	Elliott-Burke	White-Biggs	35.00	19.00
☐ MINNEAPOLIS	Teehee-Burke	Cook-Wold	60.00	32.00
☐ MINNEAPOLIS	Teehee-Burke	Cook-Young	450.00	235.00
☐ MINNEAPOLIS	Elliott-Burke	Cook-Young	65.00	35.00
☐ KANSAS CITY	Teehee-Burke	Anderson-Miller	35.00	19.00
☐ KANSAS CITY	Elliott-Burke	Anderson-Miller	35.00	19.00
☐ KANSAS CITY	Elliott-Burke	Helm-Miller	35.00	19.00
☐ DALLAS	Teehee-Burke	Talley-Van Zandt	35.00	19.00
☐ DALLAS	Elliott-Burke	Talley-Van Zandt	100.00	40.00
☐ DALLAS	Elliott-Burke	Lawder-Van Zandt	35.00	19.00

Bank	Federal Sigs.	Bank Sigs.	VF	ABP
☐ SAN FRANCISCO	Teehee-Burke	Clerk-Lynch	35.00	19.00
☐ SAN FRANCISCO	Teehee-Burke	Clerk-Calkins	35.00	19.00
☐ SAN FRANCISCO	Elliott-Burke	Clerk-Calkins	35.00	19.00
☐ SAN FRANCISCO	Elliott-Burke	Ambrose-Calkins	35.00	19.00

Two Dollars, Series 1918

Bank	Federal Sigs.	Bank Sigs.	VF	ABP
☐ BOSTON	Teehee-Burke	Bullen-Morss	125.00	65.00
☐ BOSTON	Teehee-Burke	Willett-Morss	125.00	65.00
☐ BOSTON	Elliott-Burke	Willett-Morss	125.00	65.00
☐ NEW YORK	Teehee-Burke	Sailer-Strong	125.00	65.00
☐ NEW YORK	Teehee-Burke	Hendricks-Strong	125.00	65.00
☐ NEW YORK	Elliott-Burke	Hendricks-Strong	125.00	65.00
☐ PHILADELPHIA	Teehee-Burke	Hardt-Passmore	125.00	65.00
☐ PHILADELPHIA	Teehee-Burke	Dyer-Passmore	125.00	65.00
☐ PHILADELPHIA	Elliott-Burke	Dyer-Passmore	125.00	65.00
☐ PHILADELPHIA	Elliott-Burke	Dyer-Norris	125.00	65.00
☐ CLEVELAND	Teehee-Burke	Baxter-Fancher	125.00	65.00
☐ CLEVELAND	Teehee-Burke	Davis-Fancher	125.00	65.00
☐ CLEVELAND	Elliott-Burke	Davis-Fancher	125.00	65.00
☐ RICHMOND	Teehee-Burke	Keesee-Seay	125.00	65.00
☐ RICHMOND	Elliott-Burke	Keesee-Seay	125.00	65.00
☐ ATLANTA	Teehee-Burke	Pike-McCord	125.00	65.00
☐ ATLANTA	Teehee-Burke	Bell-McCord	125.00	65.00
☐ ATLANTA	Elliott-Burke	Bell-Wellborn	125.00	65.00
☐ CHICAGO	Teehee-Burke	McCloud-McDougal	125.00	65.00
☐ CHICAGO	Teehee-Burke	Cramer-McDougal	125.00	65.00
☐ CHICAGO	Elliott-Burke	Cramer-McDougal	125.00	65.00
☐ ST. LOUIS	Teehee-Burke	Attebery-Wells	125.00	65.00
☐ ST. LOUIS	Teehee-Burke	Attebery-Biggs	125.00	65.00
☐ ST. LOUIS	Elliott-Burke	Attebery-Biggs	125.00	65.00
☐ ST. LOUIS	Elliott-Burke	White-Biggs	125.00	65.00
☐ MINNEAPOLIS	Teehee-Burke	Cook-Wold	125.00	65.00
☐ MINNEAPOLIS	Elliott-Burke	Cook-Young	125.00	65.00
☐ KANSAS CITY	Teehee-Burke	Anderson-Miller	125.00	65.00
☐ KANSAS CITY	Elliott-Burke	Helm-Miller	125.00	65.00
☐ DALLAS	Teehee-Burke	Talley-Van Zandt	125.00	65.00
☐ DALLAS	Elliott-Burke	Talley-Van Zandt	125.00	65.00
☐ SAN FRANCISCO	Teehee-Burke	Clerk-Lynch	125.00	65.00
☐ SAN FRANCISCO	Elliott-Burke	Clerk-Calkins	125.00	65.00
☐ SAN FRANCISCO	Elliott-Burke	Ambrose-Calkins	125.00	65.00

Five Dollars, Series 1915

Bank	Federal Sigs.	Bank Sigs.	VF	ABP
☐ ATLANTA	Teehee-Burke	Bell-Wellborn	225.00	110.00
☐ ATLANTA	Teehee-Burke	Pike-McCord	125.00	65.00
☐ CHICAGO	Teehee-Burke	McLallen-McDougal	125.00	65.00
☐ KANSAS CITY	Teehee-Burke	Anderson-Miller	125.00	65.00
☐ KANSAS CITY	Teehee-Burke	Cross-Miller	125.00	65.00
☐ KANSAS CITY	Teehee-Burke	Helm-Miller	125.00	65.00
☐ DALLAS	Teehee-Burke	Hoopes-Van Zandt	125.00	65.00
☐ DALLAS	Teehee-Burke	Talley-Van-Zandt	150.00	70.00
☐ SAN FRANCISCO	Teehee-Burke	Clerk-Lynch	125.00	65.00

Five Dollars, Series 1918

Bank	Federal Sigs.	Banks Sigs.	VF	ABP
☐ BOSTON	Teehee-Burke	Bullen-Morss	1000.00	450.00
☐ NEW YORK	Teehee-Burke	Hendricks-Strong	150.00	85.00
☐ PHILADELPHIA	Teehee-Burke	Hardt-Passmore	150.00	85.00
☐ PHILADELPHIA	Teehee-Burke	Dyer-Passmore	150.00	85.00
☐ CLEVELAND	Teehee-Burke	Baxter-Fancher	150.00	85.00
☐ CLEVELAND	Teehee-Burke	Davis-Fancher	150.00	85.00
☐ CLEVELAND	Elliott-Burke	Davis-Fancher	150.00	85.00
☐ ATLANTA	Teehee-Burke	Pike-McCord	150.00	85.00
☐ ATLANTA	Teehee-Burke	Bell-Wellborn	150.00	85.00
☐ ATLANTA	Elliott-Burke	Bell-Wellborn	150.00	85.00
☐ CHICAGO	Teehee-Burke	McCloud-McDougal	150.00	85.00
☐ CHICAGO	Teehee-Burke	Cramer-McDougal	150.00	85.00
☐ ST. LOUIS	Teehee-Burke	Attebery-Wells	150.00	85.00
☐ ST. LOUIS	Teehee-Burke	Attebery-Biggs	150.00	85.00
☐ ST. LOUIS	Elliott-Burke	White-Biggs	150.00	85.00
☐ MINNEAPOLIS	Teehee-Burke	Cook-Wold	150.00	85.00
☐ KANSAS CITY	Teehee-Burke	Anderson-Miller	150.00	85.00
☐ KANSAS CITY	Elliott-Burke	Helm-Miller	150.00	85.00
☐ DALLAS	Teehee-Burke	Talley-Van Zandt	150.00	85.00
☐ SAN FRANCISCO	Teehee-Burke	Clerk-Lynch	150.00	85.00

San Francisco notes dated May 20, 1914. One issue dated May 18, 1914. Scarce.

Ten Dollars, Series 1915

Bank	Federal Sigs.	Bank Sigs.	VF	ABP
☐ ATLANTA	Teehee-Burke	Bell-Wellborn	500.00	275.00
☐ CHICAGO	Teehee-Burke	McLallen-McDougal	300.00	160.00
☐ KANSAS CITY	Teehee-Burke	Anderson-Miller	300.00	160.00
☐ KANSAS CITY	Teehee-Burke	Cross-Miller	300.00	160.00
☐ KANSAS CITY	Teehee-Burke	Helm-Miller	300.00	160.00
☐ DALLAS	Teehee-Burke	Hoopes-Van Zandt	300.00	160.00
☐ DALLAS	Teehee-Burke	Gilbert-Van Zandt	600.00	325.00
☐ DALLAS	Teehee-Burke	Talley-Van Zandt	300.00	160.00

Ten Dollars, Series 1918

Bank	Federal Sigs.	Bank Sigs.	VF	ABP
☐ NEW YORK	Teehee-Burkee	Hendricks-Strong	350.00	175.00
☐ ATLANTA	Elliott-Burke	Bell-Wellborn	350.00	175.00
☐ CHICAGO	Teehee-Burke	McCloud-McDougal	300.00	160.00
☐ ST. LOUIS	Teehee-Burke	Attebery-Wells	400.00	225.00

Twenty Dollars, Series 1915

Bank	Federal Sigs.	Bank Sigs.	VF	ABP
☐ ATLANTA	Teehee-Burke	Bell-Wellborn	500.00	275.00
☐ ATLANTA	Teehee-Burke	Pike-McCord	850.00	475.00
☐ CHICAGO	Teehee-Burke	McLallen-McDougal	500.00	275.00
☐ KANSAS CITY	Teehee-Burke	Anderson-Miller	400.00	210.00
☐ KANSAS CITY	Teehee-Burke	Cross-Miller	400.00	210.00
☐ DALLAS	Teehee-Burke	Hoopes-Van Zandt	550.00	300.00
☐ DALLAS	Teehee-Burke	Gilbert-Van Zandt	750.00	425.00
☐ DALLAS	Teehee-Burke	Talley-Van Zandt	550.00	300.00

Twenty Dollars, Series 1918

Bank	Federal Sigs.	Bank Sigs.	VF	ABP
☐ ATLANTA	Elliott-Burke	Bell-Wellborn	450.00	250.00
☐ ST. LOUIS	Teehee-Burke	Attebery-Wells	750.00	425.00

Fifty Dollars — Series 1918

Bank	Federal Sigs.	Bank Sigs.	VF	UNC	ABP
☐ ST. LOUIS	Teehee-Burke	Attebery-Wells	3500.00	9750.00	2100.00

GOLD CERTIFICATES

FIRST, SECOND AND THIRD ISSUES
Issued 1865 to 1876
Signatures of Colby-Spinner, or Allison-Spinner
Countersignature and date added with pen and ink.
First Issue $20 and $100, Extremely rare.
$500 to $5000 non-collectible
Second Issue $100 to $10,000 non-collectible.
Third Issue $100 series 1875, Allison-New, Extremely rare.
$500 to $10,000 non-collectible.

FOURTH ISSUE — SERIES 1882
Twenty Dollars

Signatures	Seal	VF	ABP
☐ Bruce-Gilfillan	Brown	2000.00	1100.00

This issue countersigned by Asst. Treas. of the U.S. Thos. C. Acton, are valued at five times or more above estimate.

☐ Bruce-Wyman	Brown	750.00	400.00
☐ Rosecrans-Huston	Large brown	750.00	400.00
☐ Lyons-Roberts	Small red	150.00	85.00

Fifty Dollars

Signatures	Seal	VF	ABP
☐ Bruce-Gilfillan	Brown	2000.00	1100.00

Countersigned notes of this issue are valued at five times above estimate.

☐ Bruce-Wyman	Brown	1500.00	800.00
☐ Rosecrans-Hyatt	Large red	1500.00	800.00
☐ Rosecrans-Huston	Large brown	1500.00	800.00
☐ Lyons-Roberts	Small red	400.00	220.00
☐ Lyons-Treat	Small red	400.00	220.00
☐ Vernon-Treat	Small red	400.00	220.00
☐ Vernon-McClung	Small red	400.00	220.00
☐ Napier-McClung	Small red	400.00	220.00

One Hundred Dollars

Signatures	Seal	VF	ABP
☐ Bruce-Gilfillan	Brown	1750.00	900.00

Only one countersigned notes of above issue is known.

☐ Bruce-Wyman	Brown	1500.00	800.00
☐ Rosecrans-Hyatt	Large red	1500.00	800.00
☐ Rosecrans-Huston	Large brown	1500.00	800.00
☐ Lyons-Roberts	Small red	425.00	225.00
☐ Lyons-Treat	Small red	425.00	225.00
☐ Vernon-Treat	Small red	425.00	225.00
☐ Vernon-McClung	Small red	425.00	225.00
☐ Napier-McClung	Small red	425.00	225.00
☐ Napier-Thompson	Small red	700.00	375.00
☐ Napier-Burke	Small red	425.00	225.00
☐ Parker-Burke	Small red	425.00	225.00
☐ Teehee-Burke	Small red	425.00	225.00

$500 - $10,000 Notes
SERIES 1882 $500., $1000., $5000. and $10,000. were issued but may be considered non-collectible, although notes of each denomination do exist.

Fifth and Sixth Issues
As with the high denomination Gold Certificates of 1882, notes of Series 1888 and 1900 reportedly exist, but may be considered to be non-collectible.

Ten Dollars — Seventh and Tenth Issues

Series	Signatures	VG	VF	ABP
☐ 1907	Vernon-Treat	30.00	50.00	18.00
☐ 1907	Vernon-McClung	30.00	50.00	18.00
☐ 1907	Napier-McClung	30.00	50.00	18.00
☐ 1907	Napier-Thompson	47.50	135.00	27.50
☐ 1907	Parker-Burke	30.00	50.00	18.00
☐ 1907	Teehee-Burke	30.00	50.00	18.00
☐ 1922	Speelman-White	27.50	55.00	16.00

Twenty Dollars — Seventh and Tenth Issues

Series	Signatures	VG	VF	ABP
☐ 1905	Lyons-Roberts	225.00	1500.00	135.00
☐ 1905	Lyons-Treat	185.00	1500.00	100.00
☐ 1906	Vernon-Treat	45.00	90.00	25.00
☐ 1906	Vernon-McClung	45.00	90.00	25.00
☐ 1906	Napier-McClung	45.00	90.00	25.00
☐ 1906	Napier-Thompson	65.00	140.00	35.00
☐ 1906	Parker-Burke	45.00	90.00	25.00
☐ 1906	Teehee-Burke	45.00	90.00	25.00
☐ 1922	Speelman-White	40.00	75.00	23.00

Fifty Dollars — Ninth and Tenth Issues

Series	Signatures	VG	VF	ABP
☐ 1913	Parker-Burke	85.00	200.00	55.00
☐ 1913	Teehee-Burke	85.00	200.00	55.00
☐ 1922	Speelman-White	75.00	125.00	55.00

One Hundred Dollars — Tenth Issues

Series	Signatures	VG	VF	ABP
☐ 1922	Speelman-White	140.00	200.00	125.00

$500 and $1,000 Notes — Tenth Issue

$500. and $1000. notes were also issued in Series 1922. All are rare.

SMALL SIZE PAPER MONEY

The nation's currency demands were increasing rapidly by the 1920s, and the Treasury soon realized the obligations could be made both more handy and more economical by reducing them in size, the resulting reduction being by about one-third, from 7-3/8 by 3-1/8 inches to 6-1/8 by 2-5/8 inches.

The decision to change the size of our paper money was made in 1928 during the term of office (April 30, 1928 through January 17, 1929) of Treasurer of the United States H.T. Tate and Secretary of the Treasury A.W. Mellon. (The final issue of the old large size paper money was the one dollar Silver certificate series of 1923 signed by Walter O. Woods as Register of the Treasury and H.T. Tate as Secretary of the Treasury, who had held these offices from May 31, 1928 to January 17, 1929.) The new currency was first placed in circulation on July 10, 1929.

LEGAL TENDER NOTES

Legal Tender notes carry red Treasury seals and serial numbers, and are otherwise identified by the presence of the words United States Note in the upper border on the face side. Basically issued in $2 and $5 values from 1929 to 1966, a $1 note was also offered in th first series. In 1966 the two then circulating values were discontinued and the statutory requirement dating from May 3, 1878, that $346,681,016 worth of this obligation be maintained in circulation is now by a new series of $100 notes bearing the date 1966.

1 Dollar Notes

	Series	Signatures	VF	Unc.	ABP
☐	1928	Woods-Woodin	20.00	120.00	11.00

2 Dollar Notes

	Series	Signatures	VF	Unc	ABP
☐	1928	Tate-Mellon	15.00	30.00	9.00
☐	1928-A	Woods-Mellon	40.00	160.00	24.00
☐	1928-B	Woods-Mills	150.00	410.00	90.00
☐	1928-C	Julian-Morgenthau	7.50	35.00	4.00
☐	1928-D	Julian-Morgenthau	7.50	25.00	4.00
☐	1928-E	Julian-Vinson	15.00	45.00	9.00
☐	1928-F	Julian-Snyder	7.50	20.00	4.00
☐	1928-G	Clark-Snyder	6.00	13.00	3.50

	Series	Signatures	VF	Unc	ABP
☐	1953	Priest-Humphrey	4.50	9.00	2.60
☐	1953-A	Priest-Anderson	4.00	8.00	2.50
☐	1953-B	Smith-Dillon	4.00	7.00	2.50
☐	1953-C	Granahan-Dillon	4.00	7.00	2.50
☐	1963	Granahan-Dillon	4.00	6.50	2.50
☐	1963-A	Granahan-Fowler	4.00	7.00	2.50

	Series	Signatures	VF	Unc	ABP
☐	1928	Woods-Mellon	8.00	25.00	6.00
☐	1928-A	Woods-Mills	13.00	60.00	7.50
☐	1928-B	Julian-Morgenthau	9.00	26.00	6.50
☐	1928-C	Julian-Morgenthau	10.00	17.50	6.00
☐	1928-D	Julian-Vinson	20.00	100.00	12.00
☐	1928-E	Julian-Snyder	9.50	15.00	5.50
☐	1928-F	Clark-Snyder	8.50	15.00	—
☐	1953	Priest-Humphrey	8.50	14.00	—
☐	1953-A	Priest-Anderson	7.50	10.00	—
☐	1953-B	Smith-Dillon	7.50	10.00	—
☐	1953-C	Granahan-Dillon	7.50	10.00	—
☐	1963	Granahan-Dillon	6.50	8.00	—

100 Dollar Notes

	Series	Signatures	VF	Unc	ABP
☐	1966	Granahan-Fowler	115.00	150.00	105.00
☐	1966-A	Elston-Kennedy	120.00	165.00	105.00

SILVER CERTIFICATES

Silver Certificate notes carry blue Treasury seals and serial numbers and are otherwise identified by the presence of that designation in the upper border on the face. Originally authorized as a silver dollar backed currency on February 28, 1878, and later backed by silver bullion, this series was discontinued by an act of June 4, 1963, although they remained in substantial circulation and were redeemed in silver until June 24, 1968. No values above $10 were issued.

1 Dollar Notes

	Series	Signatures	VF	Unc.	ABP
☐	1928	Tate-Mellon	5.00	15.00	2.50
☐	1928-A	Woods-Mellon	4.00	12.00	2.00
☐	1928-B	Woods-Mills	6.00	15.00	3.00
☐	1928-C	Woods-Woodin	95.00	440.00	50.00
☐	1928-D	Julian-Woodin	100.00	290.00	55.00
☐	1928-E	Julian-Morgenthau	300.00	1000.	150.00

☐	1934	Julian-Morgenthau	4.00	15.00	2.00

☐	1935	Julian-Morgenthau	4.00	12.50	2.00
☐	1935-A	Julian-Morgenthau	—	5.00	—
☐	1935-B	Julian-Vinson	3.00	12.50	1.50
☐	1935-C	Julian-Snyder	2.00	5.00	—
☐	1935-D	Clark-Snyder (wide marg)	—	5.00	—
☐	1935-D	Clark-Snyder (narrow)	—	4.00	—
☐	1935-E	Priest-Humphrey	—	3.00	—
☐	1935-F	Priest-Anderson	—	3.00	—

☐	1935-G	Smith-Dillon w/o Motto	—	3.50	—
☐	1935-G	With Motto	—	4.50	—
☐	1935-H	Granahan-Dillon	—	4.00	—
☐	1957	Priest-Anderson	—	3.00	—
☐	1957-A	Smith-Dillon	—	3.00	—
☐	1957-B	Granahan-Dillon	—	3.00	—

5 Dollar Notes

	Series	Signatures	VF	Unc	ABP
☐	1934	Julian-Morgenthau	10.00	18.00	6.00
☐	1934-A	Julian-Morgenthau	8.00	14.00	—
☐	1934-B	Julian-Vinson	12.50	40.00	7.00
☐	1934-C	Julian-Snyder	8.00	18.00	—
☐	1934-D	Clark-Snyder	8.00	15.00	—
☐	1953	Priest-Humphrey	—	12.50	—
☐	1953-A	Priest-Anderson	—	12.50	—
☐	1953-B	Smith-Dillon	—	12.50	—
☐	1953-C	Granahan-Dillon		(Not Released)	

10 Dollar Notes

	Series	Signatures	VF	Unc	ABP
☐	1933	Julian-Woodin	650.00	4000.	375.00
☐	1933-A	Julian-Morgenthau		Unique	
☐	1934	Julian-Morgenthau	18.00	40.00	—
☐	1934-A	Julian-Morgenthau	18.00	42.50	—
☐	1934-B	Julian-Vinson	100.00	850.00	55.00
☐	1934-C	Julian-Snyder	14.00	35.00	—
☐	1934-D	Clark-Snyder	14.00	32.00	—
☐	1953	Priest-Humphrey	15.00	35.00	—
☐	1953-A	Priest-Anderson	15.00	50.00	—
☐	1953-B	Smith-Dillon	20.00	45.00	12.00

NATIONAL CURRENCY

These notes carry brown seals and serial numbers, along with the name, charter number, location, and officer's signatures of the bank of issue. Like their large size counterparts, they were backed by U.S. bonds on deposit with the Treasury.

Type 1 — Bank Number In Two Positions

Type 2 — Bank Number In Four Positions

5 Dollar Notes

	Series		Signatures	VF	Unc.	ABP
☐	1929	Type 1	Jones-Woods	15.00	60.00	8.00
☐	1929	Type 2	Jones-Woods	20.00	80.00	10.00

10 Dollar Notes

	Series		Signatures	VF	Unc.	ABP
☐	1929	Type 1	Jones-Woods	17.50	80.00	11.00
☐	1929	Type 2	Jones-Woods	20.00	100.00	12.00

20 Dollar Notes

	Series		Signatures	VF	Unc.	ABP
☐	1929	Type 1	Jones-Woods	27.50	90.00	22.00
☐	1929	Type 2	Jones-Woods	32.50	105.00	25.00

These valuations are for the most common varieties of each denomination and type. Scarcity varies greatly between banks and states of issue, and in each case the more difficult to acquire issues many be valued at ten to twenty times the prices listed.

FEDERAL RESERVE BANK NOTES

These notes also carry brown seals and serial numbers, along with the designation National Currency. They were issued as direct obligations of the various banks in the Federal Reserve System, carrying the appropriate designation thereon. Authorized on March 9, 1933, the issue was discontinued in July of 1935. Several of the banks also issued $50 and $100 notes.

5 Dollar Notes

	Series	District	VF	Unc.	ABP
☐	1929	Boston	15.00	55.00	7.50
☐	1929	New York	12.00	50.00	6.00
☐	1929	Philadelphia	15.00	65.00	7.50
☐	1929	Cleveland	12.00	50.00	6.00
☐	1929	Richmond		Not Issued	
☐	1929	Atlanta	15.00	120.00	7.50
☐	1929	Chicago	10.00	50.00	6.00
☐	1929	St. Louis	150.00	325.00	45.00
☐	1929	Minneapolis	20.00	95.00	10.00
☐	1929	Kansas City	12.00	65.00	6.00
☐	1929	Dallas	15.00	57.50	7.50
☐	1929	San Francisco	750.00	2000.	300.00

10 Dollar Notes

	Series	District	VF	Unc.	ABP
☐	1929	Boston	20.00	50.00	12.00
☐	1929	New York	15.00	42.50	—
☐	1929	Philadelphia	18.00	55.00	11.00
☐	1929	Cleveland	18.00	45.00	11.00
☐	1929	Richmond	22.00	55.00	13.00
☐	1929	Atlanta	20.00	55.00	12.00
☐	1929	Chicago	18.00	45.00	11.00
☐	1929	St. Louis	18.00	55.00	11.00
☐	1929	Minneapolis	20.00	70.00	12.00
☐	1929	Kansas City	20.00	60.00	12.00
☐	1929	Dallas	30.00	200.00	15.00
☐	1929	San Francisco	22.00	75.00	13.00

20 Dollar Notes

	Series	District	VF	Unc.	ABP
☐	1929	Boston	—	70.00	—
☐	1929	New York	—	60.00	—
☐	1929	Philadelphia	—	60.00	

	Series	District	VF	Unc.	ABP
☐	1929	Cleveland	—	60.00	—
☐	1929	Richmond	—	60.00	—
☐	1929	Atlanta	.	65.00	—
☐	1929	Chicago	—	55.00	—
☐	1929	St. Louis	25.00	85.00	22.00
☐	1929	Minneapolis	.	65.00	—
☐	1929	Kansas City	—	70.00	—
☐	1929	Dallas	25.00	105.00	22.00
☐	1929	San Francisco	25.00	100.00	22.00

FEDERAL RESERVE NOTES

Federal Reserve Note issues carry green Treasury seals and serial numbers, with the nature of the obligation being stated in the upper border on the face. The small size currency Federal Reserve Note series was launched with the 1928 issue, but the $1 note was not authorized until 1963, when $1 Silver Certificates were being discontinued. In addition to the denominations listed, Federal Reserve Notes were also issued in $50, $100, $500, $1000, $5000 and $10,000 values, but the premiums for these high face value notes are generally small. Issue of the four highest denominations was discontinued in 1969. Except the still-authorized $100 Legal Tender issue, all circulating currency is today constituted in Federal Reserve issues.

Federal Reserve Notes carry numeral and letter designation of their bank of issue on the face of each note, coinciding with the number assigned to each of the twelve Federal Reserve Districts: 1-A, Boston; 2-B, New York; 3-C, Philadelphia; 4-D, Cleveland; 5-E, Richmond; 6-F, Atlanta; 7-G, Chicago; 8-H, St. Louis; 9-I, Minneapolis; 10-J, Kansas City; 11-K, Dallas; 12-L, San Francsico. The prefix letter of the serial number is also indicative of the bank of issue.

1 Dollar Notes

	Series	Signatures	Unc.	ABP
☐	1963	Granahan-Dillon	3.00	—
☐	1963A	Granahan-Fowler	2.50	—
☐	1963B	Granahan-Barr	2.00	—
☐	1969	Elston-Kennedy	2.00	—
☐	1969A	Kabis-Kennedy	2.00	—
☐	1969B	Kabis-Connally	2.00	—
☐	1969C	Banuelos-Connally	1.50	—
☐	1969D	Banuelos-Shultz	1.50	—
☐	1974	Neff-Simon	1.50	—
☐	1977	Morton-Blumenthal	1.25	—
☐	1977A	Morton-Miller	1.25	—

5 Dollar Notes

	Series	Signatures	Unc.	ABP Unc.
☐	1928	Tate-Mellon	30.00	10.00
☐	1928A	Woods-Mellon	35.00	12.00
☐	1928B	Woods-Mellon	35.00	12.00
☐	1928C	Woods-Mills	250.00	125.00
☐	1928D	Woods-Woodin	500.00	275.00
☐	1934	Julian-Morgenthau	32.50	10.00
☐	1934A	Julian-Morgenthau	25.00	7.50
☐	1934B	Julian-Vinson	35.00	12.00
☐	1934C	Julian-Snyder	22.50	7.00
☐	1934D	Clark-Snyder	14.00	—
☐	1950	Clark-Snyder	14.00	—
☐	1950A	Priest-Humphrey	13.50	—
☐	1950B	Priest-Anderson	12.50	—
☐	1950C	Smith-Dillon	12.50	—
☐	1950D	Granahan-Dillon	12.00	—
☐	1963	Granahan-Dillon	12.00	—
☐	1950E	Granahan-Fowler	12.50	—
☐	1963A	Granahan-Fowler	10.00	—
☐	1969	Elston-Kennedy	8.50	—
☐	1969A	Kabis-Connally	8.00	—
☐	1969B	Banuelos-Connally	8.00	—
☐	1969C	Banuelos-Shultz	8.00	—
☐	1974	Neff Simon	8.00	—
☐	1977	Morton-Blumenthal	—	—
☐	1977A	Morton-Miller	—	—

10 Dollar Notes

	Series	Signatures	Unc.	ABP Unc.
☐	1928	Tate-Mellon	42.50	15.00
☐	1928A	Woods-Mellon	35.00	14.00
☐	1928B	Woods-Mellon	30.00	12.00
☐	1928C	Woods-Mills	90.00	45.00
☐	1934	Julian-Morgenthau	27.50	11.00
☐	1934A	Julian-Morgenthau	23.50	—
☐	1934B	Julian-Vinson	30.00	12.00
☐	1934C	Julian-Snyder	20.00	—
☐	1934D	Clark-Snyder	20.00	—
☐	1950	Clark-Snyder	20.00	—
☐	1950A	Priest-Humphrey	18.50	—
☐	1950B	Priest-Anderson	17.50	—
☐	1950C	Smith-Dillon	16.50	—
☐	1950D	Granahn-Dillon	16.50	—
☐	1963	Granahan-Dillon	16.50	—
☐	1950E	Granahan-Fowler	17.50	—

	Series	Signatures	Unc.	ABP Unc.
☐	1963A	Granahan-Fowler	16.00	—
☐	1969	Elston-Kennedy	15.00	—
☐	1969A	Kabis-Connally	14.00	—
☐	1969B	Banuelos-Connally	13.00	—
☐	1969C	Banuelos-Shultz	13.00	—
☐	1974	Neff-Simon	13.00	—
☐	1977	Morton-Blumenthal	—	—
☐	1977A	Morton-Miller	—	—

20 Dollar Notes

	Series	Signatures	Unc.	ABP Unc.
☐	1928	Tate-Mellon	50.00	25.00
☐	1928A	Woods-Mellon	50.00	25.00
☐	1928B	Woods-Mellon	47.50	22.50
☐	1928C	Woods-Mellon	110.00	55.00
☐	1934	Julian-Morgenthau	40.00	22.00
☐	1934	Julian-Morgenthau	40.00	22.00
☐	1934A	Julian-Morgenthau	40.00	22.00
☐	1934B	Julian-Vinson	40.00	22.00
☐	1934C	Julian-Snyder	40.00	22.00
☐	1934D	Clark-Snyder	37.50	22.00
☐	1950	Clark-Snyder	30.00	—
☐	1950A	Priest-Humphrey	27.50	—
☐	1950B	Priest-Anderson	27.50	—
☐	1950C	Smith-Dillon	27.50	—
☐	1950D	Granahan-Dillon	30.00	—
☐	1963	Granahan-Dillon	29.00	—
☐	1950E	Granahan-Fowler	30.00	—
☐	1963A	Granahan-Fowler	24.00	—
☐	1969	Elston-Kennedy	24.00	—
☐	1969A	Kabis-Connally	24.00	—
☐	1969B	Banuelos-Connally	24.00	—
☐	1969C	Banuelos-Shultz	24.00	—
☐	1974	Neff-Simon	24.00	—
☐	1977	Morton-Blumenthal	—	—

GOLD CERTIFICATES

Gold Certificate notes carry gold Treasury seals and serial numbers. The first small size Gold Certificates were released on May 29, 1929. Depreciating economic conditions caused the issue of an order on December 28, 1933, calling for the surrender of any privately held notes, and on January 31, 1934, the value of gold was raised from $20.67 to $35 per ounce. The restrictions on holding these notes were rescinded on April 24, 1964. These popular notes were also issued in $500, $1000, $5000 and $10,000 values, plus a $100,000 series 1934 issue intended for transactions within the Federal Reserve System, the latter still being restricted.

	Series	Signatures	VF	Unc.	ABP
		10 Dollar Notes			
☐	1928	Woods-Mellon	35.00	250.00	18.00
		20 Dollar Notes			
☐	1928	Woods-Mellon	50.00	265.00	30.00
		50 Dollar Notes			
☐	1928	Woods-Mellon	90.00	550.00	65.00
		100 Dollar Notes			
☐	1928	Woods-Mellon	150.00	650.00	110.00

HAWAII

As a precaution against possible Japanese invasion of Hawaii and other U.S. islands of the Pacific during World War II a special Silver Certificate and Federal Reserve Note currency bearing brown Treasury seals and serial numbers, along with overprints of HAWAII, was introduced. This precaution was invoked from June 8, 1942, to October 21, 1944, so the notes could be demonetized in the event of a successful invasion.

1 Dollar Notes

	Series	Signatures	VF	Unc.	ABP
☐	1935-A	Julian-Morgenthau	7.00	65.00	3.50

5 Dollar Notes

	Series	Signatures	VF	Unc.	ABP
☐	1934	Julian-Morgenthau	25.00	270.00	13.00
☐	1934-A	Julian-Morgenthau	14.00	190.00	7.50

10 Dollar Notes

	Series	Signatures	VF	Unc.	ABP
☐	1934-A	Julian-Morgenthau	15.00	135.00	11.00

20 Dollar Notes

	Series	Signatures	VF	Unc.	ABP
☐	1934	Julian-Morgenthau	95.00	850.00	50.00
☐	1934-A	Julian-Morgenthau	32.50	450.00	25.00

Issued for the use of American troops in North Africa during the early days of World War II, these Silver Certificates carry distinctive yellow Treasury seals, while retaining the customary blue serial numbers. The purpose of the issue was to allow for demonitization in the event of military reversals.

Series	Signatures	VF	Unc.	ABP
	1 Dollar Notes			
☐ 1935-A	Julian-Morgenthau	10.00	80.00	6.00
	5 Dollar Notes			
☐ 1934-A	Julian Morgenthau	10.00	110.00	6.00
	10 Dollar Notes			
☐ 1934	Julian-Morgenthau	1000.	5000.	600.00
☐ 1934-A	Julian-Morgenthau	17.50	125.00	12.00

EXPERIMENTAL ISSUE

In 1944 the Treasury released an experimental issue of Silver Certificates bearing red "R" and "S" overprints. The notes bearing the "R" were printed on regular paper, those with the "S" on a special experimental paper. Results of the test were inconclusive and no change in paper was carried out.

Type	F	VF	Unc.	ABP
$1 Red "R"	14.00	30.00	200.00	7.00
$1 Red "S"	10.00	15.00	180.00	6.00